The Discovery
of
Nineteenth-Century Scandinavia

Other books from Norvik Press

Anglo-Scandinavian Cross-Currents (eds Inga-Stina Ewbank, Olav Lausand & Bjørn Tysdahl)

Aspects of Modern Swedish Literature (revised edn, ed. Irene Scobbie)

Paul Binding: *With Vine-Leaves in His Hair. The Role of the Artist in Ibsen's Plays*

Centring on the Peripheries. Studies in Scandinavian, Scottish, Gaelic and Greenlandic Literature (ed. Bjarne Thorup Thomsen)

A Century of Swedish Narrative (eds Sarah Death & Helena Forsås-Scott)

English and Nordic Modernisms (eds Bjørn Tysdahl, Mats Jansson, Jakob Lothe & Steen Klitgård Povlsen)

European and Nordic Modernisms (eds Mats Jansson, Jakob Lothe & Hannu Riikonen)

Gender – Power – Text. Nordic Culture in the Twentieth Century (ed. Helena Forsås-Scott)

Nordic Letters 1870-1910 (eds Michael Robinson & Janet Garton)

Northern Constellations. New Readings in Nordic Cinema. (ed. C. Claire Thomson)

On the Threshold. New Studies in Nordic Literature (eds Michael Robinson & Janet Garton)

Ellen Rees: *On the Margins. Nordic Women Modernists of the 1930s*

Michael Robinson: *Studies in Strindberg*

Michael Robinson: *Strindberg and Genre*

Freddie Rokem: *Strindberg's Secret Codes*

Turning the Century. Centennial Essays on Ibsen (ed. Michael Robinson)

Robin Young: *Time's Disinherited Children. Childhood, Regression and Sacrifice in the Plays of Henrik Ibsen*

Knut Hamsun: *Selected Letters*, vols I and II (ed. & trans. by Harald Næss & James MacFarlane)

Erik and Amalie Skram: *Caught in the Enchanter's Net. Selected Letters* (ed. & trans. Janet Garton)

Eszter Szalczer: *Writing Daughters: August Strindberg's Other Voices*

Edith Södergran: *The Poet who Created Herself. Selected Letters* (ed. & trans. by Silvester Mazzarella)

Victoria Benedictsson: *Money* (translated by Sarah Death)

Hjalmar Bergman: *Memoirs of a Dead Man* (translated by Neil Smith)

Jens Bjørneboe: *Moment of Freedom* (translated by Esther Greenleaf Mürer)

Jens Bjørneboe: *Powderhouse* (translated by Esther Greenleaf Mürer)

Jens Bjørneboe: *The Silence* (translated by Esther Greenleaf Mürer)

Camilla Collett: *The District Governor's Daughters* (translated by Kirsten Seaver)

Kerstin Ekman: *Witches' Rings* (translated by Linda Schenck)

Kerstin Ekman: *The Spring* (translated by Linda Schenck)

Kerstin Ekman: *The Angel House* (translated by Sarah Death)

Kerstin Ekman: *City of Light* (translated by Linda Schenck)

Jørgen-Frantz Jacobsen: *Barbara* (translated by George Johnston)

P. C. Jersild: *A Living Soul* (translated by Rika Lesser)

Runar Schildt: *The Meat-Grinder and Other Stories* (translated by Anna-Lisa & Martin Murrell)

Hjalmar Söderberg: *Martin Birck's Youth* (translated by Tom Ellett)

Hjalmar Söderberg: *Short Stories* (translated by Carl Lofmark)

August Strindberg: *Tschandala* (translated by Peter Graves)

Hanne Marie Svendsen: *Under the Sun* (translated by Marina Allemano)

The Discovery
of
Nineteenth-Century
Scandinavia

edited by

Marie Wells

Norvik Press
2008

Acknowledgements

The editor would like to acknowledge the contribution of Nordisk Kulturråd, (The Nordic Cultural Council) which has made the publication of this volume possible. In 2004 their assistance was all the more appreciated because at the end of the conference it looked as if there were no funds for publication. This was because the letter from Nordisk Kulturråd offering a grant for the publication had somehow been lost in the post for seven weeks, but to the great relief of the editor, it arrived the day after the conference ended.

The editor would also like to thank all involved in Norvik Press for their willingness and enthusiasm to publish this volume.

Marie Wells
London, January 2008

A catalogue record for this book is available from the British Library.

ISBN 978 1 870041 69 0
First published 2008

Norvik Press was established in 1984 with financial support from the University of East Anglia, the Danish Ministry for Cultural Affairs, the Norwegian Cultural Department and the Swedish Institute.

Managing Editors: Janet Garton, Neil Smith and C. Claire Thomson.

Cover illustration: Geysir in Iceland.
Cover design: Richard Johnson
Layout: Neil Smith
Printed in Great Britain by Page Bros (Norwich) Ltd, UK.

Contents

Introduction

Marie Wells

This volume has its formal origins in a conference entitled *The Discovery of Nineteenth Century Scandinavia: as reflected in travel-writing, essays, letters and fiction written by Scandinavians and others* which was held at UCL in June 2004. The motives for the conference itself, however, were less formal and more personal. As a frequent visitor to Norway and teacher of Norwegian literature and culture, the editor had for many years been aware of the manifestations of the growth of tourism in Norway in the nineteenth century: the building of hotels such as the one at Balestrand, the exploits of the early British climbers who sought adventure in the Jotunheimen mountains, the fishermen who came every summer to fish for salmon, not to mention the appearance of – particularly English – travellers in Norwegian literature, ranging from the English sports hunter in Asbjørnsen's and Moe's 'The Reindeer Hunt in Rondane' to the fisherman, Sir Hugh Trevelyan, who plays a part in Hamsun's *Benoni*. The editor was also aware that travel-writing was becoming an increasingly popular genre, even given its own section in book shops. In 2002 she mentioned to a colleague that she would like to know more about Scandinavian travel-writing, and he said simply, 'well, arrange a conference', so she did. The result was something far more interesting and more diverse than anything she could have imagined.

The title and focus of the conference were chosen carefully. It was not to be 'the nineteenth-century discovery of Scandinavia' which could cover everything from the awakening interest of nineteenth century European scholars for medieval Scandinavia to the 'discovery' of one of Scandinavia's major dramatists, namely, Ibsen. These topics had in any case formed part of a joint British-Norwegian research project that culminated in the volume *Anglo-Scandinavian Cross-Currents*.[1] The aim of the title *The Discovery of Nineteenth Century Scandinavia* was to focus on the discovery of nineteenth-century Scandinavia by non-Scandinavians, but also by Scandinavians discovering their own and each other's countries.

Scandinavia had certainly been 'discovered' before the nineteenth century, a point made very clearly in respect of Sweden by Elizabeth Baigent in her contribution to this volume. One can immediately think of Robert Molesworth's *Account of Denmark* (1693) or Mary Wollstonecraft's *A Short*

Residence in Sweden, published in 1796. Molesworth and Wollstonecraft were 'outsiders' discovering Denmark and Sweden and responding to them in terms of the prevailing cultural and political concerns of the day. On the other hand, an early Scandinavian discovering his own country was the Swede, Carl von Linné or Linnaeus (1707-1778). While his writings spurred on natural historians from many countries to further work, the travel accounts that formed the background to his research were slow to reach a wider audience, not least because they were written in either Latin or Swedish. His original account of his 1732 journey through Lappland, *Iter Lapponicum* was not published till 1888, though an English translation of the manuscript journal by Sir James E. Smith was published in 1811 under the title *Lachesis Lapponica or A Tour in Lapland*. His other travel accounts: *Ölandske & Gotlandske Resa 1741* (1745), *Västgöta Resa 1746* (1747) and *Skånska Resa* (1751) could only be read by those who could read Swedish, though a German translation of *Ölandske & Gotlandske Resa* appeared in 1764.

Not only had Scandinavia been discovered before the nineteenth century, but this is far from the first volume to look at Scandinavian travel-writing, which has become the focus of much interest during the past decade. 1998 saw the publication of H. Arnold Barton's *Northern Arcadia: Foreign Travelers in Scandinavia, 1765-1815*,[2] which was the first volume 'to examine as a whole the travel literature dealing with Denmark, Schleswig-Holstein, Norway, Sweden, Finland, Iceland, and the Færø Islands'. Another volume considering the whole of Scandinavia but covering a broader period is *Northbound. Travel Encounters and Constructions 1700-1830*,[3] edited by Karen Klitgaard-Povlsen, which will appear at about the same time as this volume, and is based on a five-year research programme entitled 'Den europæiske konstruktion af Norden 1700-1820: Fra dystopi til utopi' (The European construction of the North 1700-1820: From Dystopia to Utopia) led by Povlsen. Histories of travel in individual Scandinavian countries to date are Mark Davies's *A perambulating paradox. British travel literature and the image of Sweden 1700-1865*[4] and Fjågesund's and Symes's detailed study, *The Northern Utopia: British Perceptions of Norway in the Nineteenth Century*.[5] Furthermore, one might note that in this day of numerous guide books to just about anywhere, travel-writing about Scandinavia is still being produced as Joanna Kavenna's *The Ice Museum: In Search of the Lost Land of Thule*[6] testifies.

Whereas in the seventeenth and eighteenth centuries, The Grand Tour had taken noblemen and those wishing to acquire knowledge and culture to Greece and Italy, in the late eighteenth and early nineteenth centuries various events coincided which together changed the focus and purpose of travel. Firstly, for over a decade the Napoleonic Wars put parts of Europe 'out of bounds' for the traveller. At the same time in the wake of the Romantic Movement and in reaction to urbanisation and industrialization, people were beginning to develop a taste for nature untouched by the hand of man. As a result, in the course of the nineteenth century as transport improved, and more and more people began to travel, accounts of adventures by the intrepid traveller were replaced by accounts by tourists, and Scandinavia even figured in guide books.

Travel-writing as it emerges from the pages that follow is a broad category, covering everything from official reports such as those written by Marmier for the Commission du Nord, and the *sýslumenn* for the Governor of Iceland (see the articles by Mercer and Ogilvie) to a semi fictional and fantastic journey such as that described by Hans Christian Andersen in his *Fodreise fra Holmens Kanal til Østpynten af Amager i Aarene 1828 og 1829* (see the article by Andersen). Between these two extremes are accounts of the 'discovery' of Norway by two very different British travellers, Burton and Slingsby, (see the chapter by Skarðhamar), the history of the development of travel in Finland from the days when it was an expedition 'not for the faint-hearted' to the time when it was a pleasant destination for tourists for whom 'a tour round the Isle of Wight could not be fraught with less peril' (see the article by Lurcock) and the 'discovery' and promotion of Iceland and its cultural heritage by Sabine Baring-Gould (see the article by Wawn). The contribution of foreign artists to the development of an Icelandic sense of national identity is the subject of an article by Ísleifsson.

Not all the articles in this volume are about travel-writing *per se*. Baigent's article covers the whole sweep of Anglo-Swedish contacts from the Vikings to the nineteenth century and refutes any idea of the 'discovery' of Sweden in the nineteenth century. Other articles provide background information about the countries to which the travellers travelled, and about which they wrote, and it is a real eye-opener to read the contrasting impressions of Iceland that emerge from Ogilvie's and Wawn's chapters. Travellers, of course, depend on many things to support their travels, not least places to stay, and the way parsonages in Norway were used by upper class travellers is the subject of Rogan's article.

One of the surprising aspects of the conference was that there were more papers presented on Hans Christian Andersen than on any other topic (see the chapters by Thomsen, Oxfeldt and Andersen). This may partly be attributed to the fact that in 2004 Andersen was very much to the fore in the run-up to the bi-centenary of his birth in 2005, but the conference also made it clear what a central part of his life travel was. The only other Scandinavian traveller covered in the conference and in this volume is also a Dane, namely Holger Drachmann, whose reflections on the significance of the Danish border town of Dybbøl for Danish national consciousness is the subject of van der Liet's article.

If the range of types of travel-writing covered in this volume is diverse, the treatment of the material is, if anything, even more diverse. Because research into travel-writing as a genre is still a relatively young field, it is also one that, delightfully, is open to everyone, from the person who wants to catalogue how travel and descriptions of travel in a particular country have changed over time, to the person who wants to subject a particular travel account to analysis from a post-colonial perspective.

At the level of primary research are the contributions of Wawn, Ogilvie, Rogan, Lurcock and Baigent. Wawn draws on archives in the Devon Records Office to trace Baring Gould's love affair with the history and culture of Iceland, a love affair that expressed itself in historical fiction, and ballad-type poems even before he visited the country in 1862. It was, however, a love affair that made his account of that visit, *Iceland: Its Scenes and Sagas*, a work that in Wawn's words stretches to the limits 'the traditional generic boundaries of the travel book'.

Nineteenth-century visitors to Iceland were largely interested in its heroic past or in its extraordinary landscape, but through her survey of the reports of the *sýslumenn* or District Commissioners Ogilvie in her chapter gives us a picture of what life was like for the ordinary Icelander who lived there all the time. The *sýslumenn* had to write annual reports about the state of their district to the Governor and District or Deputy Governor of Iceland, and these reports, which started in the 1700s and continued to the end of the nineteenth century, are a mine of information about the conditions, and the picture that emerges is a pretty harsh one.

Rogan has trawled church history, memoirs and local histories to trace how parsonages came to function as congenial places to stay for students and upper-class travellers. In the days when the clergy were spread through a thinly populated country, this was an arrangement that seemed to suit the clergy as much as the traveller who in exchange for board and lodging brought news of the wider world.

Lurcock too undertakes primary research, examining accounts of travel in Finland from 1830 onwards, and shows how travel changed with the advent of steam so that if one wanted something more than a comfortable boat cruise one would have to travel to the interior of Finland, where, of course, developments also eventually took place to make the visitor's life more comfortable.

For her contribution Baigent extracts information about Anglo-Swedish contacts and travel in both directions from the new *DNB* and shows how the reasons for travel changed over the centuries. In the seventeenth it seems that significant numbers of Britons left these shores to fight as mercenaries in the anti-Hapsburg war in Sweden, while in the eighteenth century scientific exchange particularly within the natural sciences seems to have been the main motive for travel and here, of course, Linnæus played a huge part. Close on the heels of natural science came applied science, instrument making and industrial spies!

As soon as one moves away from the gathering and presentation of primary information and turns to the articles on already published travel-writing documents one sees how they can be subjected to a variety of treatments. On the most straightforward level one can do a chronological comparison as Skarðhamar does when she compares accounts of Norway by two travel-writers who are separated by a span of eighty years, one writing in 1835, the other in 1904, one still writing with an Enlightenment attitude to nature, 'the natives' and the sublime, the other writing with open enjoyment of both.

Mercer's article is also based on comparisons, but in addition is influenced by the sensitivities of post-colonial theory, one of the most fruitful tools with which to examine travel-writing. She identifies in her subject Marmier some of the characteristics of the traveller-as-hero in relation to nature, but even here sees differences between Marmier's official reports and his accounts in *Lettres sur le Nord*. In relation to the inhabitants of northern Norway, however, she shows how Marmier's attitude is far from that of the ethnocentric traveller-as-coloniser.

Another contribution that uses post-colonial theory is that by Oxfeldt on Hans Christian Andersen's travelogue, *A Poet's Bazaar*. Written partly in reaction to the idealization of Andersen in the bicentenary year of his birth, Oxfeldt shows first how Andersen's æsthetic is located 'at the intersection of fantasy, feeling and reason; West and East; tradition and modernity; poetry and prose; art and commerce' with, in each case, the latter term breaking with earlier romanticism, 'i.e. the emphasis on reason, travel to the Orient, modernity, prose and commerce'. She then goes on to show with how 'uninnocent' and Euro-imperialist an eye Andersen views many aspects of life in Istanbul. This analysis again situates *A Poet's Bazaar* at an intersection, this time that of being interpreted as an expression of 'a radical postcolonial stance where all white, European, male travellers are seen as suspect imperialists', and that of a being interpreted as 'part of a national, overly self-congratulatory project on the other'.

Closely related to Oxfeldt's idea of locating Andersen's *A Poet's Bazaar* at a point of intersection is Thomsen's idea of locating Andersen's *I Sverrig* 'at a place and a text in-between', but rather than being based on post-colonial theory, his contribution is based on translation theory. Sweden, as Denmark's close neighbour is, of course, neither 'home' nor totally 'foreign', especially with regard to language, but Thomsen highlights how, as a writer of international repute whose works had already been translated into many languages, Andersen 'translates' Sweden for an international readership. However, like Oxfeldt Thomsen also sees Andersen in this travelogue as occupying a point at the intersection of the romantic and the modern, the natural and the man-made, and like Oxfeldt he also points out how Andersen does not turn his back on the modern as expressed through technology, but embraces it.

Hans Christian Andersen's contribution on his namesake is a fascinating analysis of how the nineteenth-century writer developed his talent for one aspect of his career, that of travel-writer. The journey itself, though rooted in actual geography and limited in extent, is largely a product of the imagination, and is shown to be simply the material with which Andersen already demonstrates that he knows all the conventions of travel-writing and can play with them.

By a further twist of the focus screw on the eyeglass we reach the final perspective brought to bear on Scandinavian travel-writing, that to do with travel and the creation of national identity, though the two contributions on this subject could not be more different; Henk van der Liet's article deals with Holger Drachmann's visit to Dybbøl and the effect his writing about it had on Danish self-consciousness, while Sumarliði Ísleifsson's contribution examines how it was the foreigners' celebration of Iceland and its extraordinary landscape and natural phenomena that led to the Icelanders themselves taking a pride in their own country.

Insofar as this editor thought about it, her original image of a volume of papers on travel-writing was probably of one containing chapters about resurrected and dusted off early travel accounts with quotations from particularly exciting or humorous bits. What emerged was something far more diverse and exciting, not least because in addition to what the volume contains, it also suggests all sorts of areas and aspects of travel-writing that are still to be explored, and ways of exploring them.

Notes

1. Ewbank, Inga-Stina, Lausund, Olov and Tysdahl Bjørn (eds) (1999): *Anglo-Scandinavian Cross-Currents*. Norwich, Norvik Press.
2. Barton, H. Arnold (1998): *Northern Arcadia: Foreign Travelers in Scandinavia, 1765-1815*. Carbondale, Southern Illinois University Press.
3. Povlsen, Karen Klitgaard (2007): *Northbound. Travel Encounters and Constructions 1700-1830*. Aarhus University Press.
4. Davies, Mark (2000): *A perambulating Paradox. British travel literature and the image of Sweden 1700-1865*.
5. Fjågesund, Peter and Symes, Ruth (2003): *The Northern Utopia: British Perceptions of Norway in the Nineteenth Century*. Amsterdam and New York, Rodopi.
6. Kavenna, Joanna (2005): *The Ice Museum: In Search of the Lost Land of Thule*. Viking.

Scandinavia as Seen in France Through the Findings of the Commission du Nord (1835-39).

Wendy Mercer

Prior to the nineteenth century, very little was generally known in France about the Scandinavian countries. This lack of awareness was to be addressed by the findings of a series of prestigious expeditions initiated in the 1830s. In 1833, a French gunboat, *La Lilloise*, had been dispatched to protect French fishing vessels in Icelandic waters, but in August of that year it disappeared without trace. In 1834, a further gunboat, *La Bordelaise*, was sent to search for the missing vessel and its crew, but it returned to France having found nothing. Then in 1835, a corvette, *La Recherche*, set sail for Iceland under the command of François-Thomas Tréhouart, with the same mission. This time, however, Paul Gaimard, an explorer, naturalist and medical man, and Eugène Robert, a geologist, were attached to the expedition, partly to help with the inquiries into the disappearance of *La Lilloise*, but also to explore Iceland. The expedition again failed to find any trace of the gunboat and its missing crew, but the exploration of Iceland proved to be a huge success. Gaimard and Robert returned with a large number of scientific specimens, artefacts and information which attracted a tremendous amount of attention both in the scientific world and, to a lesser extent, amongst the general public. Encouraged by the success of this aspect of the expedition, approval was given for a second expedition the following year (1836), this time to be led by Gaimard, who organised a team later to be known as the Commission du Nord; its number now included two further scientists (Victor Lottin and Raoul Anglès), the artists Auguste Meyer (or Mayer) and Louis Bévalet (as this was still before the era of photography), and a specialist in philology and literature, Xavier Marmier. The success of this expedition was such that Gaimard obtained funding for the Commission du Nord to pursue its explorations in the other Scandinavian countries over the next few years. Gaimard remained in charge, and the core members remained the same, although extra specialists, French as well as Danish, Swedish and Norwegian, were at times attached to the expeditions.[1]

Their findings were published in France in a series of volumes each of which was dedicated to a particular sphere of knowledge (geology, climate, etc.), and also to the illustrations by the artists,[2] most aimed at a fairly specialised scientific readership. The most widely read by the public at large were those produced by Marmier on history, literature and especially the travel narratives. Not only were these more intellectually accessible to a wider readership without prior specialised knowledge (e.g. of scientific terminology), but Marmier's findings and impressions also appeared in three forms: as the finished official reports published under Gaimard's direction; as articles (usually in the form of letters) published on a regular basis in some of the most prestigious reviews of the day (especially the *Revue des Deux Mondes*, but also the *Revue de Paris*, *Le Correspondant* etc.). These articles were then published in volume form as *Lettres sur l'Islande* and *Lettres sur le Nord*. The latter is very similar in content to the official report (Marmier 1844-7), although less detailed, more impressionistic, and sometimes also stylistically different. The popularity of all these accounts was enhanced by the fact that they were extremely 'readable': both unofficial and official versions are written fluently and articulately, and abound with anecdotes, personal impressions, descriptions and interesting background information.

A number of other general external factors also contributed to the public interest in these volumes. Louis-Philippe had in his youth travelled through Scandinavia; this fact would undoubtedly have contributed to the royal assent for the financial support for the expeditions having been granted so readily; it would also have stimulated the growing curiosity in France about these countries.

Perhaps even more decisive in terms of public awareness was the new interest being shown by the French in countries and cultures beyond their own borders. For various reasons they were now more open to ideas from outside. Those with an interest in literature and the arts had read Mme de Stael's *De la littérature considérée dans ses rapports avec les institutions sociales* (1800) and her slightly later *De l'Allemagne* (1810) in which she argued that the French should stop looking to the classical (Southern) literature for their inspiration, but rather seek models in Northern countries. The generation which had come of age with the advent of the July Monarchy (1830) had grown up with the influence of a Romanticism imbued with images of the 'Northern countries' and a particular predilection for snow-clad mountains, forests, lakes, and landscapes swathed in mists. As Marmier himself was quick to admit, however, these were very much received ideas, and the French remained hazy about the details: 'un rideau de brouillard enveloppe l'esprit, et le Danemark, la

Suède, la Norvège, la Laponie, le Spitzberg, la Finlande, la Russie même, nous apparaissent derrière ce brouillard avec des formes indécises et se confondent dans notre imagination' (Marmier 1841, I:73; a curtain of fog clouds the mind, and Denmark, Sweden, Norway, Lapland, Spitzbergen, Finland and even Russia appear to us through this fog as indistinct forms which become confused in our imagination). To this list, Marmier might well have added Iceland and even Scotland, which also was perceived as one of the Romantic Northern countries – mainly because of the French fascination with Ossian, although other factors such as the popularity of Walter Scott in the 1820s and an interest in Byron undoubtedly also played their part.

The other factor which had led generally to a greater interest in the outside world was of a different nature; European colonial expansion was in full swing, and France was no exception to this trend. The decade following the revolution of July 1830 saw in particular an increasing presence in Algeria under Louis-Philippe. Expansionism of course – to put it crudely – needed research about possible areas to colonise. This led to an increase in the volume of travel-writing being produced, and also led to the genre of travel-writing developing in a manner consistent with this – often unavowed – objective. People and land were increasingly described in terms of utility and profit, as dominant cultures sought to stake their claims. Because travel-writing as a genre was developing in this way, this kind of discourse was employed not only in the descriptions of distant continents most readily associated with the colonial enterprise, but also frequently applied to accounts of journeys to relatively familiar European countries. The rhetoric of subjugation which tends to typify travel-writing of this era displays a number of characteristics which can also be identified in Marmier's accounts of the expeditions.

On a number of occasions, he constructs himself and his fellow members of the Commission in the mould of the 'heroic' explorer or 'traveller-as-hero'. In 1838, after *La Recherche* had made its first – not entirely successful – expedition to Spitzbergen, Marmier and a number of his colleagues set off through Lapland, making their way south towards Haparanda and Umeå. One leg of the journey was undertaken by water, travelling in four narrow craft which could each accommodate two passengers in addition to the two oarsmen and the pilot. They passed through Kättisuvando, Ofwer-Muonio, and Muonioniska, which lay close to the Eyanpaïkka falls. Here the party were advised to leave their boats in the hands of an experienced pilot and to follow in safety on dry land; there used to be four pilots here, but one had drowned the previous year, and two others had died prematurely, worn out by the arduous nature of their work. This rang as a challenge to the ears of Marmier and Gaimard, who were tempted to make the descent in the boat. Their resolve strengthened when they were told that only a few days previously, two Englishmen had been tempted to make the descent, but had hastily reversed their decision when they had actually seen the danger of the falls. Marmier and Gaimard made the descent once, and then decided to do it again a second time for good measure. Here, Marmier presents himself in the role of 'traveller-as-hero', triumphing over the forces of nature. He also, by the references to the Englishmen, casts himself in the role of defender of French supremacy abroad. In the context of the rivalry between the two powers at that time, particularly in terms of colonialisation, the narration of this episode is clearly significant.

A very interesting example of the trope of traveller-as-hero is to be found in Marmier's account of an attempt made by a party in a rowing boat to reach the great ice barrier beyond Hakluyt, the most northerly point of Spitzbergen:

> Nous aurions voulu quitter la dernière grève sur laquelle était amarrée notre embarcation, tenter au-delà des limites extrêmes du globe une aventureuse exploration, naviguer jusqu'au bord de cet éternel rempart qui entoure le pôle, et essayer d'y pénétrer. Mais des brumes épaisses voilaient à tout instant la surface du ciel [...]. La prudence du pilote expérimenté arrêtait l'élan de nos rames: 'Vous n'irez pas même, nous disait-il, jusqu'à cette barrière que vous désirez voir de plus près; et vous courez risque d'être, dans le trajet, surpris par une brume ténébreuse qui vous empêcherait de reconnaître la direction que vous devez suivre, et de vous trouver là enserrés, écrasés par les glaces flottantes'. (Marmier 1844-7, II:351)

> (We would have liked to leave behind us the last shore where our vessel was moored, to undertake a bold exploration beyond the extreme limits of the globe; to row to the edge of that eternal barrier which surrounds the pole, and try to penetrate it. But the sky was covered by a thick veil of mist. [...] The caution of the experienced pilot calmed the vigour of our oars: 'You won't even get as far as that barrier that you want to see close up; and if you were to try and reach it, you would risk being overtaken by a thick mist; you would lose your bearings and, unable to find your way, could find yourselves trapped there and crushed by drifting ice'.)

Here Marmier again casts himself and his colleagues in the typical nineteenth-century 'explorer as hero/celebrity' role. The venture is glorified by the use of terms such as *limites extrêmes*, *éternel rempart*, etc. The narrative conforms to the tradition according to which nature is identified with the feminine, and is portrayed as something to be 'conquered', whilst the act itself is recounted in terms of active male – possibly sexual –

domination (*exploration, vigueur, pénétrer, élan*, etc.). The warnings of the pilot are referred to in terms reminiscent of an over-protective mother or nanny. The conflation of nature and the feminine, and the association of exploration and discovery with heterosexual virility is a recognised motif in the history of travel writing and is a logical consequence of the context of a capitalist patriarchy in which it is produced. Significantly, however, this episode is recounted in the official report of the expedition, but is completely omitted from Marmier's *Lettres sur le Nord*, which were published separately, but which in most other respects are very similar to the official version. The *Lettres sur le Nord* actually conclude on a completely different note:

> Je ne voyais plus devant moi que l'immense espace des flots, coupé par les trois îles [...]. L'Océan était sombre et immobile, le ciel chargé çà et là de quelques nuages lourds, et de tous côtés couvert d'un voile brumeux: seulement, sur un des points de l'horizon, on distinguait une lueur blanchâtre qui se déroulait sous les nuages comme un ruban d'argent: c'était le reflet des glaces éternelles. J'étais seul alors au milieu de la solitude immense; nul bruit ne frappait mon oreille, nulle voix ne venait m'interrompre dans mon rêve. Les rumeurs de la cité, les passions du monde, étaient bien loin. Mon pied foulait une des extrémités de la terre, et devant moi il n'y avait plus que les flots de l'Océan et les glaces du pôle. Non, je ne saurais exprimer toute la tristesse, toute la solennité de l'isolement dans un tel lieu. [...] J'ai courbé le front sous le sentiment de mon impuissance [...]. (Marmier 1841, II:117)

> (All I could see before me was the immense expanse of water, broken only by the three islands [...]. The ocean was dark and still, the sky cluttered here and there with a few heavy clouds, and covered on all sides by a shroud of mist: only, at a single point on the horizon, a whitish glow was just visible which unfolded beneath the clouds like a silver ribbon; it was the reflection of the eternal ice-field. I was alone at that moment amidst immense solitude; no sound reached my ear, no voice disturbed my dreams. The buzz of the city and worldly passions were all far away. I was standing at one of the ends of the earth; in front of me was nothing but the waves of the ocean and the ice of the pole. No, words cannot express all the sadness, all the solemnity of such a place. [...] I bowed my head in the knowledge of my impotence [...].)

This passage, apart from the final sentence, was also included in the official version *before* the account of the attempt to reach the ice barrier (thus privileging the 'traveller-as-hero' trope) and is written in Romantic terms suggesting the splendour of the spot and the emotions evoked; these include 'une terreur indéfinissable' (Marmier 1841, II:107; an unspeakable terror), 'profond saisissement' ([a] sudden and overwhelming chilling of blood), and 'mélange de terreur et d'admiration' (*ibid.*:104; a mixture of terror and admiration), which stand in strong contrast to the register of the traveller-as-hero. Even more striking, however, in the context of the vocabulary used in the official extract is the fact that the final sentence in the *Lettres* includes the phrase: 'J'ai courbé le front sous le sentiment de mon impuissance' (*ibid.*:117) – rather different from the 'élan', 'pénétration' and 'vigueur' of the official account. A possible explanation for this may be that in writing the official report, Marmier is attempting to conform to the more traditional form of travel-writing in that era, according to which natural phenomena are seen as objects to be 'conquered' and exploration is associated with strength and virility. In this context it may be that Marmier did not consider it appropriate to present either himself, or his colleagues on the expedition, as being in any way 'impuissants'!

The rhetoric of subjugation which we sometimes find in his official accounts pertaining to natural phenomena is very rarely extended in either the official or the unofficial accounts to fellow human beings. Whereas typically travel writing would present 'others' encountered in ethnocentric terms which demean or generally serve as a pretext for exploitation, this trope is largely absent from Marmier's work.

In fact, Marmier's presentation of others encountered on his travels could not be further from this cliché of ethnocentrism. When his fellow members of the Commission set off to Spitzbergen on board *La Recherche* on their first expedition in 1838, Marmier remained behind in Hammerfest to pursue his research into the language and culture of the region. His first self-appointed task was to visit some of the isolated dwellings scattered around the coast, in order to see how the people lived. To this end, he enlisted the help of Aale, the pastor of Hammerfest. Together they climbed the mountain ridge, walked down to Ryppefjord, and then on to Kvalsund, where a large crowd of Sami had gathered for one of the three annual religious services which the pastor was to celebrate there. Marmier's description of the scene in both the official report and the *Lettres sur le Nord* is used to correct a number of prejudices concerning a people about whom relatively little was known in France at that time:

En général, les pauvres Lapons ont été durement calomniés. Les voyageurs qui n'ont fait que voir de loin les sombres demeures où ils vivent, leur ont prêté bien des vices dont ils sont, pour la plupart du moins, très innocents. Il suffit de rester quelque temps parmi eux, de causer avec eux, de les suivre dans les diverses situations de la vie, pour être touché de tout ce qu'il y a de bon, de simple et d'honnête dans leur nature. (Marmier 1844-7, I:191)

(In general, the poor Laplanders have been severely misrepresented. Those travellers who have only observed from a distance the dark dwellings where they live have attributed to them many vices, of which – for the most part, at least – they are quite innocent. If you live among them for a while, chat with them, accompany them in the various situations of their lives, you cannot but be moved by all that is good, simple and honest in their nature.)

If this short extract may sound slightly patronising, it is nonetheless demonstrative of the way in which Marmier's writing differs from the more conventional travel narratives of the era. The words 'voir de loin' (to see from a distance, or to observe from a distance) summarise both the behaviour and the discourse of the typical 'traveller-as-hero' or 'traveller-as-coloniser'. The usually (although not necessarily) masculine subject in such a context seeks characteristically to preserve his or her distance from those who are 'other'. Such a strategy enables the subject to retain his or her position of superiority, which is normally already established by financial superiority, mobility, and possibly also superior physical strength, or weaponry. The apparently objective gaze – which in reality is intensely subjective – reinforces the distance and confers power on the traveller who is looking, and judging everything according to his (or her) own pre-established national or social criteria. Thus factors of difference (e.g. different types of clothes, standards of hygiene, or disease) may be used as pretexts to look (down) on others, thereby reinforcing the position of notional superiority. The refusal to relinquish the position of superiority and power implies also a failure to exchange, to empathise, to understand. Marmier for his part refuses, by and large, to 'voir de loin' (observe from a distance). The key words in his rhetoric here are conjunctions such as 'avec' (with) and 'parmi' (among), and words such as 'touché' (moved); he seeks to break down the distance between himself and others. In order to make this sharing of experience – the immersion in another culture – possible, he took great pains to learn all the languages of the countries to be visited. By partly relinquishing his own cultural identity, he is able to pass on to his French readership a different cultural experience. Marmier's refusal to 'voir de loin' actually leads him to refuse to look at all in a number of situations where exchange or involvement of any sort is impossible. At Åbo in Finland, for example, he was invited to visit the local prison, where the governor had made elaborate preparations in his honour. The prisoners were lined up for inspection, but Marmier's distress forced him to cut short his visit, 'car je ne me sentais pas le courage de contempler plus longtemps une telle infortune avec l'impuissance d'y apporter quelque adoucissement' (Marmier 1843a, I:30; because I did not have the strength to look upon such misery any longer while knowing that I was helpless to mitigate it in any way).

After attending one of the services held by Aale at Kvalsund, Marmier accepted an invitation to a jolly gathering in the local merchant's shop. From his account of the party, it would seem that the Sami were generally considered to be the lowest of the low in social terms, and were excluded from any such gathering; their only contact with the merchant was for business, begging for credit when they had no other means to purchase necessities. One such man, who was moved by curiosity, put his head round the door, and Marmier soon engaged him in conversation. The man, Ole Ollsen,[3] came from near the Russian border, but brought his herd of reindeer to Kvalsund every summer. He told Marmier about his life, and invited Marmier to visit him in Kitell the following year. The following day, just as Marmier was preparing to leave, Ollsen came to find him and made him a gift of a Norwegian coin in memory of their meeting. Marmier further records that Ollsen and his wife came to look him up at Hammerfest the following year on his return from Spitzbergen, when he was able to invite them on board *La Recherche* to take a glass of eau-de-vie. Here we see reciprocity and evident mutual respect. Marmier hardly ever casts himself as the distant outsider, travelling only to observe and judge others by his own norms. He enters into relationships and gives the individuals a certain stature in his narratives by recording their names, life stories, opinions, hopes and anxieties. On occasion, his sympathy for the peoples encountered leads him to speak out in a manner which would have been controversial at the time. Thus, for example, he is forthright in criticising the Danish monopolies in Iceland and the Faroe Islands.

Little sympathy for 'others' encountered, however, is to be found in another 'unofficial' account of the Spitzbergen expedition: the travel narrative of Léonie d'Aunet. D'Aunet was the companion and later wife of the painter Biard, who accompanied the second expedition to Spitzbergen in 1839:[4] she published an 'unofficial' account of this expedition under the title *Voyage d'une femme au Spitzberg* in 1854. D'Aunet's narrative draws much more strongly on the more common traditions of travel writing of this era. In it, she consistently distances herself from the objects of her observations, offering a classic example of the rhetoric of traveller as oppressor/exploiter, and constructing herself firmly as the representative of the French expansionism and capitalism of the era. Far from entering into relationships of mutual respect and reciprocity with the Sami she encounters, she subjects them in her text to a process of dehumanisation and bestialisation, referring to them as being devoid of 'normal' sexual characteristics (e.g. d'Aunet 1872:148, 271); they are described variously as 'ugly' (the adjective *laide* and the noun *laideur* are frequently applied to Sami women by d'Aunet; see e.g. pp.147, 148, 243); 'dirty' (*sales*, p.147);

'hideous' (*hideuse* is another frequently used epithet, e.g. pp.243, 259); 'horrible' (pp.148, 259); 'repulsive' (*repoussant*, p.147); 'monster[s]' (*stryge*, p.259); 'ogre's daughter[s]' (*filles de l'ogre*, p.147); 'large grey bears walking on their hind legs' (*de gros ours gris marchant sur leurs pattes de derrière*, p.140) and 'monkey[s]' (*singe*, p.259). The hands of an elderly woman are described as 'abominable little claws' (*abominables petites griffes*, p.259); the woman herself resembles a 'heap of animal hides' (*amas de peaux de bêtes*, p.259). In general terms, d'Aunet concludes that:

> Les Lapons de Kautokeino laissent une autre impression que les Lapons d'Hammerfest, et ce sont les mêmes hommes, mais les deux faces du sauvage: à Hammerfest, le sauvage en fête est ivre, hébété, hideux; à Kautokeino, dans sa vie de famille, il est doux, paresseux, borné. Hors de lui, il inspire le dégoût; chez lui, il fait naître la pitié. (d'Aunet 1872:267)

> (The Laplanders of Kautokeino leave a different impression from those at Hammmerfest; they are the same people, but the two faces of the savage. At Hammerfest, the savage on holiday is drunken, vacant, hideous; at Kautokeino, in his family life, he is docile, lazy and simple-minded. Outside the home, he is disgusting; at home, he is pitiful.)

Although d'Aunet reserves her most offensive outpourings for the Sami, she also writes in pejorative terms about others met on her travels – particularly women. In Kiel, she claims that the 'frightful' ('affreux'; p.28) and 'horrible' (p.28) hats worn by the women are an eyesore fit for use only by scarecrows; Swedish women are tall, blonde and fresh-complexioned, but have rotten teeth and large feet (p.53); whilst the Norwegian women are taller than their male counterparts and have a magnificent complexion which makes them appear to be pretty when they are not: they have a lot of children and look old before their time (p.74).[5]

It is also significant in the context of traveller as exploiter/coloniser that great attention is paid in d'Aunet's text to material acquisition and the bargains to be had. Shopping sprees are described with minute detail of purchases and prices (see, for example, pp.12, 277, 349); every opportunity is seized to purchase a bargain, often with a view to trade: in Hjerkinn, for example, we are told that she acquires three white wolf skins for 35 francs, which she will be able to sell at a good profit in France (p.87). Ironically, she elsewhere castigates the entire Sami race for their supposed avarice, claiming that their desire to make money overrides any human considerations in their relationships (pp.248-9). Details of potential trade or financial transactions (other than benign anecdotes such as Ollsen's gift of a coin – which cannot be viewed as exploitative) are notably absent from Marmier's texts. Thus d'Aunet's text displays an attitude to 'others' which is much more in keeping with the rhetoric more generally employed in travel writing of the era. It should be emphasised, however, that her particular account of the expedition was completely unofficial, was published some fifteen years after the event, and would have been much less widely read than those by Marmier (despite its 'succès de scandale').

Although some of these less sympathetic tropes may be identified in Marmier's writing, they are few; they are limited by and large to his 'official' reports, and are more than outweighed by positive features. On the whole, his accounts are sensitive and very positive. He frequently comments, for example, on the fact that education, literacy and general cultural awareness are far more developed in the Scandinavian countries than in France. Much evidence is offered to support this view. Anecdotally, he cites, for example, a fisherman's daughter in Reykjavik making the weekly fish delivery who is able to show him the finest passages of *Njal's Saga*, and he remarks that it would be virtually impossible to find a fisherman's daughter with the same level of erudition in France. He reports having seen a very poor woman in Uppsala spending what appeared to be her last worldly wealth to purchase a canto of *Frithiofs Saga* badly printed on a sheet of cheap paper. His more formal publications include the systematic presentation of the educational systems in the different countries, the collections of the major libraries, and the strengths of the local universities. This respect for the Scandinavians is of course enormously enhanced by the fact that he did not only publish the travel narratives in their various forms: he also produced volumes on the history of Iceland and on Icelandic literature, histories of the Scandinavian countries and comprehensive surveys of the literatures of the individual countries, and numerous translations, mainly of poetry and short stories, but also a volume of *Chants populaires du Nord*. Even the *Lettres sur l'Islande*, Marmier's account of the Iceland expedition, contains a remarkable survey of Icelandic literature encompassing eddic and skaldic poetry, Icelandic mythology, the sagas, and a history of the Icelandic language. It received enthusiastic reviews from the *Revue des Deux Mondes* and the *Revue germanique* amongst others. It was reprinted at least five times between 1837 and 1855, and translated into a number of different languages. Pirate Belgian editions appeared as early as 1837. His work on Swedish, Danish and Norwegian literatures appeared first of all in 1839 in a volume of *Histoire de la littérature en Danemark et en Suède*; an *Histoire de la littérature scandinave* came out in 1848; and the official version of his findings, published under Gaimard's direction along with all the other scientific data, under the title *Littérature scandinave* appeared in 1849. All of these were translated into other languages, so their influence extended well beyond the borders of France.

The surveys of history and literature are outstanding for their time in a number of ways. Apart from the considerable importance of their novelty in France, they are extremely erudite. They are the result of careful and comprehensive documentation, and contain lengthy bibliographies, quite rare at the time. Yet they are readable and accessible to a general public. In addition to consulting written sources in their original languages, Marmier also made contact with a significant number of the major literary figures of the day. Thus, for example, his presentations of the life and works of Oehlenschläger, Andersen, Ingemann, Grundtvig, Heiberg; or Tegnér, Geijer, Atterbom, and Frederika Bremer, are based not only on his own appreciations of the written works, but on detailed conversations with the authors themselves. His surveys were therefore not only comprehensive from a historical point of view but also very up-to-date. In addition to these critical presentations, Marmier translated a significant number of literary works (e.g. by Oehlenschläger, Holberg, and numerous others from Danish, Swedish and Norwegian). His interest did not diminish over the years, and collections of short stories featuring Scandinavian authors continued to appear in translation until shortly before his death in 1892.

It is hard to gauge the full impact of this work in France, but we have some indications of how important it was. It was certainly very widely read: quite apart from the material published in the influential reviews of the time, all the volumes mentioned were sold in several reprints and some had new editions. Already by the time he was appointed to the Iceland expedition in 1836 Marmier was very well known for his work on things German, and by 1839 he was a full-blown celebrity. Prior to the Spitzbergen expeditions, he had been appointed to a chair in foreign literature at the newly-established faculty of letters at the University of Rennes. His lectures, which drew widely on his knowledge of the literatures of the Northern countries, established the discipline of comparative literature in all but name, as well as the study of folklore. They were reported in great detail in both local and national press, as much for their content as for the fact that Marmier by this time had the kind of celebrity status that we would now associate with a pop star or a film actor. No room in the university was big enough to hold all the people who wished to attend his lectures, and more spacious accommodation was found at the town hall. A scandal was created when he was mobbed by a crowd of over-enthusiastic young women, an episode which greatly displeased the university authorities (Sainte-Beuve 1935-66, III:85). Interesting anecdotal evidence of the impact of his work is to be found in the diary of Hans Christian Andersen, who recalls a visit to the Paris opera in March 1843. He entered into conversation with the man sitting beside him, who asked him where he came from. When Andersen replied that he was Danish, his neighbour told him that he knew of two great Scandinavian writers, Tegnér and Andersen – from his reading of Marmier (Andersen 1971-7, II:322).

Marmier's presentation of Scandinavia and its literature also left its mark on the development of French literature of the era. Again, this is too vast a subject to deal with in any depth here, but two aspects may be mentioned which have already been the subject of published research. During Marmier's short academic career at Rennes (one term – he resigned in order to join the expeditions to Spitzbergen and Lapland with the Commission du Nord) Leconte de Lisle was a law student there. Alison Fairlie, in her excellent study of *Leconte de Lisle's Poems of the Barbarian Races* (1947), demonstrates convincingly that Marmier's work on Iceland (particularly the *Lettres sur l'Islande* and the *Chants populaires du Nord*) provided an important source of inspiration for the *Poèmes barbares*. The novelist Jules Verne, a writer of a very different kind, also owes a great deal to Marmier; Daniel-Henri Pageaux has shown a number of ways in which the famous novel *Voyage au centre de la terre* (*Journey to the Centre of the Earth*) draws on Marmier's *Lettres sur l'Islande* (Pageaux 1980).

It is possible therefore to conclude that thanks to the findings of the Commission du Nord, Scandinavia was no longer perceived in France *solely* in terms of its snow-capped mountains and Romantic landscapes. Though the 'unofficial' account published by d'Aunet gives a less informed and less sympathetic view of the countries, and though she cannot rightly be described as a member of the Commission, her work being only an indirect consequence of the expedition, analysis of her text serves to highlight the extraordinary achievement represented by the other publications. By and large, both the encounters occasioned by the expeditions and the resultant publications served to promote understanding between France and the Scandinavian countries on a number of levels. In addition to the scientific data provided for specialist research, the general public and especially the literary world became aware of the existence of the mythology, the culture, and the literary and scholastic traditions of those countries. This new knowledge was to enrich intellectual life in France – and indeed beyond its borders – immeasurably.

Bibliography

Andersen, H. C. (1971-7): *Dagbøger 1825-1875*, 12 vols. Copenhagen: GECGAD.

d'Aunet, L. (1872 [1854]): *Voyage d'une femme au Spitzberg*. Paris: Hachette.

Fairlie, A. (1947): *Leconte de Lisle's Poems of the Barbarian Races*. Cambridge: Cambridge University Press.

Knutsen, N. M., & Posti, P. (2002a): *La Recherche: en ekspedisjon mot nord: une expédition vers le nord*. Tromsø: Angelica.

—— (eds) (2002b): *La Recherche: en ekspedisjon mot nord: bilder fra Norge og Spitsbergen: une expédition vers le nord: illustrations sur la Norvège et le Spitzberg*. Tromsø: Angelica.

Marmier, X. (1837): *Lettres sur l'Islande*. Paris: Bonnaire.

—— (1839): *Histoire de la littérature en Danemark et en Suède*. Paris: Bonnaire.

—— (1840): *Voyage en Islande et Groënland, exécuté pendant les années 1835 et 1836 sur la corvette 'La Recherche' [...]. Histoire de l'Islande*. Paris: Arthus Bertrand.

—— (1841): *Lettres sur le Nord (Danemark, Suède, Norvège, Laponie et Spitzberg)*, 2 vols. Brussels: N.-J. Grégoir, V. Wouters et Cie.

—— (1842): *Chants populaires du Nord*. Paris: Charpentier.

—— (1843a): *Lettres sur la Russie, la Finlande et la Pologne*. Paris: Delloye.

—— (1843b): *Voyage en Islande et Groënland, exécuté pendant les années 1835 et 1836 sur la corvette 'La Recherche' [...]. Littérature islandaise*, 2 vols. Paris: Arthus Bertrand.

—— (1844-7): *Voyages de la commission scientifique du nord en Scandinavie, en Laponie, au Spitzberg et aux Feroë pendant les années 1838, 1839 et 1840 sur la corvette La Recherche commandée par M. Paul Fabvre, publiés par ordre du roi sous la direction de M. Paul Gaimard. Relation du voyage*, 2 vols. Paris: Arthus Bertrand.

—— (1848): *Histoire de la littérature scandinave*. Paris: Arthus Bertrand.

—— (1849): *Voyages de la commission scientifique du nord en Scandinavie, en Laponie, au Spitzberg et aux Feroë pendant les années 1838, 1839 et 1840 sur la corvette La Recherche commandée par M. Paul Fabvre, publiés par ordre du roi sous la direction de M. Paul Gaimard. Littérature scandinave*. Paris: Arthus Bertrand.

—— (1854): *Voyages de la commission scientifique du nord en Scandinavie, en Laponie, au Spitzberg et aux Feroë pendant les années 1838, 1839 et 1840 sur la corvette La Recherche commandée par M. Paul Fabvre, publiés par ordre du roi sous la direction de M. Paul Gaimard. Histoire de la Scandinavie*. Paris: Arthus Bertrand.

Mequet, E. (1852): *Voyage en Islande et Groënland, exécuté pendant les années 1835 et 1836 sur la corvette 'La Recherche' [...]. Journal de voyage*. Paris: Arthus Bertrand.

Mercer, W. S. (ed.) (1992): Léonie d'Aunet, *Voyage d'une femme au Spitzberg*. Paris: Le Félin.

—— (1993): 'Léonie d'Aunet (1820-1879) in the shade of Victor Hugo: talent hidden by sex', in *Studi Francesi*, CIX, 31-46.

—— (1999): 'Gender and genre in nineteenth-century French travel writing: Xavier Marmier and Léonie d'Aunet', in *Travel Writing and Empire: Postcolonial Theory in Transit*, ed. Steve Clark. London and New York: Zed, 147-163.

Pageaux, D-H. (1980): 'Voyages aux sources du voyage au centre de la terre', in *Revue de littérature comparée*, LIV, 2, 202-12.

Sainte-Beuve, C. A. (1935-66): *Correspondance générale, recueillie, classée et annotée par Jean Bonnerot*, 15 vols. Paris: Stock.

Notes

1. For further information on the participants and organisation, see Marmier 1837:xiii and 1844-7, I:3; also Knutsen & Posti 2002a.
2. A number of the beautiful engravings of Norway and Spitzbergen have been reproduced in a modern edition (Knutsen & Posti 2002b).
3. Marmier writes Ollsen, but Thomas Munch-Petersen kindly informs me that 'Olsen' would be a more common spelling.
4. In previous publications (see Mercer 1993 and the introduction to my 1992 edition of the text), I have suggested the scope of d'Aunet's achievement and highlighted salient positive features of her text; I have further demonstrated that she was at a considerable disadvantage when travelling (in terms of age, social status, gender, lack of education etc.). Although these factors may to a certain extent explain her prejudices, they do not alter the specificity of the text (see Mercer 1999) nor the image that it would have projected in France of the Scandinavian countries.
5. Although I make the point (Mercer 1999:159) that such pronouncements probably to a certain extent reflect d'Aunet's own insecurities, she is writing, to use Mary Daly's term, as a 'fembot'.

Sabine Baring-Gould and Iceland: A Re-Evaluation.

Andrew Wawn

An Islands Man

Sabine Baring-Gould's credentials for inclusion in a volume of essays about Scandinavian travel and travel writers are not immediately obvious. Though he travelled with his parents over much of western and central Europe as a boy, and though he revisited many favourite haunts in later years, there is no evidence that he ever set foot in mainland Scandinavia. He certainly never wrote a travel book about Norway, Sweden or Denmark, whereas he wrote several such volumes about Germany and France. Moreover, though Baring-Gould's impressive private library, now preserved at Killerton House near Exeter, has copies of works such as Olaus Magnus's pioneering *Historia de gentibus septentrionalibus* (1555), and Samuel Laing's agenda-setting *Journal of a Residence in Norway during the Years 1834, 1835, 1836* (London, 1837; reading Laing 'gave me an incredible craving to know Icelandic and to travel to Scandinavia', Baring-Gould 1923:127), it is the Icelandic and Faroese items that feature more prominently, as if to confirm that Baring-Gould was at heart a north Atlantic islands rather than a mainlands man. As we shall see Baring-Gould certainly relished his brief stay in the Faroe Islands, but that rare glimpse of Tórshavn and Kirkjubøur was a bonus. Iceland was the main focus of the voyage, the only one he ever undertook in those waters. He went at a time when, again as his library confirms, travel to Iceland was beginning to enjoy significant popularity in Britain and beyond. Indeed it was in no small measure due to his *Iceland: Its Scenes and Sagas* (1863) that the cold coasts of Iceland became a place of pilgrimage for saga-reading Britons. Baring-Gould's book established him as one of Victorian England's most distinctive and influential commentators on life and literature at sixty-six degrees north. And the published volume tells only half the story. The present essay, drawing on previously unexamined and unpublished manuscripts, seeks to re-evaluate the significance of Baring-Gould's 1862 Icelandic travels and of his lifelong infatuation (Baring-Gould 1876:561; 1900:82-3; [1913]:146) with that island's culture.

The apparent paradox of an Icelandophile un- or under-engaged with Scandinavia is typical of the man. Sabine Baring-Gould's life was full of contradictions (general accounts of his life include Purcell 1957, Kirk-Smith 1998, Lister 2002; see also Baring-Gould 1923, 1925): the sickly child who lived to be ninety; the largely home-educated boy who became a public schoolmaster; the pious young clergyman who shocked his Yorkshire parishioners by marrying an uneducated mill girl half his age; the Anglo-Catholic zealot intrigued by ancient paganism; the law-abiding squarson who wrote enthusiastically about the outlawed saga hero Grettir Ásmundarson; the provincial English folklorist with international scholarly instincts; the prolific popularising philologist whose most important work (some sixteen accomplished translations of Old Icelandic sagas: Devon Record Office [hereafter DRO] 5203/M, Box 5) remains unpublished and unstudied; and, not least, the conventional Victorian traveller whose 1863 Iceland travelogue defies convention at every turn.

One constant element among the paradoxes of Baring-Gould's hectic life was his fascination with ancient and modern Iceland. He opened himself up to Iceland, projected himself onto it, and sought himself in it. A letter to his mother before he journeyed north (DRO 5203/M, Box 25a, undated [?1860]) identifies the very personal nature of his travelling agenda:

> I had found out some time ago that the Barings were descended from a Bæring the Beautiful, King of the Saxons, but I did not know his origins and had written to Iceland for the saga about him [....] Bæring was the son of the famous Ragnar Loðbrok and I have made out the pedigree from the Hervarar saga, Ragnar Loðbrok saga, Eyrbyggja saga and Laxdæla saga, up as far back as *Odin*!! And am in raptures to find that Iceland was first colonised by a family related to us [...] I really believe the Baring family to be one of the most antient in Europe [...] If I were to go to Iceland I should claim relationship with the descendants of those who settled there if I could find them.

That Baring-Gould's claims were based on moonshine matters not (the first editor of *Bærings saga* appears to refer to Baring-Gould's interest in the work and to his contacts with Jón Sigurðsson in Copenhagen: Cederschiöld: 1884, cxcii). His faith in their veracity clearly energised his Old Icelandic language learning, book collecting, saga reading and translating – and his immediate travel plans. Baring-Gould's northern odyssey was thus no mere day trip to the culture. The young Anglican priest was, in more than one sense, a man with a mission in 1862 and remained so for the rest of his long life.

Preliminary contexts: Eric, Thorkell and Sverrir

Three representative passages written at different stages during that life offer us a preliminary glimpse of the variety of contexts within which Baring-Gould's Icelandic thoughts developed. Firstly, we may consider the opening of his historical novel *Öraefadal: An Icelandic Tale* (1858-62; see also 1894), a medieval melodrama set at the cathedral school at Skálholt and in the volcanic wastes of Öræfasveit. The work, published serially in the magazine of Hurstpierpoint School, tells of the torrid rite of passage of Eric, a Skálholt student torn between the Christian values of his education and the Viking-Age vengeance culture of his family. He struggles to resolve the conflict between love for Ingebjorg, daughter of the worthy Gregorius, and loyalty to Gudruda, his fiery pagan mother. Gudruda had mistakenly interpreted Gregorius's possession of her husband Gunnar's ancestral sword (a creation of Völundr the smith) as evidence of murder, rather than (as was the case) of a chance find, after Gunnar had been devoured by predatory wolves. The story ends bleakly for Gudruda, but more hopefully for the wounded young hero, thanks to the ministrations of a gifted physician attached to the Kirkjubær community. Eric's future (importantly for the pious Baring-Gould) lay in communion with the Catholic church.

Some of this Gothic gloom is anticipated in the tale's atmospheric opening paragraph:

> A cold night in Norway; the moon had just been clouded over by piles of grey mist, which rolled through the sky, sending out arms of vapour; and she, haggard and ghastly, seemed to steel over her course, swathed in corpse-clothes. Now and then, some crags caught a straggling gleam and flashed forth, but directly after were again blotted out; while, far below, a frozen fiord was shining like steel, till the shadow turned it to lead. An uncertain light flickered down the mountain side over the pine forests, which raved and bent, as the wind poured through them (Baring-Gould 1858-62, 1/1 May 1858:6)

This is among Baring-Gould's earliest literary responses to the old north. The only earlier ones known to me are a novelistic expansion of the first two chapters of *Kristni saga*, which tell of the conversion of Iceland (Baring-Gould 1856; 1863:157-8), and an 1857 ballad about Völundr, the legendary smith (DRO 5203/M, Box 8), which was soon incorporated into the *Öraefadal* tale, where it is performed at a Kirkjubær *kvöldvaka* (Baring-Gould 1894:177-80). These two early works also begin in the bleak midwinter, with eerie moonlight, swaying woods, and 'raving' storms. Thus, though *Öraefadal* was a pioneering narrative in its day, the first historical novel in English to be set exclusively in Viking-Age Norway and Iceland, the formulaic *sturm und drang* atmospherics of its opening recall the default stylistic mode of several late-eighteenth-century British poets who sought to depict old northern myth and legend (Clunies Ross 1998). The opening paragraph of *Öraefadal* also reveals that Baring-Gould's Viking-Age vision was pointing from Norway towards Iceland, as the reader follows the fortunes of a volatile Norwegian emigré community in the new colony. This same transition from mainland to island came to be reflected in mid-nineteenth-century north Atlantic travel and travelogues, as Frederick Metcalfe, for example, the eponymous hero of *The Oxonian in Norway* (1856), soon became *The Oxonian in Iceland* (1861). Baring-Gould's *Iceland: Its Scenes and Sagas* played a major role in this re-location of many old northernists' interests.

The second representative Baring-Gould passage derives from 'Thorkell-Mani' (1896), a poem that voices a conversion theme in a semi-balladic mode. Its origins can be traced to the brief *Landnámabók* reference in which Þorkell máni Þorsteinsson, a dying pagan law-speaker, asks to be carried out into the sunshine, there to commit himself into the care of 'þeim guði, er sólina hafði skapat' (that God who had created the sun) (Jakob Benediktsson 1968:46). Baring-Gould's poem is an Icelandophile Victorian clergyman's gloss on the scene. Just as Matthew Arnold's dead Balder had no wish to return to life in Valhöll, so Thorkell finds the prospect of endless war-games and relentless jollity in that same stronghold of the gods deeply unappealing. He is content to make a righteous pagan's more peaceful proto-Christian end:

> I am dying, O my children! Come around my bed.
> My feet are cold as ashes, heavy is my head;
> You see me powerless lying – – – I, who was of old
> The scourge of evil-doers, Thorkell, stout and bold.
> I cannot mount my war-horse, now I cannot wield
> My great blue sword there hanging, rusting by my shield.
> But He the sun who fashioned in the skies above,
> And who the moon suspended, surely must be love;
> Now therefore, O my children, do this thing I ask,
> Transport me through the doorway in the sun to bask.
> Upon that bright globe gliding through the deep blue sky
> Gazing – thus, and only thus, in comfort can I die.
> For chambered here in darkness on my doubts I brood,
> But in the mellow sunlight I feel that God is good.
> A God to mortals tender, the very Fount of light –
> Not Odin, whose whole glory is to booze and fight. (Wright 1896:28)

Baring-Gould was clearly impressed by Thorkell's death-bed decision to reach out to the Christian god whose message was just reaching Iceland at the end of the tenth century. On his return to England from Iceland he himself was soon labouring mightily, like some latter-day Þangbrandr, in missionary work among the sometimes godless mining communities around Wakefield in south Yorkshire, where in 1864, he became parish priest. Unsurprisingly, he was attracted to other tales of righteous Viking pagans converting to Christianity – notably *Vatnsdœla saga*. He painstakingly translated the whole of this work from the 1860 Leipzig edition of Guðbrandur Vigfússon and Theodor Möbius (DRO 5203/M, Box 25a), and introduced English readers to that saga's finest scene by including a translation in his *Iceland* volume (Baring-Gould 1863:138-47).

Indeed *Vatnsdœla saga* offers several verbal echoes of Thorkell's 'He the sun who fashioned in the skies above' line cited above (Einar Ól. Sveinsson 1939:97, 125). No wonder that Baring-Gould, while in Iceland, had made a point of journeying far from such beaten tourist tracks as there were in order to explore Vatnsdalur in the distant north: 'I started with my guide and an extra hour, leaving the others to fish [...] I could not wait for them and there are several things I want to see in Vatnsdal [...] [notably] an old fort which in times of yore was erected by a man-sacrificer and which was stormed and taken by some of the chieftains of Vatnsdal' (DRO 5203/M, Box 25a, letter from Grímstunga, 27 June 1862; see *Vatnsdœla saga*, ch. 30). Thereafter Baring-Gould often drew on the saga in his writings about English folklore (as in Baring-Gould 1865:29, 41-2, 50; Henderson 1879:61). With its witches, wizards and waifs, and its spells, spooks and soothsayers, the saga proved to be an inexhaustible bran-tub of lore and legend for him. Its dramatisation of the clash across several generations between exotic but destructive sorcery and (first) righteous paganism and (later) muscular Christianity ideally fitted the eye of the Anglo-Catholic clergyman who inspired his own flock at Horbury Brig by marching them up the hill to the Whitsun service in 1865, carrying the Cross, and singing the hymn that he had composed specially for the occasion: 'Onward Christian soldiers, / Marching as to war, / With the Cross of Jesus, / Going on before'.

To the *Öraefadal* paragraph and the 'Thorkell-mani' poem, we may add a brief passage written in the last year of his life, relating not to Iceland, but to the Faroese childhood of King Sverrir of Norway. In the first of two volumes of lightly-urged reminiscence, Baring-Gould recalls visiting the site of Sverrir's home at Kirkjubøur. It may have been sixty-one years since he had trekked over the hills from Tórshavn to visit that tiny hamlet ('as like Dartmoor as possible, the same brawling brooks, plunging harum scarum over piles of rock and diving among bogs of vivid green moss': DRO 5203/M, Box 25a, Vestmannaeyjar, Trinity Sunday 1862, to his mother), but the memories remained vivid and lyrical:

> On Stromsoe, near the southern point, is a terrace little raised above the high-tide level, frowned down upon by belted crags, red and black striped; here are the ruins of a cathedral, that was never more than a shabby little parish church in size and structure, and beside it a small farm. The low walls and roof never enclosed any crowd, for there were no neighbours [...] the only song of white-robed choristers ever heard there was the scream of the gulls, and the only organ-note the piping of the wind. (Baring-Gould 1923:308)

This was the small farm of the bishop, whose chaplain's brother had married a young woman called Gunnhildr – and Sverrir, the future King of Norway, was their son.

Baring-Gould remembered the haunts of Sverrir the boy, and drew inspiration from the values of Sverrir the man. He celebrated the twelfth-century hero, who, from Baring-Gould's unyielding perspective, had defied an imperious Pope (Innocent III), and thereby maintained the independence of the early Norwegian church. These images had a powerful resonance for Baring-Gould, who held fast to the values of the true Ecclesia Anglicana, and scorned the threats and decrees of manipulative (as he viewed them) modern popes such as Pius IX. Sverrir, like Þorkell máni, was a medieval hero with a modern meaning for Baring-Gould's life and Christian witness (Baring-Gould 1923:309-13).

Judging a Book by its Cover

Three literary moments, then: each based on medieval images or texts; each linked to a specific north Atlantic location visited by Baring-Gould in the summer of 1862; each reflecting an aspect of his devotional, intellectual or political sensibility; and each casting light on cultural boundaries and continuities that constantly engaged him – between paganism and Christianity, medieval and modern, oral legend and written saga, Iceland and England. It was Baring-Gould's awareness of such continuities that may help to explain why, when writing about Iceland, he continually challenged the traditional generic boundaries of the travel book in order to give the fullest expression to his wide-ranging vision. For him wildlife observation could end up as philosophical reflection; folklore could dissolve into theology; landscape could trigger saga translation. In this way Baring-Gould signals that every moment and memory has its place within the 'one stupendous whole' of Iceland, as created by God. The first hymn that the present writer ever learnt at Sunday School, half a century and more ago, began: 'God who made the earth, / The air, the sky, the sea, / Who gave each life its birth, / Careth for me'. The author and promoter of such an inclusive vision was, unsurprisingly, Sabine Baring-Gould.

This distinctively broad agenda informs the whole of *Iceland: Its Scenes and Sagas*. Indeed we need only examine the volume's front cover and title-page to see how Baring-Gould was redefining the nature of Iceland travel writing. To begin with the runic lettering on the cover. This was no empty designer-chic gesture by the publisher, but rather a proud display of the author's effortfully-acquired runic knowledge. In transcribed form the inscription reads *skrifuð (a)f sabini barinki koult isl(e?)ntinka sk(e?)nur ok sokur*, 'written by Sabine Baring-Gould of the Icelanders scenes and sagas' (I am grateful to Professor Judith Jesch of Nottingham University for help in reading the runes). It did not matter that few if any of Baring-Gould's readers would have understood or appreciated his efforts. In the runic representation of Baring-Gould's name we may read a coded celebration of his family's putative old northern origins, as well as a statement of the volume's ambitious production values.

The title-page itself offers other indications of the changing face of nineteenth-century old northernism. Firstly, the page features a Shakespearean quotation – 'Farewell heat, and welcome frost', from *The Merchant of Venice* (2.ii.75). A century earlier the title-page of *Five Pieces of Runic Poetry* (1763) saw fit to cite lines from Lucan's *De bello civili*, celebrating the barbarian northern warriors' eager embrace of death in battle (Clunies Ross 2001:20-1). Baring-Gould clearly no longer felt the need reverentially to touch any traditional Graeco-Roman cultural base. Encouraged by the liberating insights of early nineteenth-century German philology (Boesche 2002, Shippey 2005), the texts and bardic figures of other vernaculars could now provide title-page filigree for old northern volumes. Secondly, Baring-Gould dedicates the volume to his uncle, Major-General Edward Sabine, President of the Royal Society. This recalls a bygone Enlightenment Age when expeditions to Iceland had invariably been driven by natural science, notably geology. While Baring-Gould did not turn his back on such perspectives (see DRO 5203/M, Box 25a, 19 November 1862, to his brother Willy, theorising about Geysir, based on his own miniature working model!), by the time of the publication of *Iceland: Its Scenes and Sagas* the newer disciplines of philology, folklore, and ethnology had earned the right to a voice in the volume. Indeed, Baring-Gould's title seems to represent at least a partial rejection of the priorities signalled by the title of Captain Charles Forbes' newly published *Iceland: Its Volcanoes, Geysers and Glaciers* (1860).

Thirdly, the title-page verso quotes four lines by a modern Icelandic poet (Jónas Hallgrímsson, 1807-45), who, though he had already achieved iconic status among many of his fellow-countrymen, was virtually unknown in Britain. Carefully quoted and translated by Baring-Gould, the lines provided Victorian readers with their first glimpse of Jónas's poetry:

Ísland, far-sœldar frón,
Ok hag-sœldar hrím-hvíta móðir!
Hvar er þín fornaldar frœgð,
Frelsið ok manndáðin bezt'?

(Iceland, thou fare-blessed spot,
Thou use-blessed rime-whitened mother!
Where are thine olden fame,
And freedom, and manliness best?) (Baring-Gould 1863:vi)

Even the relatively literal style of translation adopted for these now famous lines from 'Ísland' (1835) tells its own tale. In retaining the compound adjectives and nouns of the original, and following the inverted word order at the end of the fourth line, the style seems to signal the translator's delight at the capacity of the all-conquering English language to embrace its neighbouring north-Atlantic tongue and afford it crisply equivalent expression. It also suggests that he regards such compatibility as indicative of deeper links between the two communities and cultures, a perception which, as we have noted, helped to motivate Baring-Gould's Iceland travels in the first place.

We might add that the actual meaning of the quotation (and of the poem that it introduces) will have seemed particularly congenial to Baring-Gould. The four-stage thematic structure of Jónas's 'Ísland' is clear – Viking-Age Iceland was a place of beauty; its early settlers were energetic and creative; modern Iceland retains its medieval beauty; but the land's heroic inheritance has been squandered, leading the poet to ponder the future anxiously. That fear of a more general cultural decay – of what the great Icelandicist George Webbe Dasent, who met Baring-Gould during his own 1862 Iceland travels (Baring-Gould 1923:263), called 'melancholy presentiments of dissolution' (Dasent 1903:lxxi) – was very Baring-Gouldian. It finds expression in his novels (Baring-Gould 1894:107), sermons, folkloristic writings, and even in press interviews, in which he can often be found lamenting the disappearance of the rich oral traditions of rural Britain (as in Baring-Gould 1895). Such anxieties served to keep Baring-Gould close to his church, his faith, his missionary work – and, not least, to his local folklore data collecting, as he attempted to hold the cultural line in an unstable world.

Lastly, the title-page reveals that Baring-Gould was a Fellow of St Nicholas College, Lancing, in Sussex, having also taught at the neighbouring Hurstpierpoint College, where his *Öraefadal* tale was first published in the school magazine, as was his re-telling of *Hrafnkels saga* (*Hurst Johnian* V, 1862). The cloistered calm of these institutions suited Baring-Gould's pious sensibility, and the school's undemanding pedagogical regime (Edwards 1914:31-2) afforded him ample opportunity to learn the Icelandic language, read the sagas, and plan his travels. That same pious sensibility governed the selection of material for his travelogue. At a time of hectic non-conformist evangelical activity in England, modern berserkerism in Baring-Gould's view, he was always on the lookout for reassuring evidence of High Church observance wherever he went: his *Iceland* book is full of Pevsner-like detail about ecclesiastical architecture, vestments, furnishings, music, and missionary activity (as with Baring Gould 1863:158-9, 158-60, 172, 235-40, 291-6).

As we shall see, these various title-page resonances and agendas inevitably find fuller expression in the main body of the *Iceland* text. We might signpost three of them in advance. Firstly, the spirit of Baring-Gould the missionary can be sensed in at least one of the saga scenes he selects for translation. The death of Ingimundr episode in *Vatnsdæla saga* (chs 22-26) dramatises both the external conflict between the godly and the godless within the turbulent communities of Settlement-Age Iceland, and the internal battles between good and evil within the hearts of even the most virtuous settlers. Secondly, we see Baring-Gould the folklorist recording Icelandic customs and superstitions, and then associating them with the equivalent elements in the regions of England in which he had lived, and in the countries of Europe through which he had travelled. He believed that such traditions were often the residuum of a long-lost old northern paganism: they were 'the apples of Sodom, fair cheeked, but containing the dust and ashes of heathenism' (Baring-Gould 1876:318). By explaining them as such Baring-Gould sought to promote the cause of Anglo-Catholic revival by divesting the true faith of its unsustainable superstitions and extravagant supernaturalism, re-assigning such elements to their pagan origins, and to challenge popular Wesleyan practices, which, he believed, were themselves responsible for recycling long-forgotten features of old northern paganism. And, thirdly, the *Iceland* volume reveals the dialect enthusiast at work. Parallels between English and Icelandic local usage recorded from oral sources on his travels were explained in ways that we might describe as a kind of popular Grimmianism. Baring-Gould is keen to show how the newly revealed patterns of Indo-European linguistic development could explain the Icelandic terms for features of natural landscape and supernatural tradition (Baring-Gould 1863:148-9: discussion of 'Old Nick').

'Making a Book'

The missionary, the folklorist, the dialectician: this interdependent triple perspective consistently informed Baring-Gould's vision of Iceland, and thus provided *Iceland: Its Scenes and Sagas* with a significant competitive advantage in an Iceland travel book market that had suddenly become very crowded around 1860. Rival volumes included Lord Dufferin's *Letters from High Latitudes* (1857), A. J. Symington's *Pen and Pencil Sketches of Faroe and Iceland* (1862), along with the works by Forbes (1860) and Metcalfe (1861) already mentioned. Baring-Gould sent a copy of the latter volume to his mother, noting that while it would give her 'a fair notion of the island', it was 'disfigured with much coarseness of writing and attempted wit which is simply vulgar' (DRO 5203/M, Box 25a, Hurstpierpoint, 23 May 1862). In this competitive atmosphere Baring-Gould needed to identify a gap in the market:

> My chances of making a book are rather diminished as I find that Dr Dasent, the well-known Icelandic scholar, was out there last year and is going again this year, and is at work on a volume of his travels.

His fall-back strategy was an enterprising one:

> If no publisher will take my travels I shall get one to take a series of tales from the sagas, not servile translations, but worked up with descriptions of the scenery and locale, and with sketches.

Either way, Baring-Gould's 'pitch' to the publishers was that his volume would offer undiluted Iceland – none of the Spitzbergen, Jan Mayen Islands, and Norwegian interludes favoured by his competitors. In the event, Dasent (exasperatingly) never produced the anticipated travel book, leaving Baring-Gould free to show his paces. He wrote about the north of the island while others focused mainly on the south-west; he understood (some) modern Icelandic, while his rivals just shouted louder in English; he included the first colour pictures in any Iceland travel book since Sir George Mackenzie's *Travels in the Island of Iceland* (1811), and his black and white illustrations are more numerous and revealing than those in earlier volumes. And, finally, as we have noted, he included translations of saga scenes – and published others subsequently in periodicals ('Hrolfe Krake', *Once A Week*, 14 May 1864:585-8; 'Thorgunna's Ghost' [from *Eyrbyggja saga*], *ibid.*, 19 January 1867:74-8). Moreover, complementing the book's innovative spirit were Baring-Gould's personal contacts with influential Icelanders, as exemplified by his frequent use of a letter of introduction from Oddur Hjaltalín, a prominent physician (DRO 5203/M, Box 25a, Grímstunga, 29 June, to his mother, is written over Oddur's original letter), and his association with Sveinn Skúlason (Baring-Gould 1863:180), a cosmopolitan local journalist, publisher and politician, who had escorted the great German scholar Konrad Maurer in 1858 (Baldur Hafstað 1997:143-6).

No wonder that Baring-Gould, anticipating the spirit of Sir Richard Burton's *Ultima Thule; or, a Summer in Iceland* (1875), occasionally directs gentle disdain towards those rivals whose published responses to Iceland too often sounded too awed about too little. Travel to Greece and Italy had long been regarded as a kind of serious cultural performance for English folk of a certain age and status, as participants searched anxiously for the fugitive essence of each celebrated natural marvel and sculpted antiquity (Buzard 1993:10). Baring-Gould helped to educate the gaze of those drawn to the alternative, more northerly Grand Tour. He redefined the essence of Iceland for the Britons who followed in his wake.

Saga, Legend and Lava

We can examine key aspects of that essence via three moments from the 1862 *Iceland* volume: about a saga, a legend, and a lava field. To take first the chapters Baring-Gould translated from *Vatnsdæla saga*. These include the greatest scene in the saga, and one of the finest narratives in the entire *Íslendingasögur* corpus. The saga, a manuscript copy of which Baring-Gould had purchased in Akureyri from a weeping farmer 'reduced to great poverty' (Baring-Gould 1863:225; BL Add. MS 24972), tells of the birth, development, and manifest destiny of a pioneering community in Vatnsdalur – of the innate nobility of its heroes and the acrid hostility of its villains. Overall the saga dramatises the process whereby a righteous pagan community prepares its soul for conversion. In the translated *Vatnsdæla saga* scene the sons of the valley's venerable patriarch Ingimundr clash over local fishing rights with Hrolleifr, malevolent son of the malign witch Gróa. Ingimundr makes his way to the river, as ever in the role of peace-maker, but is mortally wounded by the sour-spirited Hrolleifr. After unobtrusively journeying home, Ingimundr asks to be set in his high-seat, and for the lights to be extinguished. Eventually realising that their father has left the scene of the fight, the sons set off anxiously in search of him. In the dark of the homestead, the eldest son, Þorsteinn, stumbles and feels a dampness on the floor. When the lights are kindled, this proves to be the blood of his father, who sits, dignified and dead, in his high-seat.

Baring-Gould prefaces the translation section (1863:138-47) with a striking print of the valley, dominated in the foreground by a well-appointed modern farmstead, its Danish flag fluttering briskly in the breeze, with smartly dressed figures standing outside, and the river in the middle distance. As for the translation itself we may recall Baring-Gould's claim that the treatment of any saga scenes included in *Iceland: Its Scenes and Sagas* would not be 'servile'. The DRO Baring-Gould archive affords us the opportunity to assess the relative levels of servility in two versions of his *Vatnsdæla* translation – that prepared for the *Iceland* volume, and its unpublished original. First, the relatively literal manuscript version:

> The boy came to the river and saw a fine salmon which Hrolleif had caught. Said the youth – 'On my word you are the greatest hound of a man! You have done that for which no mulct will be demanded, in giving Ingimund the bonder his death: he bade me tell you not to bide at home tomorrow morning, for he reckoned that his sons would be on the look out to avenge their father. Now I have brought you this message from his command and not because I should regret to see you under the axes of the brothers'. (DRO 5203/M, Box 25a)

And now the published translation:

> The boy ran to the river, and saw Hrolleifr draw out a fine salmon, which he had just caught.
> 'Dog of a fellow!' shouted the exasperated boy. 'You have done a deed for which no mulct will be asked. Now, reluctantly, I bring you a message from the dying lips of him whom you have slain. Fly at once, before the brothers are after you; yet, on my honour, I long to see their axes rattling about your skull.' (Baring-Gould 1863:142)

The additional colour in the latter version is immediately obvious: '*kom* til árinnar' becomes '*ran* to the river'; *mælti*, 'said', is intensified into 'shouted', while the boy is now 'exasperated'; the cool 'he bade me tell you' re-emerges as the more emotive 'I bring a message from the dying lips of him whom you have slain'; the measured tread of 'he reckoned that his sons would be on the look out to avenge their father' dissolves into the racier 'Fly at once, before the brothers are after you'; and the more laconic 'nor should I regret to see you under the axes' is winched up into 'I long to see their axes rattling about your skull'. Baring-Gould's unpublished version is fastidiously cautious, whereas the published one is daringly dramatic, with its arresting camera angles and microphone positions. There were few nineteenth-century British Icelandicists with the philological fleetness of foot successfully to have shifted registers in this way. The translator's desire to engage the sympathies of a potentially inexperienced readership is obvious. And, moreover, unlike George Dasent, William Morris and other celebrated saga translators, Baring-Gould appears to have worked without the assistance of learned Icelanders.

After the saga, the legend. Baring-Gould learns from an oral source of the local Icelandic belief that Óðinn rides on horseback at night with his hell-hounds, blowing his horn and raising mayhem, followed by assorted spirits and the souls of unbaptised children (Baring-Gould 1863:199-204). In a much-quoted discussion (as in Henderson 1879:132-6) Baring-Gould sets this wisp of legend in a broader context, by linking it with similar legends in England (notably Yorkshire and Devonshire) and Western Europe (Schlesvig, Norway, Sweden, Normandy, Netherlands, regions of Germany, and France). He then offers his readers a Jacob Grimm-derived philological explanation of the phenomenon, nuanced by current mythological theory. He claims that the legend had arisen out of attempts by early Indo-European man to describe storms. The sequence was as follows: the Old Norse verb *vaða*, 'to storm/rush', had an irregular preterite singular form *óð*; the primitive mind personified the force of the rushing wind as a deity, to which they gave the name Óðinn, derived from the verb. The Indo-European tribes eventually migrated, along with the legend; this, in time, attracted additional elements, as when, in Christian lands, Óðinn's wild followers were interpreted as unbaptised souls howling in agony (see also Baring-Gould 1876:27; 1900:232; 1904:44-5).

Baring-Gould relished the fact that his basic knowledge of spoken Icelandic had afforded him a measure of direct access to oral lore of this kind; and also that his familiarity with nineteenth-century German mythological scholarship meant that, unlike the hapless Edward Casaubon in *Middlemarch* (Nuttall 2003:26-71), he had an up-to-date intellectual framework into which he could fit such narratives. Baring-Gould had spent lengthy periods in Germany in his youth, and had developed, while at school in Mannheim in the early 1840s, a taste for old northern myth and for modern German theories concerning its development (Baring-Gould 1923:83). In turn, he lost no opportunity to pass on to his many readers this new hierarchy of learning, which embraced orality as well as literacy, Gervase of Tilbury as well as Cicero, the rural as well as the urban, the popular as well as the scholastic.

And, lastly, the lava; our third and final glimpse of Baring-Gould's redefined Icelandic essence takes us from saga and legend to landscape. Visiting a Catholic mission in Iceland he is told by the Abbé that 'there is the magnificence of Satan imprinted deep in the face of this land' (Baring-Gould 1863:42). Though some of the plates in the book seem almost to confirm this, as with the craggy features of Hörgárdalur (Plate 11, opposite p.228), for Baring-Gould it was too naive a notion. For him, landscape was like language and legend – each had developed according to principles identified by nineteenth-century theorists, and each had undergone definable processes of formation and fragmentation, reduction and reformation. Nowhere was this more true than in Iceland. Baring-Gould's travels there had confirmed to him that in every lava flow the processes of God's Creation were being replayed on a daily basis:

> Everywhere one sees [...] jaws which have gnashed together till they have ground their teeth to powder; horns, spikes, shavings, polygons of inky rock, slivered, ripped, spurned aside, welted and crushed, as the fiery mass [...] has mangled itself in its writhing. See! The work of regeneration and restoration has

begun. On yon tilted block, one tremulous saxifrage has taken root, and lifts its white face to God and man; the forerunner of other plants, which are to subdue and reduce to powder this iron rock, to fill its grizzly hollows, and make the rough places plain. The rains will honeycomb its shoulders, the frosts chip off its angles, the winds fret its sides; the birds will bring seeds to it, plants will spring up and dissolve its tissues, willow will take root in its crannies, birch plant itself and shed leaves into its crevices, and the wilderness becomes a fruitful field. (Baring-Gould 1863:207-8)

The manner of this testimony is part of its meaning: the soaring lyricism, the darting imagery, the telling blend of syntactic energy and control. It is as if Baring-Gould himself, like one of the pre-historic Indo-European tribes that fascinated comparative mythologists of his day, has observed nature with such a passionate immediacy that it has come alive as a kind of pious metaphor. Here is that 'magnificence of Satan' overwhelmed by the forces of God's creation. Here is the message of *Vatnsdæla saga* – and of the Horbury Brig Mission – distilled in a geological metonymy.

'Not a great author'

How, then, may we sum up Sabine Baring-Gould's traveller's vision of mid-nineteenth-century Iceland? One obituarist claimed that his life was of interest primarily by virtue of his having lived so long and written so much, but that ultimately '[he was] not a great author or a great scholar' (anonymous, Leeds University Brotherton Library MS M298, f. 17). This seems too dismissive a judgement; it is challenged by the annotated volumes in his impressive library, by his unpublished saga translations, by much of his published work, and by the evidence of the DRO Baring-Gould holdings. It would be fairer to say that he was an energetic, versatile and outward-looking philologist, ever eager via journalism, editing, novel writing, and lecturing (Lister 2002:33; DRO 5203/M, Box 25a, 25 October 1866, letter to his mother), to promote the insights of continental linguistic and mythological learning within the shires of Middle England. These were the instincts that made Sabine Baring-Gould the best-informed, most ambitious and most innovative Victorian English traveller in and champion of Iceland.

A final thought. Baring-Gould included in his Iceland travelogue detailed accounts of his expedition expenditures. Oscar Wilde was later to remind us that a cynic is someone who knows the price of everything and the value of nothing. *Iceland: Its Scenes and Sagas* reveals on every page that Baring-Gould knew the value of Iceland; and Appendix E (Baring-Gould 1863:445-7) confirms that he also knew its price – £100-16s-8d for the entire trip.

Bibliography

Manuscript Sources:

BL [British Library] Add. MS 24969, 24972
Devon Record Office [DRO] 5203/M
University of Leeds, Brotherton Library, MS M298.
Killerton House, Exeter, Devon. Baring-Gould library.

Printed Sources:

Anon. (1895): 'The Rev. S. Baring Gould at home', *Sunday Magazine* 24, 11-15.
Baring-Gould, Sabine (1856): 'The Rock of Thor (A.D. 981)', *The Churchman's Companion* 19, 285-94.
—— (1858-62): 'Öraefadal: An Icelandic Tale', *The Hurst Johnian* I 6-12, 36-44, 67-82 etc.
—— (1863): *Iceland: Its Scenes and Sagas*. London.
—— (1876): *Curious Myths of the Middle Ages*. Revised edition. London.
—— (1890): *Grettir the Outlaw: a Story of Iceland*. London.
—— (1892): *Strange Survivals*. London.
—— (1894): *The Icelander's Sword; or, The Story of Oraefadal*. London.
—— (1900): *A Book of Dartmoor*. London.
—— (1904): *Siegfried: A Romance*. London.
—— ([1913]): *A Book of Folk-Lore*. London.
—— (1923): *Early Reminiscences, 1834-1864*. London.
—— (1925): *Further Reminiscences, 1864-1894*. London.
Benediktsson, Jakob (ed. 1968): *Íslendingabók, Landnámabók*. Íslenzk fornrit 1. Reykjavík.
Bosche, Laurens P. van den (2002): *Freidrich Max Müller: A Life Devoted to the Humanities*. Leiden.
Burton, Sir Richard F. (1875): *Ultima Thule; or, A Summer in Iceland*. 2 vols. London and Edinburgh.
Buzard, James (1993): *The Beaten Track: European Tourism, Literature and the Ways to Culture, 1800-1918*. Oxford.
Cederschiöld, Gustav, (ed. 1884): *Fornsögur Suðrlanda*. Lund.
Clunies Ross, Margaret (1998): *The Norse Muse in Britain, 1750-1820*. Trieste.
—— (ed. 2001): *The Old Norse Poetic Translations of Thomas Percy: A New Edition and Commentary*. Turnhout.
Dasent, George Webbe (trans. 1903): *Popular Tales from the Norse*. Revised edition. Edinburgh.
Edwards, Rev. D. (1914): *Reminiscences*. London.
Forbes, Charles S. (1860): *Iceland: Its Volcanoes, Geysers, and Glaciers*. London.
Hafstað, Baldur (trans. 1997): *Konrad Maurer, Íslandsferð 1858*. Reykjavík.
Henderson, William (1879): *Notes on the Folk-Lore of the Northern Counties of England and the Borders*. London.
Kirk-Smith, Howard (1998): *Now the Day is Over: The Life and Times of Sabine Baring-Gould*. Boston, Lincs.
Lister, Keith (2002): *'Half my Life': The Story of Sabine Baring-Gould and Grace*. Wakefield.
Mackenzie, George S. (1811): *Travels in the Island of Iceland in the Summer of the Year MDCCCX*. Edinburgh.
Metcalfe, Frederick (1856): *The Oxonian in Norway*. 2 vols. London.
—— (1861): *The Oxonian in Iceland*. London.
Nuttall, A. D. (2003): *Dead from the Waist Down: Scholars and Scholarship in Literature and*

the Popular Imagination. New Haven and London.

Purcell, William (1957): *Onward Christian Soldier: A Life of Sabine Baring-Gould, Parson, Squire, Novelist, Antiquarian, 1834-1924*. London.

Shippey, Tom (2005): 'A Revolution Reconsidered: Mythography and Mythology in the Nineteenth Century', pp. 1-28, in Tom Shippey (ed.), *The Shadow Walkers: Jacob Grimm's Mythology of the Monstrous*. Tempe, Arizona.

Sveinsson, Einar Ólafur (ed. 1939): *Vatnsdœla saga, Hallfreðar saga, Kormáks saga*. Íslenzk fornrit 8. Reykjavík.

Wawn, Andrew (2000): *The Vikings and the Victorians*. Cambridge.

Wright, W. H. K. (ed. 1896): *West-Country Poets: Their Lives and Works*. London.

Environmental Images of Nineteenth-Century Iceland from Official Letters (*Bréf Sýslumanna og Amtmanna*).

Astrid E. J. Ogilvie

Introduction: The Origin of the Letters

Immediately after New Year, the inconstant and changeable weather which had prevailed for the last 2 months of the previous year was supplanted by a quite severe frost, partly caused by strong northeasterly storms and heavy snowfalls. This weather lasted, not just to the end of the month (January) but continued almost unchanged for the next 2 months, February and March. Although the wind occasionally changed to a southerly or southwesterly direction, this did not last for more than 1 to 2 days at a time before it began to blow again from the north with increased strength. Both the frost and the snow were much more severe than they usually are, even at this time of year. However, it was the snow that was much more than usual as in most places the ground was covered by such amounts of snow that all transport by horse was impossible and even people on foot had difficulty. Communication by sea also ceased completely on account of the ice which filled up all bays and fjords. As a consequence, for all this time, all livestock needed to be kept in and given fodder, as not even horses were able to seek their food outside... (Letter from District Governor, Bergur Ólafsson Thorberg, dated 31 August 1866, Stykkishólmur, Snæfellsnessýsla.)[1]

It was in the nineteenth century that the medieval literature of Iceland, in particular the *Sagas of Icelanders*, really began to be 'discovered' by the outside world. At the same time, travellers to Iceland, who had started to visit the island in the eighteenth century, began to increase in numbers. While many nineteenth-century travel and other writings concerning Iceland were published and enjoyed by a relatively large audience, certain other, detailed, descriptive writings exist which have been seen by very few. These include official letters that were written from all of the districts or counties in Iceland to the Governor and District or Deputy Governor of Iceland. These letters, or reports, were written annually from the early 1700s and the practice was continued to the end of the nineteenth century. The officials responsible for the reports were called *Sýslumenn* (plural) or, in the singular form

Sýslumaður. (*Menn* meaning, of course, 'men', and *maður*, 'man'.) The term *Sýsla* was originally used in both Norway and Denmark to mean 'work', 'business' or 'activity'. It also came to refer to an official of the government; in particular, one who 'does the work or business of the king' and was used as early as the tenth century (Benediktsson 1884:1-2). It has been suggested that the term *Sýslumaður* arose out of the practice of kings to send trusted men to carry out a task or mission (*sýsla*), especially in outlying regions (Lehmann 1888). It subsequently came to mean a jurisdictional area; an example is 'Vendsyssel' in Denmark. In Norway, the term is no longer used except in regard to just one official, the *Sysselman*, on Spitsbergen. The word more commonly used in Norway for the same kind of official is *Lensmann*. In Iceland, however, the term is still contained in the names of all the jurisdictional counties or *Sýslur* in the country (see *Figure 1*) as well as for present-day officials.

The origin of the term *Sýsla* as it was used on Iceland may be traced back primarily to the events of the years 1262-64 when Iceland became part of the Norwegian kingdom. Subsequently, according to the late-thirteenth century Icelandic code of laws, commonly called *Jónsbók*,[2] Iceland was divided into 12 jurisdictional regions. These were known literally as 'things'; the Icelandic word is *þing*, often translated as an 'assembly' or 'meeting' and referring both to the event and the place where it occurred. The word *Sýsla* is to be found in *Jónsbók* (33, 325) in the meaning of an administrative region, but was not generally used in this way until the middle of the sixteenth century when the administrative system was reorganized after the Reformation (Þorsteinsson 1972). Thus, around this time, the name of the districts changed from *þing* to *sýsla* and the man who represented the king in a certain jurisdictional region came to be known as a *sýslumaður* (Þórarinsson 1994). The title *sýslumaður* is also to be found in Jónsbók (Laxness 1995:84).

The Kalmar Union, effected in 1397, united Norway with Denmark and Sweden. At that time, Iceland, Greenland and the Faroes were still regarded politically as part of Norway. In 1523 the Union came to an end, but some elements remained until 1536 when the Danish privy council unilaterally declared Norway to be a Danish province. Although Norway kept some separate institutions, Iceland, Greenland and the Faroes came directly under the Danish crown. Although it was only in 1814, with the Treaty of Kiel, that Iceland became formally subject to the Danish crown, in practice, Danish administration was directly imposed on Iceland in 1662 with the initiation of the Danish absolute monarchy. At that time, for administrative purposes, the Danish kingdom became divided into separate districts, each called an *Amt*. Iceland in entirety was considered to be one 'Amt'. The 'Amt' was to have a

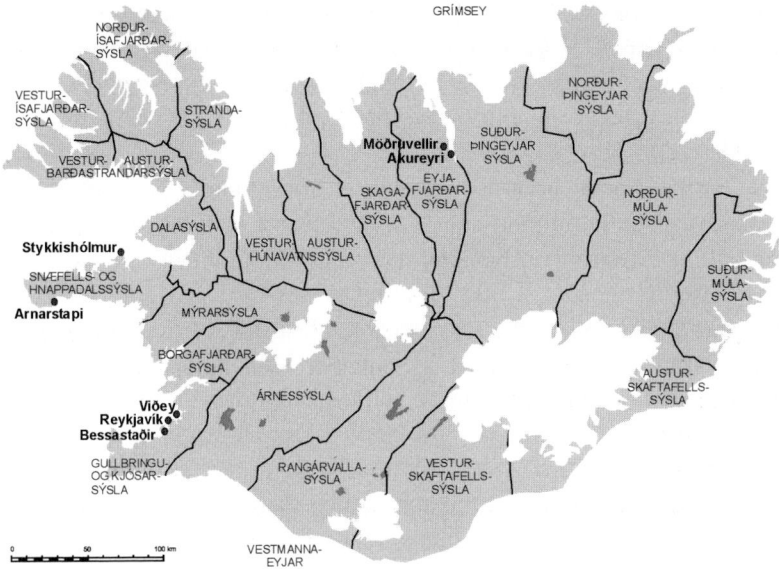

Figure 1: This map shows different districts (*sýslur*). It should be noted that this is to give a general guideline only. Nineteenth-century boundaries varied slightly from the present. Also shown are the residences of the District Governors and the Governor, as mentioned in the text.

Governor or *Stiftamtmaður* in charge of it. The first appointed *Stiftamtmaður* over Iceland was the five-year-old illegitimate son of King Christian V, Ulrik Christian Gyldenløve. As he was clearly unable to perform his appointed duties, another official was required to do this (Laxness 1995:38). He was termed an *Amtmaður* and was first appointed in 1688. This title may be translated as 'District' or 'Deputy Governor'. The *Stiftamtmaður* was the highest representative of the king on Iceland.

In 1770, the *Amt* of Iceland was divided in two, with the southern and western areas now comprising one *Amt*, and the northern and eastern regions another. Later, the former was also divided in two in order to create a separate southern and western *Amt*. The District Governor for the north and east traditionally lived at Möðruvellir in the Hörgárdalur valley in Eyjafjarðarsýsla (see *Figure 1*). After a fire there in 1874, the seat of the District Governor was moved to Akureyri. The District Governor for the western district was usually based either at Arnarstapi or Stykkishólmur on the Snaefellsness peninsula. Prior to 1770, the Governors rarely visited Iceland. After that time, they were generally resident, and also held the title of District Governor for the south. They were then based at Bessastaðir on

Álftanes close to Reykjavík (the current residence of Icelandic presidents) or else lived in Reykjavík, or nearby, in particular on the island of Viðey. In 1872, the position of *Stiftamtmaður* was eliminated and replaced by the *Landshöfðingi* who was now to be the highest-ranking representative of the Danish king on Iceland. This title also may be translated as 'Governor' but will be referred to here as 'Governor General' in order to avoid confusion. The last *Stiftamtmaður* became the new *Landshöfðingi*. The position of *Amtmaður* was kept until home rule was established in 1904.

Most of the Governors of Iceland were Danish, but many of the District Governors were Icelandic. Under the authority of the Governors and the District Governors were the *Sýslumenn*, 'District Commissioners' or 'Sheriffs'. For the most part, one sýslumaður held jurisdiction over one county or district (*Sýsla*), but there were exceptions to this. Thus, for example, Gullbringa and Kjós districts were together generally the responsibility of one sheriff. The Sheriffs were almost all Icelandic, and they were the main representative of the law in their districts. They collected the taxes and other moneys due to the king, kept an eye on how trade was going and tried to make sure that items were weighed and measured correctly (Laxness 1995:85). They also had policing and judicial powers. They were supposed to attend the *Alþing*, the National Assembly, every year. They sometimes failed in this duty, however; the journey could be long and arduous and the Sheriffs frequently stated that they could not afford it. Another heavy burden for them was having to look after the 'criminals' (*sakamenn*) or, as they are sometimes named, *delinquentar*, for a period of time, pending trial. The Sheriffs were also required to bring them to the *Alþing* at their own expense. Hard times in the mid- to late-eighteenth century meant that stealing increased greatly and the Sheriffs had to spend even more time keeping order (Ogilvie 1982). This was the context of the building of a prison in Reykjavik. It was built during the years 1761 to 1771 and used as such to 1816.[3]

It was, however, a further duty of the Sheriffs that is of particular interest here. The *Stiftamtmaður*, or the *Amtmaður* as his representative, was required to send the Danish government annual reports on the economy of the country (Laxness 1995:38). In order to adequately fulfil this duty, the *sýslumaður* in each district of Iceland was, in turn, charged with the task of drawing up a report on conditions in the district for which he was responsible. From the early 1700s, these reports were usually written annually. From around 1780, they were written more frequently, often two to three times per year. The different sheriffs interpreted this duty in different ways; some wrote comparatively briefly; others gave fuller accounts. On the whole, the letters from the nineteenth century contain far more detail than those of the eighteenth.

These letters written by the Sheriffs were usually in Danish, occasionally in Icelandic, often in Gothic script, and they are all in manuscript form. They are located in the National Archives of Iceland (*Þjóðskjalasafn Íslands*) in Reykjavík. The letter quoted at the start of this chapter is a typical example: it was written in 1866 by the District Governor for the western district, Bergur Thorberg (1829-1886; he was appointed *Landshöfðingi*, Governor General of Iceland, in 1882). The letters contain information on weather and climate, other environmental conditions, fishing catches, the growth of grass and the hay harvest, health and diseases, trade, and other items of interest. Letters arrived from Denmark to Iceland with trading and other vessels, usually in early summer, and were sent to Denmark and elsewhere when the ships departed, usually in September. In order to place the letters in perspective, a short excursion on the location, climate, history, and economy of Iceland follows below.

Iceland: Location, Climate, Settlement History

Iceland's central location in the North Atlantic means that the island has a very interesting and variable climate. The country lies at the intersection of cold Polar and mild Atlantic air and ocean currents, and this makes its climate very changeable. The effect of the relatively warm Irminger current makes human habitation possible, even though the island is marginal for agriculture. An important feature of Iceland's climate is the sea ice which drifts from East Greenland on cold marine currents and affects the coasts, especially the north of Iceland (Ogilvie and Jónsdóttir 2000; Ogilvie and Jónsson 2001). The island is also subject to volcanic activity. The climate of Iceland has a profound influence on all aspects of the country's economy and society (Ogilvie 2001; Ogilvie and McGovern 2000).

The settlement of Iceland began in the last decades of the ninth century (Vésteinsson 1998). At that time, the settlers brought with them a farming economy based on animal husbandry with sheep, pigs, cattle and horses as the main domestic animals. Although barley was grown during the first few centuries after settlement, the climate, on the whole, has not been suitable for grain-growing. An economic transition took place some time around AD 1150 to 1200 with the cessation of the raising of pigs, and a greater emphasis on sheep rather than cattle (Ogilvie *et al.* 2005). The origins of this transition were undoubtedly partly the result of climatic conditions as pigs require a relatively mild climate, and cattle consume far more grass and hay than sheep. From the end of the Commonwealth Period in Iceland, until the mid-twentieth century brought prosperity and a high standard of living, the population of Iceland can only be described as extremely poor. There were mitigating factors, however. In comparison with peasant classes in other parts of Europe, Icelandic farmers enjoyed some measure of freedom. The population varied from around 30,000 to 60,000, with declines in population frequently coinciding with famine years. There were no towns or villages to speak of until the end of the eighteenth century when Reykjavik began to take form. Instead there were scattered farmsteads with a few fishing stations on the coasts. The large majority of the inhabitants were tenants of the Danish King or the Church. As animal husbandry formed the lynchpin of the Icelandic economy it was the grass and hay for the livestock that has traditionally been the most important crop in Iceland. The grass for the hay crop came from two sources: the homefield (*tún*) close to the farm, and from outlying pastures. The reaping of the grass was by hand, and was a continuous process, from early July to late September. Hay-making was often a difficult and laborious task undertaken by all able-bodied members of the community. If there was insufficient hay for winter fodder, then domestic animals could die, and the human population, in turn, could be subject to famine and death. This chain of events occurred many times in Iceland's history.

Iceland in the Nineteenth Century

The nineteenth century began with a difficult legacy from the past. Severe years and famines occurred in the mid- to late-eighteenth century, and these, compounded with the major volcanic eruption of Lakagígar in 1784, together with difficult economic conditions, meant a large loss of life amongst both humans and domestic animals (Ogilvie 1986; Demarée and Ogilvie 2001). In 1703, the first census taken showed a population of 50,358. In 1801 it had dropped to 47,852 (*Hagskinna Íslands* 1997). The nineteenth century was undoubtedly a time of great change in Iceland, and may be seen as a time that was deeply rooted in the past, as well as a time that contained the seeds of the developments that were to come with the twentieth century. It was during the nineteenth century that nationalism grew in Iceland and the *sjalfstæðisbarátta*, the 'struggle for independence' resulted in the granting of home rule from Denmark in 1918 and the establishment of a free republic in 1944. In the meantime, Iceland, until the 1880s, was relatively untouched by the urbanization and industrialization that characterised much of the rest of Europe and the Icelandic economy remained very limited, with a major focus on farming. However, the industrial revolution in Europe did have effects in Iceland. From 1855, free trade was established in Iceland and this brought about better conditions. This, in turn, caused the Icelanders to increase their foreign trade and to produce more goods for sale, including both fish and meat products. The standard of living improved somewhat, and by 1870 the population had reached 70,000 (Nordal and Kristinsson 1996:85). However, most people still lived on farms in rural districts, and towns were virtually non-existent. In the last quarter of the century, changes occurred more rapidly; in particular, fishing increased and the traditional Icelandic emphasis on farming instead of fishing began to give way before a new economic way of life where fishing became the basis of the economy. There was a move away from the rural districts, and, by 1900, Reykjavik had a population of 6,000 (Nordal and Kristinsson 1996:86). A little over one hundred years before, in 1786, when Reykjavik received its municipal charter it had a total of 167 inhabitants. These many changes that occurred during the nineteenth century are reflected in the letters of the Sheriffs and District Governors of Iceland.

Environmental Images of Iceland from the Letters of the Sheriffs and District Governors

The images of Iceland presented by the Sheriffs' letters show a country where life was a constant struggle. Success meant survival, not much more, and failure could mean death. The letters often begin with a statement to the effect that conditions in the country, 'Landets Tilstand', are very difficult. The letters reflect the economic as well as the natural world. The letters usually begin with an account of the weather over the past year, giving descriptions of each season. Sometimes these are very detailed and sometimes even include quantitative meteorological observations. In addition, examples are given of perceptions of economic activities in an environmental context; in particular, the all-important grass crop and hay harvest as well as fisheries catches. The letters illustrate just how central the weather was to the lives of people living in Iceland in past centuries. Descriptions of other aspects of the environment such as volcanic eruptions, glacial phenomena and floods also occur. Several examples of these are given below, as well as examples of descriptions of individual seasons, and the perceived impacts on the farming and fishing communities. This discussion of the environmental images of Iceland through the eyes of the Sheriffs begins with an extract from a letter written by Gunnlaugur Pétursson Blöndahl (1834-1884) giving details of the autumn of 1867:

> During the first days of September the weather was calm and favourable. However, during the rest of the month there were lasting severe storms from the north and northeast with cold and night frost. During all of October the weather was mainly unsteady with alternating storms and rains. During the last days of this month a severe frost occurred with snows and continual strong northeasterly winds. This weather lasted almost unbroken to the last days of November when the weather again became milder with southerly winds and rain, so that the snow,

for the most part, thawed... (Letter from Gunnlaugur Pétursson Blöndahl, dated 31 December 1867, Barðastrandarsýsla.)

It was the winter season, however, that was often crucial for the well-being of both people and animals:

> The winter so far has been very severe and unpleasant for this district. At the end of September, and occasionally in October, foggy weather occurred with sleet and easterly winds. The earth thus eventually became covered with a thick and hard crust of ice, impenetrable to horses as well as sheep from early in November (1824) to 6 January (1825) when the first winter thaw occurred. This lasted a week and melted the ice layer. Now we have frost and snow again, with northwesterly storms [...] In a sudden and raging snowstorm on 6 December, three people lost their lives, and sheep were also lost in various places... (Letter from Sheriff Þórður Björnsson, dated 22 January 1825, Garður, Suður-Þingeyjarsýsla.)

This letter, written by Þórður Björnsson (1766-1834) in Suður-Þingeyjarsýsla in northeastern Iceland, highlights the changeable nature of the weather and describes a situation that is especially dangerous for the livestock: a succession of freezes and thaws. This renders the ground virtually impenetrable to the animals, and they need to be given supplementary fodder. The real danger of sudden snowstorms is illustrated by the fact that three people lost their lives as well as a number of sheep. Stories abound of people who died in blizzards as they were going from one farm to another; a sudden severe snowstorm could make it impossible to see anything at all:

> This spring was everywhere in the north, and, as far as I know, in the east too, among the colder ones, although not actually severe. However, some people, especially in Húnavatn and Skagafjörður, did lose a considerable number of their sheep, especially the so-called year-old sheep (*gemlingar*)[...] After the cold spring, the air began to get milder in the beginning of June. The weather became very dry up to around mid July... (Letter from District Governor Stefán Þórarinsson, dated 9 September 1820, Möðruvellir, Eyjafjarðarsýsla.)

A severe spring season could be potentially even more hazardous for the livestock than a severe winter, as it would mean an additional period of time with little new grass. The sheep were also more vulnerable then as lambing occurred in late spring/early summer. Stefán Þórarinsson (1831-1892), quoted above, was District Governor in the Northern and Eastern districts from 1783 to 1823 (Ólason 1951:340).

> [...] From St Hans day (24 June) there was continual dry weather. It was also dry throughout August. After that the weather became more damp with southerly winds to mid October... (Letter from Sheriff Jónas Scheving, dated 31 December 1816, Leirá, Borgarfjarðarsýsla.)

This letter from Sheriff Jónas Scheving (1770-1831) in Borgarfjord district in the west of Iceland describes a dry summer in that area in 1816. Unusually dry or wet weather during the summer could both negatively impact the grass growth and harvest. This year is also of special interest as it has become known as the 'Year Without A Summer' (Stommel and Stommel 1979). The very cold weather that year in many parts of the world was caused by the eruption of the volcano Tambora in Indonesia in April 1815. The weather in Iceland in 1816 was not of an extreme nature, but it was severe in most parts (Ogilvie 1992).

Very cold years undoubtedly did play a part in social stress which manifested itself in the desertion of farms, begging and petty crime. When the livestock died for lack of food, it could happen that human beings also died. Such problems were not widespread in 1816, however, and just one district, Snæfellsnessýsla, reported difficulties of this kind:

> Great lack of food among inhabitants. People pressed by beggars from here and also from other districts. The majority of the district's populace has already got into debt at the trading places in previous years, and have scraped together all that they could in order to pay. So now they have to give all the best fish to the merchants and have little left for themselves except for flatfish and cod's heads. This is poor winter provision, particularly on the coast among the poor fishermen who do not earn sufficient during the summer to buy other necessary foodstuffs from the farmers, and who therefore live in the greatest misery... (Letter from Sheriff Sigurður Guðlaugsson, dated 18 February 1817, Gröf, Snæfellsnessýsla.)

The lack of food may be attributed to adverse economic trading conditions as well as climate. Elsewhere in this letter, the Sheriff states that the trading places were very poorly supplied with cereals and other imported foodstuffs. However, the fishing, of great importance to the district, largely failed this year, due directly to climate impacts. The Sheriff, Sigurður Guðlaugsson (1764-1840) noted that 'although there should have been fishing in the latter part of the winter months, the severe frost and layers of ice far out to sea, frequently prevented the fishermen from getting out to sea for many days on end'. As Snæfellsnes and other nearby areas were important fishing centres, they attracted people whose inland sources of food had failed.

As well as the sea freezing off the western coasts as in the example above, another climatic phenomenon which affects Iceland is the sea ice which drifts to its shores on the East Greenland Current. The causes of the presence of ice are complex, but sea ice off Iceland is usually associated with very cold weather. The ice most commonly reaches the northwest, north and east of Iceland. It is rare for it to reach the southern coasts. The advent of ice was mostly feared as it brought cold and hunger in its wake. The image of the ice undoubtedly conjured up fear and it was personified as a dreaded enemy (Ogilvie 1995):

> [...] the winter was among the best, but the spring was very cold, especially after the sea ice, which lay here for some time, had embraced the coasts. In the similarly cold summer, the grass growth was thus very poor. The hay harvest, which began in mid August, was hindered by frost, fog and cold chills as well as much snow on occasion, especially around 18 August and again from 19 to 26 September. It was also difficult to harvest the hay in the constant and severe rain in late September and early October [...] In the spring the inhabitants caught several sharks, and in the autumn a considerable number of cod and halibut [...] However, on 19 October the fishing stopped due to encroaching drift ice. The two whales washed up in the jurisdictional areas of Broddanes and Bær by the sea ice in June, helped much in preventing hunger deaths in the dearth at that time... (Letter from Sheriff Jón Jónsson, dated 3 January 1816, Bær, Hrútafirði, Strandasýsla.)

This further example from the year 1816 written by Sheriff Jón Jónsson (1747-1831) in the western fjords area gives an interesting description of the nature of the ice, which often brought fog as well as cold temperatures. It illustrates the negative impacts of the ice, including the disruption of fishing. It frequently also prevented trading vessels from landing and bringing vital goods. However, the ice could, on occasion, also have some favourable impacts. In this case, two whales were washed ashore in the ice and this extra food supply was a great help at a time of famine.

A minor volcanic eruption also occurred in 1816. This is known from a letter written by Sheriff Lýður Guðmundsson (1728-1812) at Vík in Vestur-Skaftafellssýsla. According to this, the eruption began under Skaftafellsjökull (glacier) in the southeast some time in May. In June, the eruption was visible over 16 miles (24 km) away, with an enormous column of rising vapour. 'This later divided itself into clouds, and caused a bitingly sharp, cold drought until the clouds finally dispersed, and fell as a malignant, cold, severe and lasting heavy rain.' The eruption did not appear to have any serious effects, although the vegetable and hay crops were adversely affected. This Sheriff also reported flooding of the River Skeiðará on 17, 18 and 19 July. He described the river as 'flowing out of the bowels of the Skaftafell glacier'. The river now runs adjacent to the neighbouring Skeiðarárjökull, and the glaciers today are smaller and of a different shape than they were in the early nineteenth century. The Sheriff noted that the river flooded a large part of Skeiðarásandur (a stretch of sandy plain) and cut off all passage over a much greater distance. The flood is likely to have been caused by ice melting during the volcanic eruption.

In the year 1831, there is another extremely interesting account from the neighbouring district of Austur-Skaftafellssýsla. The Governor at the time, Lorenz A. Krieger, noted the advance of the glacier Breiðamerkurjökull, an outlet glacier of the great Vatnajökull which dominates the region. Having had an oral report from the local Sheriff, Magnús Stephensen, Krieger requested a written report, which the Sheriff provided. He noted that the glacier had been advancing for some time. In 1824, for example, he had been aware of an area of pasture land which he says has now (1831) been completely covered by the glacier. He is concerned that soon the glacier will reach all the way to the sea:

> If the glacier reaches the sea, I do not think one will be able to travel on foot. Even if it does not, then calving icebergs will make it impossible even by horse. As this will have considerable consequences for communication with the greater part of Austur-Skaftafellssýsla, I have not dared to omit giving my report concerning this natural phenomenon... (Letter from Sheriff Magnús Stephensen, dated 3 June, 1831, Höfðabrekka, Austur- Skaftafellssýsla.)[4]

One of the most severe winters of the nineteenth century occurred in 1880-1881. In fact, the period ensuing, to around 1888, has come to be known as the 'Dire Years'. The letter below comes from the Húnavatn district in the north:

> The extremely severe weather which began in earnest in the middle of November (1880) lasted until the beginning of April (1881). It was the general opinion, that no one now living had experienced such long-lasting and severe frost. This was frequently between 12 and 30 degrees Réamur and was often around 20 degrees. There was frequent fog due to the sea ice, and the bay of Húnaflói was full of sea ice. The spring was cold and dry and the grass growth was of the poorest quality. The summer was also cold and dry and there was also night frost... (Sheriff Lárus Blöndahl, dated 1 October 1881, Kornsá, Húnavatnssýsla.)

Similar accounts of severity are found in the east.

> The weather during this time (1 January to 30 September 1881) has been one of the most severe, with the most snow and frost that people remember. The sea ice came to the east before Christmas and lay fast to the coasts until the spring, filling all bays and fjords. The summer has been cold and wet, and hence with much damage to the grass... (Letter from Sheriff Einar Thorlacius, dated 1 October, 1881, Norður-Múlasýsla.)

Accounts such as this are to be found all over Iceland for the 1880s. For the year 1882, in a combined account for Snæfellsnes and Hnappadalssýsla in the west, some temperature measurements are given (although it may difficult to determine their accuracy). Although the Sheriff here emphases the severity, in most parts of Iceland this winter was not as harsh as 1881, but the spring and summer were very cold.

> From the New Year to 1 April (1882) it must be called a severe time, mainly with frosts from minus 10 to minus 15 degrees Celsius. During March they were from minus 18 to minus 25. The weather then improved, but with the onset of May, the weather became cold again, and there was so much frost at night that all growth (of grass) was prevented... (Letter from Sheriff Sigurður Jónsson, dated 20 March 1882, Stykkishólmur, Snæfelsnessýsla.)

The 1880s continued with several further cold years with sea ice. A succession of poor summers caused consecutive hay-crop failure. It was during the 'Dire Years' that emigration to the United States and Canada reached a peak. Many people abandoned their homes and left Iceland. Beginning in 1883, over the next few years, approximately 1215 Icelanders, from a total population of 69,722 left the country to go to the US and Canada (Ponzi 1995). Iceland's last great subsistence famine occurred during the 'Dire Years'. During the twentieth century, the only comparable period of severe cold and sea ice occurred in the latter part of the 1960s (1965-1970) which are known as the 'ice years'. Icelanders had then long since ceased to have the same vulnerability to climatic conditions as they did in the nineteenth century and earlier.

Conclusion

The Sheriffs and District Governors of Iceland often complained in their letters that their circumstances were very difficult, and not significantly different from the populace at large. Sometimes they wrote letters to the Governor or the King of Denmark with requests of one kind or another to improve their lot. It frequently appears that the letters were not answered, or at least not for many years. Nevertheless, they continued to perform their duties, their complaints held in restraint, in spite of the hard life they often led. Clearly they must be applauded as both dedicated civil servants and meticulous observers of nature. A combination of a great respect for the written word together with an acute awareness of the importance of the natural world, especially the weather, seems to have produced in Iceland many such careful recorders of a variety of elements of climate and other natural phenomena. Such information is invaluable in constructing records of variations in past climate (Ogilvie 2005; Ogilvie and Jónsson 2001).

The images of Iceland as seen through the eyes of the Sheriffs and District Governors show a land of cold, hunger, and sometimes misery. At the same time, there are shafts of sunlight, literally, as a mild winter or a successful hay harvest is recorded with evident pleasure. When they did their duty, year after year, recording events and situations that may, at times, have seemed commonplace and humdrum, they could have had no idea what a wealth of treasure they left behind for modern historians of climate and society in the form of the vivid images they so faithfully recorded.

Acknowledgements

The research described here is supported by RANNÍS (The Icelandic Centre for Research) and by the US National Science Foundation. Part of this paper was written in 2006 at *Stofnun Árna Magnússonar á Íslandi* in Reykjavik, and at *Snorrastofa* in Reykholt. Their hospitality was greatly appreciated. The staff of *Þjóðskjalasafn Íslands*, especially Jón Torfason, are warmly thanked. I am also grateful to Ingibjörg Jónsdóttir for the map of the districts of Iceland and to Trausti Jónsson who made useful comments on the manuscript.

Bibliography

Manuscript sources:

Sheriffs' Letters from *Þjóðskjalasafn Íslands* (National Archives) Reykjavík.

Published works:

Benediktsson, Bogi (1881-1884): *Sýslumannaæfir eptir Boga Benediktsson Með skýringum og viðaukum eptir Jón Pétursson.* Reykjavík, Einar Þórðarson.

Demarée, G. R. and Ogilvie, A. E. J. (2001): '*Bon baisers d'Islande*: climatological, environmental and human dimensions impacts in Europe of the *Lakagígar* eruption (1783-1784) in Iceland', in *History and Climate: Memories of the Future?* (eds P. D. Jones, A. E. J. Ogilvie, T. D. Davies and K. R. Briffa). New York, Boston, Dordrecht, London, Moscow, Kluwer Academic/Plenum Publishers pp. 219-246.

Hagskinna Íslands Icelandic Historical Statistics (1997): Reykjavík, Statistics Iceland.

Jónsbók og Réttarbætr (1904): Kong Magnus Hakonsson Lovbog for Island vedtaget paa Altinget 1281 de for Island givne Retterbøder af 1294, 1305 og 1314. Copenhagen, Ólafur Halldórsson.

Laxness, Einar (1995): *Íslands saga I-III.* Reykjavík, Alfræði Vöku-Helgafells.

Lehmann, K. (1888): *Der Ursprung des norwegischen Sysselamtes*, Abh. Z. germ., insbes. Nord. Berlin and Leipzig, Rechtsgesch.

Nordal, Jóhannes and Kristinsson, Valdimar (1996): *Iceland the Republic*, Handbook published by the Central Bank of Iceland, Reykjavík.

Ogilvie, A. E. J. (1982): 'Climate and Society in Iceland from the Medieval Period to the Late Eighteenth Century', Unpublished PhD thesis. School of Environmental Sciences, University of East Anglia, Norwich, UK.

—— (1986): 'The climate of Iceland, 1701-1784', *Jökull* 36, pp. 57-73.

—— (1992): '1816 – A year without a summer in Iceland?' in *The Year Without a Summer? World Climate in 1816* (ed. C. R. Harrington). Ottawa, Canadian Museum of Nature, pp. 331-354.

—— (1995): '"The country's ancient enemy": Sea-ice variations in Iceland in historical times and their social impact', in *International Conference on Past, Present and Future Climate* (ed. P. Heikinheimo), Proceedings of the SILMU conference held in Helsinki, Finland, 22-25 August, 1995. Publication of the Academy of Finland 6/95, 176-178.

—— (2001): 'Climate and farming in northern Iceland, ca. 1700-1850', in *Aspects of Arctic and Sub-Arctic History* (eds I. Sigurðsson and J. Skaptason). Reykjavík, University of Iceland Press, pp. 289-299.

—— (2005): 'Local knowledge and travellers' tales: A selection of climatic observations in Iceland', in *Iceland – Modern Processes and Past Environments, Developments in Quaternary Science 5* (eds. C. Caseldine, A. Russell, J. Harðardóttir and O. Knudsen). , Amsterdam, Boston, Heidelberg, London, Elsevier, pp. 257-287.

Ogilvie, A. E. J. and Jónsdóttir, I. (2000): 'Sea ice, climate and Icelandic fisheries in historical times', *Arctic* 53 (4), pp. 383-394.

Ogilvie, A. E. J. and Jónsson, T. (2001): '"Little Ice Age" research: A perspective from Iceland', *Climatic Change* 48, pp. 9-52.

Ogilvie, A. E. J. and McGovern T. H. (2000): 'Sagas and science: climate and human impacts in the North Atlantic', in *Vikings: The North Atlantic Saga* (eds W. W. Fitzhugh and E. I. Ward). Washington, Smithsonian Instititution Press, pp. 385-393.

Ogilvie, A. E. J., McGovern, T. H. and Jónsson, T. (2005): 'Global issues, local concerns: syntheses of climate and human-dimensions issues in Mývatnssveit, northern Iceland', in *Conference Book for The 6th Open Meeting of the Human Dimensions of Global Environmental Change Research Community*. Bonn, University of Bonn, p. 105.

Ólason, Páll Eggert (1951): *Íslenzkar Æviskrár Frá Landnámstímum til Ársloka 1940*, IV Bindi. Reykjavík, Hinu Íslenzka Bókmenntafélags.

Ponzi, Frank (1995): *Ísland fyrir aldamót: harðindaárin 1882-1888. Iceland: the dire years: 1882-1888, úr ljósmyndum og dagbókum Maitland James Burnett og Walter H. Trevelyan.* Brennholt, Mosfellsbær.

Stommel, H. and Stommel, E. (1979): 'The year without a summer', *Scientific American* 240 (6), pp. 1191-1198.

Þórarinsson, Hjörtur E. (1994): *Saga sýslunefdar Eyjafjarðarsýslu 1874-1989*, Akureyri, Héraðsnefn Eyjafjarðar.

Þorsteinsson, Björn (1972): Syssel: Island, *Kulturhistorisk Leksikon for nordisk middelalder fra vikingetid til reformationstid* Bind XVII. Reykjavík, Bókaverzlun Ísafoldar.

Vésteinsson, Orri (1998): 'Patterns of Settlement in Iceland. A Study in Pre-History', *Saga-Book of the Viking Society* XXV, pp. 1-29.

Notes

1. All the letters quoted have been transcribed and translated from the original Danish and Icelandic by the author.
2. The Icelandic code of laws, commonly called 'Jónsbók', was instituted by the *Alþing* or Parliament in 1281 and was named for one of its authors, Jón Einarsson. It is based on the law of King Magnús Hákonarson of Norway. The 'Jónsbók' was Iceland's principal law code until it began to be superseded by Norwegian laws in the 1720s, and a few articles remain in force to this day.
3. In 1819 it was converted to a dwelling house and used as such for many years, and also notably as an office for the Governor and later the Governor General. *Stjórnarráðshúsið*, as it is now termed in Icelandic, is currently the office of the Prime Minister.
4. The glacial lagoon formed by the melting of Breiðamerkurjökull in the present warm climatic regime has now become a tourist attraction.

Foreign Visual Art and Changing Attitudes to the Icelandic Landscape in the Nineteenth and Early Twentieth Centuries.

Sumarliði Ísleifsson

The Icelandic writer Halldór Laxness once described how the Icelanders' attitude to their landscape had changed during the nineteenth and twentieth centuries: 'as late as the nineteenth century the Icelanders regarded mountains as ugly. It wasn't enough that Búlandstindur [in eastern Iceland] was "extraordinarily ugly", but the Mývatn district [in northern Iceland] with its ring of mountains and lake was considered "an abominable place".' Of the situation in the twentieth century, however, Laxness can write:

> In our century it is considered the done thing for townspeople of a certain class to acquire profiles of their favourite mountains to hang above the sofa, and such prized possessions are referred to as 'sofa pieces' in the Danish fashion. People looked at these landscapes on their walls for such a long time that many of them began to want to go there. (Laxness 1978:5; SÍ translation)

This raises the question of when the opinion of the Icelanders, that is of the upper classes, educated people and general public, changed with regard to their country's scenery. Why did they start putting Icelandic landscapes on their walls in the form of paintings? What factors contributed to this? Were foreign artists in any way responsible for the transformation that took place in attitudes to Icelandic scenery in the nineteenth and twentieth centuries? How did their works come to the attention of the locals? Was the development in Iceland similar to that in neighbouring countries? These questions will be explored in the following article.

Most people are astonished when it is pointed out to them that well into the nineteenth century Icelandic nature had the reputation in domestic and foreign writings of being violent, evil and even satanic.[1] The following description is found in an English translation of the travelogue by the Icelanders Eggert Ólafsson and Bjarni Pálsson who carried out their travels and research between 1752 and 1757:

> From the situation of this country, it is often threatened and damaged by disruptions of the mountains [*sic*], which generally happen after heavy rains in summer; but principally when these occur in spring and autumn, they undermine and detach from the mountains enormous masses of rock, which only adhere to them by a small portion of cemented gravel or mould. The inhabitants are also much exposed in winter by the rapid fall of vast conglomerations of snow, which are formed on the glaciers. When these heaps accumulate on the summits of the mountains, they appear like arches above the vallies, into which they are at length precipitated by their own weight. From the ancient and modern chronicles of this country, we learn of many periods when men and cattle have been destroyed by such accidents. (Olafsen and Povelsen 1805:5-6)

And one foreign publication declared in the late eighteenth century:

> The country does not afford a pleasing view to the eye of a traveller, for it is uneven, covered with rocks and rugged mountains, and continually cloathed with ice and snow, with barren fields between them, destitute of wood, and encrusted with lava for many miles. (Trusler 1788:104; see also Vaughan 1988:132 ff)

Making images of Iceland

But times were changing and foreign scientists and scholars were becoming interested in the nature and culture of Iceland. The first foreign exploratory and scientific expeditions visited Iceland in the late eighteenth century. Sir Joseph Banks sailed for the north in 1772, followed by John Stanley in 1789. Stanley's expedition resulted in pictures that were to have a major impact on descriptions of Iceland in the nineteenth century. The best known is the engraving of Geysir after an oil painting by the British artist Edward Dayes who painted the picture from Stanley's sketches and account but never actually visited Iceland himself.

Stanley considered Geysir 'sublime', in the spirit of the British philosopher Edmund Burke, a sentiment that is interpreted in the picture. Such ideas were in keeping with the radical changes that were taking place as classical attitudes and demands for harmony and order gave way to an appreciation of the natural wilderness. Romantic ideas gradually gained ascendancy in the intellectual life of the upper and middle classes in the cities of Western Europe. Feeling and insight, together with a sense of religious and philosophical meaning, came to dominate thinking. Landscapes gradually took precedence over other genres of painting. All over Europe people began painting lofty mountains, mighty waterfalls and endless vistas, at first mainly in the Alpine regions but later in the Nordic countries.

Figure 1: Geysir (1796). An engraving by F. Chesham after a painting by Edward Dayes. (From the library of the Central Bank of Iceland.)

The British botanist William Hooker visited Iceland in 1809, on the same ship as Jörgen Jörgensen, known as the 'Dog-day King' for his short-lived *coup d'état* in Iceland. Hooker later achieved fame as a botanist and became Director of the Royal Botanical Gardens at Kew in London. During his trip to Iceland he presented Ólafur Stephensen, the former governor-general, then resident on Videy Island in the neighbourhood of Reykjavík, with an engraving of Edward Dayes' picture of Geysir (see *figure 1*, above), a gift from Joseph Banks. The picture was the first 'profile' of an Icelandic natural phenomenon to be hung in an Icelandic home. After Stephensen died it was inherited by his son, Chief Justice Magnús Stephensen, and subsequently by his daughter Thórunn and her husband the Rev. Hannes Stephensen from Ytri Hólmur. Around 1900 the picture adorned the drawing room of Thórunn's granddaughter and namesake, Thórunn, and her husband Chief Physician Jónassen. The Geysir picture remained in the possession of Ólafur Stephensen's descendants for nearly a century and a half until it was acquired by the National Museum of Iceland in

1944. It is the first example of how new, changed images of nature reached Iceland in pictorial form and remained ever after in the most influential homes in the country, which were visited by many people and emulated as a model of fashionable living.

Several other copies of this engraving found their way to Iceland and references to it were common.[2] The picture also became a model for many of the images of Geysir that were later produced in Iceland. It was, for example, the model for the picture of Geysir in the missionary and Bible-distributor Ebenezer Henderson's book about his sojourns in Iceland in 1814 and 1815. In the book he describes Geysir in high-flown terms as a symbol of Icelandic nature. His words are a good example of how much attitudes to the landscape had changed by this time: Iceland's landscape was no longer diabolical but a vision of the Lord's might:

> The water rushed up out of the pipe with amazing velocity, and was projected by irregular jets into the atmosphere, surrounded by immense volumes of steam … The first four or five jets were inconsiderable … these were followed by one about fifty feet, which was succeeded by two or three considerably lower; after which came the last, exceeding all the rest in splendour, which rose at least to the height of seventy feet. [...] The whole scene was indescribably astonishing [...] While the jets were rushing up towards heaven, with the velocity of an arrow, my mind was forcibly borne along with them, to the contemplation of the Great and Omnipotent JEHOVAH, in comparison with whom, these, and all the wonders scattered over the whole immensity of existence, dwindle into absolute insignificance [...] Such scenes exhibit only 'the hiding of His power.' It is merely the surface of His works that is visible. (Henderson 1818:45-48)

Foreign travellers and artists did not begin visiting the island in any numbers until around the mid-1830s. In 1834 Frederik, the heir to the Danish throne, travelled there, accompanied by the German-Danish painter Frederik Kloss who produced several oil paintings following the trip. Lithographs of Kloss's pictures were published in a book called *Prospecter fra Island* (Views of Iceland) and were also sold separately, gaining a fairly wide circulation in Iceland itself.

The Frenchman Paul Gaimard mounted a famous expedition to Iceland in 1835-6. Among his party was the French painter Auguste Mayer who made numerous sketches during the visit. And his lithographs later appeared in four 'atlases', part of a 12-volume series about the expedition. Mayer's pictures glorify the country's spectacular scenery and praise the primitive life of the inhabitants.[3] The atlases were available in Iceland and in addition Mayer's pictures were widely copied in foreign travel accounts of the island and in illustrated newspapers and journals that were circulated there.

Figure 2: Goðafoss (1856). An engraving by A. Nay, after a painting by Emanuel Larsen. (From the library of the Central Bank of Iceland.)

In 1845 the volcano Hekla drew attention to itself in dramatic style after a long period of dormancy. The eruption attracted a great deal of interest in Europe, since wind bore the ash far to the south, and motivated a young Danish artist, Emanuel Larsen, to journey to Iceland. He produced numerous drawings, graphic artworks and several paintings, including pictures of celebrated sites such as Almannagjá, Geysir, Hekla, Snæfellsjökull and Goðafoss (see *figure 2*, above). They later appeared as lithographs in the work *Danmark*, published in 1856. They were also available as separate prints and were repeatedly reprinted in books and papers whenever Iceland received a mention. However, the pictures were to gain their widest circulation as illustrations on bank notes issued by the Bank of Iceland after 1900.

Illustrated newspapers and journals first made their mark in Europe during the 1830s. The 1840s and 1850s saw the launch of major papers such as *Illustrierte Zeitung* in Germany, *The Illustrated London News* in Britain and *Illustreret Tidende* in Denmark. News and articles about Iceland often appeared in these papers, accompanied by hundreds of images of the country. These newspapers also turned up in Iceland, with *Illustreret Tidende* the most common, but other illustrated papers were also seen there. Towards the end of the nineteenth century a group of influential citizens in Reykjavík clubbed together to subscribe to the *Illustrierte Zeitung* and the paper was passed around among them.

The National Gallery of Iceland was founded in 1884 and by the turn of the century had acquired over one hundred paintings and graphic artworks by foreign artists. The pictures were on display in Parliament House and some were hung in the Ministerial Residence when it was taken into use after the turn of the century. Members of Parliament and parliamentary staff had the pictures before their eyes on a daily basis, while the public could view them at weekends.[4]

The development in Iceland was in some ways similar to that in neighbouring countries. In Scandinavia, foreign artists, or Scandinavian painters who lived abroad for their entire careers, played a considerable role in changing people's attitudes to their country's natural scenery and image. A good example is the well-known Norwegian painter, Johann Chr. Dahl, who worked mainly in Germany during the first half of the nineteenth century. Dahl painted a mountainous northern landscape, generally inventing places to fit in with prevailing conventions and ideas of picturesque Nordic scenery. His pictures were to have a major impact on his countrymen. The Swedish-American scholar, Kenneth Olwig, expressed it as the creation of:

> idealised images of the Nordic natural landscape. The people in the Nordic countries came to adopt these notions of the landscape as their own. From this perspective one might claim that the Nordic scenery was invented in Central Europe. The process, however, could sooner be described as dialectical. (Olwig 1992:162; SÍ translation)[5]

The Icelander's 'utmost indifference'

But while John Stanley, Ebenezer Henderson and other foreign travellers around 1800 could scarcely find words to express their enthusiasm for the Icelandic landscape, it was rare to find an Icelander waxing lyrical about his own scenery. George Mackenzie, who visited the country in 1810, was surprised at how little interest the Icelanders showed in such magnificent natural phenomena as Geysir, and how even men of education had little regard for the hot spring:

> At the present day, the number of natives who have visited these springs is comparatively very small; and by those who live near them, their extraordinary operations constantly going on, are regarded with the same eye as the most common and indifferent appearances of nature. (Mackenzie 1812:219-220)

William Hooker made a similar point, commenting that the Icelanders were astonished by the fact that he had come to their country 'for the sake of seeing the Geysers, which they are accustomed to look at with the utmost indifference' (Hooker 1813:174).

But as the century progressed this attitude slowly changed, initially among poets and the educated classes. What had previously seemed menacing and malevolent now became a source of pride and enthusiasm. The poem by Jónas Hallgrímsson (1807-1845), 'To M. Paul Gaimard', composed on the occasion of the traveller's visit to Copenhagen, includes the lines, 'Þú stóðst á tindi Heklu hám/og horfðir yfir landið fríða, /þar sem um grænar grundir líða/skínandi ár að ægi blám'[6] (Standing on Hekla's lofty head / you surveyed the beauteous plain, / where shining rivers thread green meads / on their way to the deep blue main).

The leaders of society now started to turn against those voices that were so insolent as to declare in the latter half of the nineteenth century that Iceland's landscape was 'so far from deserving the title of spectacular or awe-inspiring that it should rather be called underwhelming'.[7] The famous British explorer Richard Burton went furthest in these declarations. In his *Ultima Thule* he states that:

> we have all drawn for ourselves our own Iceland – a distorted and exaggerated mental picture of what has not met, and will not meet, the eye of sense. Moreover, the travellers of the early century saw scenes of thrilling horror, of majestic grandeur, and of heavenly beauty, where our more critical, perhaps more cultivated, taste finds very humble features. [...] even the hard-headed Scot gallops between Reykjavik and Thingvellir along the edge of a 'dreadful precipice,' where I saw only the humblest ravine; and travellers to the age-weary, worn-out Geysir rise at midnight in their excitement to sing those 'grand old psalm-tunes, such as York and the Old Hundreth'. (Burton 1875:ix-xi)

The Icelandic newspaper *Þjóðólfur* was at pains to point out that honourable men, both at home and abroad, had responded to the explorer's slights, one of them claiming that 'nothing anywhere else in the world can surpass Iceland when it comes to peculiarly wild and dramatic natural beauty' (21 January 1873:48; SÍ translation).

But how general and deep-rooted was the tendency among Icelanders around 1900 to admire and extol the wonders of the Icelandic landscape? Poets lauded the mountains, and Icelandic artists had begun to paint them instead of leaving the task to foreigners. Icelandic photographers travelled around the country taking pictures, which they then sold to the tourists and showed to the public. One of these was the photographer Magnús Ólafsson. He held a slideshow in 1912 in which he 'simply shows us our Icelandic scenery from all the most strikingly beautiful places in the country with such captivating colours that it inspires awe in the beholder', to quote the Icelandic newspaper *Lögrjetta* (17 April 1912:85; SI translation). Ólafsson's pictures included places that foreign artists had made famous in the nineteenth century. And soon it became popular for people to hang photographs of landscapes, tinted with colour, on the walls of their homes.

The poets certainly lauded the mountains, as the German Andreas Heusler pointed out in a German newspaper after a trip to Iceland in 1895. Nevertheless he found it odd that 'Icelandic literature makes much of the beauty of the mountains and these poems are on every man's lips', yet the locals never actually walked in those mountains; this activity remained the sole preserve of foreign visitors.[8] So it was around 1900 that the Icelandic poets praised the landscape and their countrymen echoed them but they had not yet reached the stage of wanting to subject their shoes to unnecessary wear and tear by actually hiking in these mountains.

A similar view emerges in the travel journal of the well-known Swedish draughtsman and author, Albert Engström, who travelled around Iceland in 1911. He maintained that the Icelanders 'still hadn't discovered their country, were not sufficiently captivated by its majestic, imposing beauty'. He added 'I believe that their patriotism has hitherto had its deepest roots in their history. But as they come to discover Europe better they will gladly, gratefully and proudly return to their homeland and then the world will see some art...'[9]

Andreas Heusler and Albert Engström are here writing about the educated classes but they were probably aware of differing opinions dictated by education, domicile and social status. Around 1900 over 80% of the population still lived in the countryside. While this was so, people's attitude to nature was principally influenced by practical considerations. But swift-moving changes in the twentieth century led to a social transformation and by the middle of the century over 70% of Icelanders were residents of towns or villages, an influential urban middle class had formed in the towns and education progressed by leaps and bounds. This was accompanied by rapid technological changes, including more diverse and powerful means of disseminating new ideas. Postcards were a significant medium for images in this context, as well as the Icelandic bank notes already mentioned; illustrated Icelandic magazines made the landscape familiar through photographs, and slideshows became increasingly popular. As the century progressed still more powerful media were introduced, but this development will not be discussed here.

Many aspects of this process remain to be studied. Yet one can conclude that the work of foreign artists had a lasting effect when it came to transforming the Icelandic population's attitude to their own scenery.

As I have pointed out in this article, their influences were not always direct or obvious, and were often filtered by intermediaries. It is hard to assess their impact but what is clear is that by the mid twentieth century a large number of Icelandic homes contained pictures that indicated their appreciation of their native landscape. And these pictures were frequently of places that had been popularised by foreign travellers in the nineteenth century.

Bibliography

Atlas historique. Lithographié d'après les dessins de M.A Meyer 1-2. Paris s.a.

Burton, Richard F. (1875): *Ultima Thule; or A Summer in Iceland* I. London.

Danmark (1856): Copenhagen.

Engström, Albert (1913): *Åt Häcklefjäll. Minnen från en Islandsfärd.* Stockholm.

Gaimard, Paul (1838-1852): *Voyage en Islande et au Groënland exécuté pendant les années 1835 et 1836 sur la corvette La Recherche* [etc.]. Paris [12 vol.]

'Guðmundar saga Arasonar eftir Arngrím ábóta'. *Byskupa sögur* III (1948): Hólabiskupar. Reykjavík.

Hand-Book for Travellers in Denmark, Norway, Sweden and Iceland (1858): London,

Henderson, Ebenezer (1818): *Iceland; or the Journal of a Residence in that Island, During the Years 1814 and 1815* [etc.] I. Edinburgh.

Hooker, William Jackson (1813): *Journal of a Tour in Iceland in the Summer of 1809*, I. London.

Ísafold (newspaper) 1896.

Hallgrímsson, Jónas (1989): *Ritverk Jónasar Hallgrímssonar* I. Ljóð og laust mál. Reykjavík.

Kloss, Frederik Theodor (1835): *Prospecter af Island malede efter Naturen paa den, i Fölge med Hans Kongelige Höjhed, Prinds til Danmark Frederik Carl Christian's i Sommeren 1834 foretagen Reise* [etc.]. Copenhagen.

Laxness, Halldór (1978): 'Formáli', in Kjartan Júlíusson, *Reginfjöll að haustnóttum.* Reykjavík.

Lögrjetta (newspaper) 1896, 1912.

Mackenzie, George Steuart (1812): *Travels in the Island of Iceland, during the Summer of the Year MDCCCX.* Edinburgh.

Nordal, Bera (1994): 'Stofngjöf Listasafns Íslands'. *Stofngjöf Listasafns Íslands.* Afmælissýning. Reykjavík.

Olwig, Kenneth (1992): 'Den europeiska nationens nordiska natur', in *Frihetens Källa. Nordens betydelse för Europa: en Antologi* (ed. Sven Olof Karlsson). Stockholm.

Ólafsson, Eggert and Pálsson, Bjarni (Olafsen and Povelsen) (1805): *Travel in Iceland: Performed by Order of His Danish Majesty* [etc.]. London.

Þjóðólfur (newspaper) 1873.

Trusler, John (1788): *The Habitable World Described, or the Present State of the People in All Parts of the Globe, from North to South* [etc.] I. London.

Vaughan, William (1988): *Romantic Art.* London.

Notes

1. See, for instance, a mediaeval description of the Icelandic landscape in 'Guðmundar saga Arasonar eftir Arngrím ábóta'. *Byskupa sögur* III, pp. 160-161.
2. See *Hand-Book for Travellers in Denmark, Norway, Sweden and Iceland*, p. 97.
3. Gaimard, Paul, *Voyage en Islande et au Groënland 1838-1852*.
4. Nordal 1994:7-17.
5. Olwig 1992:162; the original text is as follows: 'idealiserade bilder av det nordiska naturlandskapet. Dessa föreställninger om landskapet kom folken i de nordiska länderna att själva tillägna sig. Ur den synvinkel kunde man hävda att naturen i Norden uppfanns i centrum av Europa. Processen kan emellertid snarare beskrivas som dialektisk'.
6. Hallgrímsson 1989:104.
7. *Þjóðólfur* 3 Jan. 1873.
8. Heusler was quoted in the newspaper *Lögrjetta*, 19 Feb. 1896:38.
9. Engström 1913:317; the original text is as follows: 'Men isländarne ha tydligen ännu icke upptäckt sitt land, icke lärt sig rysa tillräcklig inför dess våldsamma, sublima skönhet. Jag tror att deras forsterlandskärlek tillsvidare har sina rötter i historien. Men då de en gång upptäckt Europa, skola de med glädje, tacksamhet och stolthet återvända hem, och världen skall få se en konst.'

'Beneath the Mountain's Lofty Frowning Brow' – British Descriptions of Mountain Adventures in Norway.

Anne-Kari Skarðhamar

Introduction: William Cecil Slingsby and his predecessors

William Cecil Slingsby (1849-1929) is no doubt the most famous of the British mountaineers who visited Norway in the nineteenth century. His book, *Norway. The Northern Playground. Sketches of climbing and mountain exploration in Norway between 1872 and 1903* (1904) has been translated in an extended and revised version under the title *Norge. Den nordlige arena – skisser fra tindebestigninger og oppdagerferder i norsk natur mellom 1872 og 1921* (1998).

Slingsby may have been the most famous British mountaineer in Norway, but he was not the first, and in his work he gives a brief account of the books written by five of his travelling predecessors, or the 'true pioneers' as he calls them, all of whom had previously introduced the Norwegian wilderness and mountains to an English public. Of the five, Lieutenant William Henry Breton of the Royal Navy was the first, with his book *Scandinavian Sketches or A Tour in Norway* (1835). The next British travel-writers mentioned by Slingsby among the 'true pioneers' are Thomas Forester and Michael S. Biddulph, who wrote and illustrated *Norway in 1848 and 1849. Rambles among the Fjelds and Fjords of the Central and Western Districts* (1850) and introduced the mountain chain Hurrungane to an English public – however, as Slingsby adds, 'at a respectful distance' (Slingsby 1904:8).

Breton and Forester seem to have similar intentions in their writing. Breton's double intention was to entertain his readers and to present a travel guide for future visitors. The subject of Thomas Forester's descriptions is the unexplored parts of Norway. A different motive for writing is represented by a Scotsman, professor James David Forbes (1809-1868), who was a physicist, geologist and glaciologist, in his *Norway and its Glaciers. Visited in 1851* (1853). The intention of his book was scientific: Forbes' exploration of glaciers was research, not only play. Slingsby claims that *Norway and its Glaciers* is 'undoubtedly one of the great mountain classics', and 'much the best book ever yet written on Norway' (Slingsby 1904:8).

In 1861, Francis M. Wyndham wrote a handbook on reindeer hunting in the Jotunheimen, entitled *Wild life in the fields of Norway* (Norwegian translation *Villmarksliv i norske fjell*, 1870), which, according to Slingsby was followed by 'other sportsmen and travellers, good, bad, and indifferent' (Slingsby 1904:8). Lieutenant-Colonel John Robert Campbell, an old friend of Slingsby's, wrote a series of articles in *Alpine Journal* which later appeared in the book *How to see Norway* (1871).

Slingsby says about the authors of these five travel descriptions that they were the true pioneers, although none of them except Campbell made any actual ascents. They are credited with having paved the way for other English travellers, among them Slingsby himself, who some years later could then benefit from the experience of the pioneers (Slingsby 1998:19).

The aim of this article is to throw light on the description of nature and the inhabitants of Norway in one travel account from the first half of the century, William Henry Breton's *Scandinavian Sketches or A Tour in Norway* and compare his book with Cecil Slingsby's, which appeared sixty-nine years later. With support from theories about nature in literature (Klaus P. Mortensen 1993, 1996) and about travel accounts (Pratt 1992/2003), the following questions will be discussed:

1. What made Norway an attractive 'playground' for British adventurers in the first half of the nineteenth century?

2. What ideas and attitudes towards nature are expressed in the accounts of travel in the Norwegian countryside and its wilderness?

3. What attitudes to 'the natives' or 'the other' do the descriptions express?

On travel writing and Norway as an attraction to explorers. Ethnographic travel writing

William Henry Breton's *Scandinavian Sketches or A Tour in Norway* (1835) and William Cecil Slingsby's *Norway. The Northern Playground* (1904) are ethnographic, in the sense that they are texts by which British writers represent to themselves the nature and the inhabitants ('the others') of a foreign country. In contrast to ethnographic texts, Mary Louise Pratt in her book *Imperial Eyes. Travel writing and Transculturation* (1992) introduces the term *autoethnographic* texts. These are constructed by 'the others' in response to, or in dialogue with, the metropolitan representations of the upper classes or imperialists (Pratt 1992/2003:7).

The difference between the travel descriptions of Breton and Slingsby may be regarded as expressions of what Pratt calls a shift in European 'planetary consciousness'. By 'planetary consciousness', Pratt understands 'an orientation toward interior exploration and the construction of global-scale meaning through the descriptive apparatuses of natural history' (Pratt 1992:15). This shift coincides with many others including 'the consolidation of bourgeois forms of subjectivity and power' (Pratt 1999/2003:9), and one might add: the bourgeois attitude to nature. However, there is no 'imperial eye', or colonizing intention attached to the explorations of the Norwegian wilderness. When an implicitly condescending attitude can be traced in some of the texts, it may be socially conditioned as a result of subjugating the 'lower orders' who may be regarded as ignorant and primitive.

Who were the writers of travel literature, and what sources did they draw on?

Breton was a globetrotter who had travelled in Asia, Africa, all over America and of course in Europe, Switzerland in particular, and he frequently compares what he sees in Norway to what he has seen elsewhere (Breton 1835:225). According to Slingsby, Breton describes 'with the modesty nearly always associated with naval men' his remarkably adventurous journey through the Jotunheimen and other wild regions of Norway in 1834 (Slingsby 1904:8). This appears to be a highly inaccurate statement. Slingsby may either be too polite or not have read Breton thoroughly, as Lieutenant Breton's modesty is hard to spot. His attitude in a number of passages gives the impression of being more condescending and ironic than modest.

Breton prepared himself well for his travels by reading. He frequently refers to travel writing and to descriptions of Norway and the northern part of Europe, mentioning, for instance, Pliny the elder, 'the first writer who expressly mentions the north by the name of Scandinavia' (Breton 1835:21), though several of his other sources are anonymous, quoted only as 'one who wrote' etc. He is critical to his sources and often expresses a different view. He refers to descriptions of Trondheim by Christian Leopold von Buch (*Reise durch Norwegen und Lappland* (1810)) and others 'who seem to have considered it the most charming place under the sun, and thought it equal to the Bay of Naples' and remarks drily that these have 'employed too much of the *couleur de rose* in their representations' (Breton 1835:115).

William Cecil Slingsby opens his travel accounts of the mountains of Norway by explaining his interest in the country as a playground for adventures and exploration: 'Norway is one of the most mountainous countries in the world, and is to-day recognised as being one of the most delightful of our Alpine playgrounds' (Slingsby 1904:1). Or again:

> From the earliest childhood when, under the guidance of a governess, I acquired some inaccurate information about the Dovre Fjeld, to the advanced period of existence when Miss Marthineau's charming little book, *Feats on the Fjord*, lay open before me, I longed to go to Norway more than to any other country (Slingsby 1904:17).

Slingsby was the young, upper-class Englishman who was looking for a playground for activities that by most Norwegians would be interpreted as exclusive leisure pastimes. Great concern was caused by Slingsby's insufficient awareness of the possible dangers he might be faced with in his *playground*. He was not familiar with the precautions which were demanded for responsible mountain excursions, and people in the valleys found it irresponsible to put one's life at stake for mere pleasure. They claimed that Slingsby and his companions often escaped from their adventures in one piece thanks to mere chance. Slingsby represented a kind of British self-sufficiency, and advice from others ran off him like water off a duck's back. Like his countrymen, he practised the art of listening politely, but then going his own way. By this he confirmed the saying which was common in the Norwegian countryside: 'Anten er han spikande galen, eller so er han engelskmann' (Either he is completely mad, or he's an Englishman) (Slingsby/Schwarzott 1998:8).

First and foremost Slingsby became famous for his mountain climbing and glacier explorations in Hurrungane (1874), Store Skagastølstind, the highest peak in the Hurrungane (1876/1908) and Kjenndalsbreen (1881). Slingsby did not call himself a rock-climber, but a mountaineer. Jan Schwarzott explains the difference: to a rock-climber the climbing is the priority, but to a mountaineer it is *the mountains* (Slingsby/Schwarzott 1998:9).

Slingsby has been called the father of Norwegian mountain climbing. His aim was to explore the Norwegian mountains and glaciers and make their abundance of challenges and beauty known to the Norwegians themselves (Slingsby/Young 1998:11). He climbed in Norway, the Swiss Alps and in Great Britain. The historically most important rock wall in England on Scafell was named after him, the *Slingsby Chimney* (1888) and two sections of Store Skagastølstind, the *Slingsby Glacier* and the *Slingsby Peak* (1876). His enthusiasm was infectious to other climbers, his friends and even his own family. Slingsby's sister came with him on one tour, his cousins on others, and his wife was the first female mountaineer to ascend Lodalskåpa and Romsdalshorn, while their youngest daughter ascended Store Skagastølstind and followed her father's track to please him when he was not able himself to take part in the fiftieth celebration of his first ascent.

Slingsby was widely read in history, travel writing and poetry (Slingsby/Young 1998:12), and the title of his book alludes to the title of Leslie Stephen's *The Playground of Europe* (1871) which deals with the Swiss Alps. When

Slingsby added *The Northern Playground* after *Norway* it was an assertion to Stephen that there were other playgrounds just as challenging.

In the introduction to his book Slingsby writes that Norwegian peasants made the first ascents of mountains like Galdhøpiggen, Lodalskåpa, Romsdalshorn, Slogen and Gaustatoppen, but that mountaineering as a noble sport was not recognized until it was reintroduced by British adventurers. Lieutenant Breton was the first British adventurer and the first pioneer of the five mentioned by Slingsby. However, Breton was not a mountaineer, even if he ascended Snøhetta in the Dovrefjell, and he preferred to travel by horse.

For whom did they write their travel accounts?

Breton's book is a handbook for tourists and contains information on a number of topics and fields that would be of interest to an educated reader. For instance on topography and physical geography he refers to theories explaining why the sea level is lower than it once was. He also explains the tide, sea currents and whirlpools and possible alteration in the climate (Breton 1835:22, 136, 13, 19). He gives a long and fairly thorough account (twelve pages) of the history of Norway. He explains the constitution and political, judicial and ecclasiastical administration of the country, and informs the reader about exports, population, census, mortality rates, temperatures, depths of fjords and other kinds of information which can be measured and mathematically described.

As Breton is addressing gentlemen travellers, he sees the need to prepare them for the various kinds of trial ahead. He finds a lot of things to complain about. One of them is the food available at the post-houses, 'beef or mutton the traveller must not expect, except in the towns, unless smoked, and even then not always at the mere post stations (...) Of a verity, this is no "land of flesh-pots" and every person should take provisions with him' (Breton 1835:66).

Slingsby says in his preface to *Norway. The Northern Playground* that he is writing for the tourist about the possibilities of mountain sport in Norway. He does not address his book exclusively to rock-climbers or mountaineers. Almost as a contradiction to this statement the Norwegian climber Ferdinand Schjelderup in his obituary of his friend Slingsby concluded the description of Slingsby's mountain adventures: 'by achievements like this he taught us that mountains were created to be climbed' (Slingsby/Schwarzott 1998:353).

How did they write? Structure and style

Breton's book opens with descriptions of topography, vegetation and fauna. He reflects on travel writing and sets down his chief criteria for an interesting account: variation of landscape and houses, wild and cultivated nature. The great disadvantage with Norway is the lack of towns, for 'the reader must eventually become tired of perusing remarks on the scenery alone, unvaried by accounts of edifices, monuments of antiquity, and objects of interest, so constantly observed in other countries, and so conducive to rendering a journal more amusing' (Breton 1835:182).

Breton regularly employs allusions and references to classical Greek, old English and Norse literature; for example when describing the danger and violence of the Saltstraumen whirlpool, he refers, evidently ironically, to the story of a man who was taken down to the bottom of it, 'this man has outdone Nicholas the Fisherman, who explores the dark recesses of Charybdis' (Breton 1835:14). Another reference to Charybdis is attached to the description of the Malstrøm, which other authors have attempted to prove was the place where Ulysses met with Scylla and Charybdis (Breton 1835:139). In the region of Trøndelag Breton mentions historic chiefs renowned in arms, and quotes from the songs of Ossian: 'it howls in thy empty court, and whistles round thy half worn shields' (Breton 1835:156). He also refers to old Norse literature and quotes a passage in prose translation from Ragnar Loðbrok's Death-Song, which affords 'a specimen of the Norsk poetry' with notions of life after death, and shows the character of Ragnar Loðbrok who invaded Northumbria about AD 860 (Breton 1835:24). He likewise refers to the poetry of the 'skalds' and to the *Elder Edda* as well as to Snorri's *Edda* (Breton 1835:112ff).

Irony and understatement are figures of speech frequently employed by Breton as the following two examples show:

> Cowper exclaims for some vast wilderness, some boundless contiguity of shade! He should have visited the North, where his utmost wishes would have been gratified.' (Breton 1835:46)

> I have strong a objection to this detestable system of depasturing cattle upon the graves of our forefathers, which ought to be left in tranquility and repose; but some may perhaps think that, as 'all flesh is grass', those of us who are of no utility during our lives, may as well be converted to some purpose when dead. (Breton 1835:67)

Slingsby based his travel writing on his diaries in order to preserve his first impressions and prevent reinterpretation by memory and reflection, and he was aware that he wrote best when the incidents could be described chronologically. Jan Schwarzott, who edited and translated Slingsby's travel accounts for a Norwegian public in 1998, gave in his preface a characteristic of Slingsby's style, stating that his 'archaic arabesques and Victorian ornament' were flexible instruments for his 'alliterations, poetic phrases and musicality' (Slingsby/Schwarzott 1998:5; author's translation).

Each chapter in Slingsby's *Norway. The Northern Playground* starts with a few quotations from poems or words of wisdom in prose. Longfellow, Shakespeare, Wordsworth, Virgil, Samuel Johnson and others are represented, as for instance, Coleridge, in three lines from a poem which forms part of the title of this article:

Beneath the mountain's lofty frowning brow,
Ere aught of perilous ascent you meet,
A mead of mildest charms delays the unlabouring feet. (Slingsby 1904:358)

In Slingsby's text poems are also sometimes interwoven. When he reflects on the difference in the standard of comfort in mountain huts in his young days and fifty years later, he exclaims, 'Ah! now is the time of prose and plenty. We had the poetry and hunger. Fortunately each condition represents much thorough enjoyment, and probably the balance is well adjusted'. He then proceeds to quote a pastoral romantic poem (Slingsby 1904:39).

Nature: the ugly, the beautiful – and the challenging

In his book *The Time of Unrememberable Being* (1996), Klaus P. Mortensen compares passages by Ludvig Holberg and Thomas Gray to illustrate the changes taking place in the interpretation of nature in the eighteenth century. These may act as a useful backdrop to discussions about descriptions of nature in nineteenth-century travel literature. Holberg writes in his first *Levnedsbrev* from 1728 about his experiences of the Alps in 1716. He finds the rough, wild and uncultivated landscape ugly, while beauty is to be found in civilization where man has tamed and cultivated the wilderness. A few years later Thomas Gray writes a letter about his experiences in the Alps. To Gray the wild and inaccessible Alpine landscape is impressive, attractive and romantic. Nature gives a double impact of threatening danger and joyful elevation (Mortensen 1996:19).

Holberg's and Gray's contrasting views of alpine nature illustrate not only a difference in their individual temperaments, but also a general change in the view of nature in Europe and in England in the latter half of the eighteenth century. Klaus P. Mortensen argues that the growing appreciation of wild nature was connected to the growth of the urban middle-class culture. When people moved from the country to the towns, they lost their closeness to nature. The notion of nature as a lost paradise developed. The movement out of towns and into nature which the travel accounts of ramblers and mountaineers described may be seen as a desire for liberation and the restoration of a link to a lost origin (Mortensen 1996:21).

This change in interpretation and attitude to nature can be seen in poetry and in art, and it goes further in order to try to see the power behind a particular landscape. Poets, artist and travellers with this concept of nature turn to it to be absorbed or to internalize their experiences of nature, and not only to regard it as a physical and geographic phenomenon at a distance.

From Breton's point of view the Norwegian countryside 'wears such a look of neglect', and he gives one reason for this: there are hardly any gentlemen's country houses as 'persons of property reside for the most part near the towns' (Breton 1835:15). He misses interesting pieces of architecture which give a break to the landscape: 'we met with neither the remains of feudal magnificence nor monastic architecture; and this is one reason why travelling becomes, after a time, so wearisome' (Breton 1835:16).

The standard for an admirable landscape may be set by what Breton appreciates in his own country as a combination of fields and mild scenery with a river winding through it, or what he experienced in Switzerland. Thus 'wild and romantic' may be a positive characteristic when it reminds him of the Alps, as does Fillefjeld, which is 'in many respects equal to Simplon itself'; it has such a 'bold and savage grandeur (...) that the mind can scarcely conceive any thing more strikingly wild' (Breton 1835:216). A highly positive description is also given of the scenery at Hovie near Reien:

> The scenery is extremely grand, and as wild as possible, the mountains rising abruptly, and reminding me, though on a much smaller scale, of the Jungfrau and of Lauterbrun, in Switzerland. Hence ascending a pass, the sides of which are naked crags, I was delighted with some wonderfully fine imagery, Nature being seen in one of her most interesting forms. At Thune, the situation of which, on the Mose Vand, is perfectly alpine, we perceive farms and saeters. (Breton 1835:212)

Breton judges by the standards of educated English taste. His ultimate criteria for a beautiful landscape are variations upon open cultivated and fertile areas with mountains. But even when such scenery is found, Breton does not hesitate in suggesting improvements: 'there is most charming scenery, but of a less alpine nature than the preceding part of the route, and it might be infinitely improved by greater attention to agriculture' (Breton 1835:183).

Breton's view of nature proves him to be much more of an eighteenth-century classicist, a son of the Enlightenment, than an early nineteenth-century romanticist. He does not appreciate the wild and rugged, and when he applies the term 'romantic' it refers to a landscape which is mildly curved and undulating rather than wild. Breton's ideals seem to be clarity, harmony, and unity with well composed variety. In his opinion the epithets 'wonderful' and 'fine' should not be employed to describe broken and irregular scenery with hills around and 'houses scattered over its surface' (Breton 1835:183). Such disharmony does not satisfy the admirer as regards sublimity or beauty of nature (Breton 1835:184, cf. 210). He perceives a landscape as an aesthetic construction, more or less successfully made, and seems to read elements of nature as 'requisites' of a tableau, 'waterfalls conduce to the general effect, but the essential requisite, a large body of water, is wanting in all' (Breton 1835:217). The same criteria are applied to the construction of a farm and the situation of the buildings. Breton demands 'some kind of regularity' instead of 'a cluster of from five or ten to even twenty-five huts of all sorts and sizes, sometimes scattered, at others jumbled together without any regard to order' (Breton 1835:188).

The admiration of nature in the eighteenth century required that nature became a landscape, a composed unit – simultaneously individual and universal. Not until an aesthetic distance was achieved would it be possible to establish the extract of nature which was a landscape. The aesthetic point of view demanded distance, alienation. The bourgeois observer had been liberated from the force of nature and is not dependent on it for his existence (Mortensen 1996:27).

Slingsby does not share Breton's criteria of regularity and harmony, and praises Bergen even if he observes a certain disharmony in its architecture:

> Bergen, Bjørgvin – the mountain pastures – of the old, overlooked by its seven fjelde, is, even yet, in spite of the ruthless substitution of prosaic stucco buildings for picturesque wooden houses each with its gable end towards the front, one of the most beautiful cities in the world. (Slingsby 1904:18)

Breton's use of the term 'sublime' corresponds to Joseph Addison's concept of the sublime as comprising three elements: the great, the uncommon and the beautiful. Sublimity is connected with the object or scenery observed. Addison's external greatness is followed by a greatness of the observer's mind. A wide horizon in contrast to a narrow mountain passage elevates the human mind and represents freedom. This is probably why Breton prefers the wide, open landscape on the banks of the river Glomma.

Slingsby also observes the sublime as the great in nature and with uncommon and beautiful details, and he sometimes enthusiastically expresses his impressions in metaphors:

> To our intense delight there was a huge rainbow, or rather a rain ring, (...) the sublimity of this scene was unique. It suggested the idea that fairy hands had woven the oval frame of the pictures whose subject was the mighty Vøringsfoss and its wonderous surroundings. (Slingsby 1904:24)

In his philosophy on the sublime and beautiful Edmund Burke puts the emphasis on the psychological aspects of the sublime. To Burke, the human experience of nature as overwhelming is suspended between pain and delight. The sublime is experienced on the brink of the abyss. The sublime delight is attached to the disapperance of danger and fear (Mortensen 1993:98-104 and

1999:115ff.). Only at one point in his description does Breton approach a sublime experience in Burkes's sense of the word. Breton passes through a valley near Gudvangen where overhanging rocks give an impression of threatening danger and a 'feeling of insecurity that can hardly fail to make the traveller reflect upon the uncertainty of human existence', but even in this situation the aesthetic assessment prevails: 'this caused an undefinable sensation as of haste to reach a spot more free from danger, and yet the magnificence of the scenery was such, that my apprehensions were not sufficient to hurry me away from the contemplation of it' (Breton 1835:222).

Slingsby responds emotionally to nature, as is evident in his opening quotation from Ruskin's 'The Mountain Glory' from *Modern Painters* (1843):

> For to myself, mountains are the beginning and the end of all natural scenery; in them, and in the forms of inferior landscape that lead to them, my affections are wholly bound up. (Slingsby 1904:xviii)

Slingsby is challenged by the inaccessable peaks and is wild with excitement when his expeditions are successful. He appreciates the grandeur of the mountains, and he experiences that nature gives a double impact of threatening danger and joyful elevation. His descriptions illustrate Burke's theory that the sublime is experienced on the brink of the abyss, suspended between pain and delight. On descending the Kjenndalsbreen Slingsby describes his route:

> The ledge, mere groove cut into the face of the rock, twelve feet deep, two feet wide, and about twenty-five yards long, was no myth, and we crawled along it without difficulty, and in perfect safety, though a regular avalanche track was just a few feet above our heads and a frightful abyss was below us. (...) We had now turned our precipice, waterfall, and third ice-fall. Surely now we were safe. (...) Now we began to admire the grandeur of our surroundings. (Slingsby 1904:301)

Descriptions of 'the natives'

In contrast to English travellers before him, Slingsby was cheerful, open and friendly in his manner towards 'the natives'. He appreciated the local inhabitants of the mountain valleys, mingled with them and in his book refers to them by their names as individuals and equals, not as a collective or a subordinate category of natives as we shall see that Breton does. Ferdinand Schjelderup wrote in his obituary of Slingsby that 'he took a keen interest in the conditions of life of the farmers, in bygone days and now – their hunting and "sæter" life and in short, the ways in which they managed to acquire their means of living where nature is severe and overwhelming' (Slingsby/ Schwarzott 1998:353). Slingsby also preferred to climb with local people, and they accepted him as one of their own. It is perhaps for these reasons that

Wyndham Young, who wrote a preface to a later edition of Slingsby's book, could refer to a remark made by Slingsby's cousin, Alfred Hopkinson, who said that Slingsby alternated with Saint Olav as the patron saint of Norway (Slingsby/Schwarzott 1998:11). Even today it seems that Slingsby draws comparisons of the highest order, being compared by Jan Schwarzott to Fridtjof Nansen:

> Begge oppnådde å bli folkekjære her på berget, en heder bare de færreste nordmenn forunt og eksepsjonelt for en utlending. Sant nok hadde klatrerbragdene gjort Slingsbys navn kjent av alle, men de rørte ikke ved hjertene. Slikt forlanger mer, og kanskje fortrinnsvis noe annet, enn å være flink til å fly på toppene. (Slingsby/Schwarzott 1998:8)

> (Both of them achieved the status of being loved by the Norwegian people, an honour only few Norwegians enjoy, and which is even more exceptional for a foreigner. True enough, his climbing achievements brought fame to the name of Slingsby, but rock climbing alone could not touch the hearts of the people. That demands more and maybe something quite different from the ability to ascend a lot of peaks.)

With Breton, names never occur, except those of clergymen and members of a social class in whose company he feels at ease. Breton discriminates between the clergy and the peasants. He advises other English gentlemen to meet the clergy, who are always ready to assist and open their homes to visitors, but he warns his countrymen against ridiculing and 'treating their entertainers with scorn and derision' in their travel descriptions, as has been done by a writer who is not mentioned by name. The consequence may be that the clergymen will cease to show hospitality to travellers (Breton 1835:55).

Breton does not expect much civilization or culture from the inhabitants of Norway. According to his reading, 'all the old historians' describe the inhabitants as 'ignorant, and almost exclusively occupied in war or in the chase' (Breton 1835:23). Nor has he much to say in favour of the hygienic conditions of the country. The tourist must be prepared to 'pass the night amidst vermin and dirt' (Breton 1835:52). Very few of the post-houses (inns, 'skyssstasjoner') where he spent a night satisfy his demands as to standards of hygiene and price:

> Of post-houses a very small number are good, others are tolerable, but far the greater proportion are dirty and wretched, one of our little country inns being superior to the best of them, and less expensive. (Breton 1835:64)

In contast to the complaints of Breton, Slingsby takes the vermin like a good sport and explains with a great portion of humour about the usefulness of a Scottish plaid as a protection against unwanted blood-suckers:

> Without a plaid one must keep all one's clothes on, excepting boots and coat. With a plaid one can take most of them off, wrap one's feet well, and leave a good length for the head, then roll up almost like a chrysalis and fasten the folds securely with safety pins, and after drawing over oneself the skins and saying to one's companions, 'God nat, drøm behagelig', can boldly defy the attacks of the evil creatures whose saltatory attainments are proverbial, and which show such a decided preference for a well-washed Englishman. In the north of England we still call this foe to midnight slumbers a 'lop'. (Slingsby 1904:47)

Breton complains of the peasants being dirty. The man or the boy who goes with him in the carriol 'brings his dirty person into too great a propinquity with yourself, and transfers to your custody sundry of those animals familiar to man, but not less disagreeable' (Breton 1835:60).

He also strongly dislikes the Norwegian habit of shaking hands. When the peasants are given money, they shake hands with the donor, 'a custom common throughout Norway, but not very agreeable to a person who regards cleanliness, as the greater number of the lower orders are not over particular in respect to ablutions' (Breton 1835:86).

Breton's attitude to what he considers the lower classes is not only condescending, but frequently contemptuous. The peasants are described as stupid and curious and completely unaccustomed to strangers: 'each article they could not comprehend excited a chuckle of admiration; and they would stand gaping with astonishment' (Breton 1835:86). Much is said by Breton in praise of Norwegian women. They are not only good-looking, but pretty with a high colour and remarkably beautiful teeth. 'The dress of the women was frequently slovenly and indecent but when clad in their holiday costumes their appearance was greatly improved; ornaments of silver are common among them: and some of these were curious, as well as antique' (Breton 1835:195). But even women are dirty and 'in their personal habits they are often most disgusting (...) and covered with vermin' (Breton 1835:196). Nevertheless, Breton's concluding remarks about the natives of Norway are that he considers:

> the Norwegians a happy race of people, and never observed among them that wretchedness so often witnessed in the United Kingdom; but so it is in most alpine regions, the inhabitants of which seem more contented, and to all appearance far less subjected to privations than those of other countries. (Breton 1835:203)

Breton travelled all over Norway and is moderate or negative in his assessment:

> Thus ended an excursion of 700 miles, during which I saw much to gratify, and not a little of an opposite character. That a degree of monotony prevails in the scenery is indubitable, and there are likewise prospects of remarkable beauty; but unfortunately the effect is often marred by that neglect as regards agricultural improvements. (Breton 1835:184)

Slingsby opens his introduction to *Norway. The Northern Playground* by praising the 'characteristics and sterling good qualities of a race to which I am proud to believe that we are nearer akin than to any other in Europe' (Slingsby 1904:16), and he ends his book with a recommendation and a challenge to his mountaineering readers:

> Then away to the mountains, away, away, and glean more health and strength of mind and body to enable you to combat the difficulties of life, and to lay up a rich store of happy memories from which you can always draw, yet can never exhaust. (Slingsby 1904:422)

Conclusion

Mary Louise Pratt claims there is a shift in the aims and the manner of travel writing after 1735 with Carl Linné's *Systema naturae* and the first international scientific expeditions to other parts of the world than Europe. Travel writing shifts from maritime to interior explorations, and the travellers have scientific purposes.

Although written in 1835, Breton's book can in a sense be regarded as a 'pre-shift' work. He collects information on natural and social history, climate, geology, physical oceanography etc., though he is far less systematic and is less specialist in a scientific sense than David Forbes (1853), who was a scientist in the field of glaciology and wrote about his excursions to the Norwegian glaciers. Breton's descriptions may be seen as an example of the attitude of the enlightenment. He is a globetrotter, is in no hurry, is curious and wants to cover as much ground as possible. His aim is to give advice, warnings and recommendations to future tourists. He travels for the sake of his own pleasure, not as a natural and social scientist, and he feels free to criticize, ridicule and appreciate as he pleases. However he has a well-developed sense of style and rhetoric and frequently employs allusions, references, understatement, often with an elegant tinge of irony. He reveals his classical criteria for a beautiful landscape. Beauty has to do with form, variation and cultivation. He celebrates the classical ideas of clarity, order and harmony, and his attitude is rational with no traces of metaphysics or an inner nature beyond the physical forms of the mountains. He allows outbursts of emotion only when he is annoyed. In these respects he is closer to Ludvig Holberg than to Thomas Gray, though at one point he expresses a certain ambiguity. Wild and rocky nature may be called beautiful on certain conditions and as long as they are not monotonous:

> there exist for me no charms in the melodious roaring of torrents, nor howling winds, nor even in the aspect of frowning mountains, although they may delight the eye for a time. (Breton 1835:215)

Slingsby's aim as a travel writer was to collect information on the nature of Norwegian mountain peaks and glaciers and the access to them, and to combine this with a broad survey of the country and the people. In his obituary of Slingsby, Ferdinand Schjelderup writes of his love for adventures and:

> his insatiable curiosity. In every field he was equally keen to enlarge his experience and enhance his knowledge. (...) Nothing was indifferent to him. Along with the ascents themselves he was no less engrossed in every aspect of nature, in birds and animals, trees and flowers, and geology. Similarly he was interested in history, folklore, folk-music. (Slingsby/Schwartzott 1998:353)

Breton spent one summer in Norway, whereas Slingsby kept coming back for years adding new information about glaciers and mountains before he wrote his book.

Neither Breton's nor Slingsby's books are scientific travel-writing in the sense that Marie Louise Pratt describes in *Imperial Eyes*. Nevertheless there is a difference between the two that is more than the difference of individual temperaments. Breton resembles in many respects the imperialist. What he observes in Norway is mostly inferior to what he has experienced in Britain and other cultivated countries. Like Ludvig Holberg and the travel writers of the Enlightenment, Breton regards the mountains from a distance as an aesthetic object, a constructed landscape, 'there is a rugged grandeur about the mountains, and if they were rather less frowning the scenery would be improved' (Breton 1835:177).

Where Breton's attitude is condescending, Slingsby's is enthusiastically and actively exploring and he is a 'frolicsome boy again', a romanticist with an almost religious attitude.

Slingsby gains strength, joy and sublime experiences from life in the mountains:

> No man, however callous he may be by nature, can be much amongst the high mountains without gaining strength of character as well as physical strength. King David knew this when he wrote Psalm cxxi: 'I will lift up mine eyes unto the hills, from whence cometh my help.' (Slingsby 1904:421)

Bibliography:

Breton, William Henry, (1835): *Scandinavian Sketches or A Tour in Norway*. London, J. Bohn.
Mortensen, Klaus P. (1993): *Himmelstormerne. En linje i dansk naturdigtning*. København, Gyldendal.
Mortensen, Klaus P. (1996): *The Time of Unrememberable Being. Wordsworth og det sublime*

1787-1805. København, Litteraturkritikk & romantikkstudier.

Mortensen, Klaus P. (1999): 'Naturens spejl – fra gudbilledlighed til naturlighed' in *Naturhistorier. Naturoppfatning, menneskesyn og poetikk i skandinavisk litteratur*. Eds Lærkesen, Bache-Wiig, Lombnæs. Oslo, LNU/Cappelen Akademisk forlag.

Pratt, Marie Louise (1992/2003): *Imperial eyes: travel writing and transculturation*. London and New York, Routledge.

Slingsby, William Cecil (1904): *Norway. The Northern Playground. Sketches of climbing and mountain exploration in Norway between 1872 and 1903*. Edinburgh, David Douglas.

Slingsby, William Cecil (1998): *Norge. Den nordlige arena. Skisser fra tindebestigninger og oppdagerferder i norsk natur mellom 1872 og 1921*. (Ed. Jan Schwarzott.) Oslo, Grøndahl Dreyer.

From a Haven for Travellers to a Boarding House for Tourists: The Vicarage in the History of Travelling and Hospitality in Norway.

Bjarne Rogan

Among the basic needs for travellers are lodging and meals – a roof and a bed for the night, and food and drink at fairly regular intervals. Closely related to these necessities is hospitality, a concept which also implies attention, generosity and a sense of responsibility towards the stranger.

The present chapter discusses the lodging and care of travellers in private homes, as experienced by early travellers. Seen through the eyes of foreigners, Norway had found a rather special solution to these practical issues, by making demands on one specific professional group: government officials and especially vicars. I shall discuss the origin of this renowned hospitality as well as its myth of origin, its heyday in the eighteenth and early nineteenth centuries, and the decline around the middle of the nineteenth century.

Old myths and post-Reformation vicarages

The infrastructure for travelling in Norway was weak in the late Medieval Age and the first centuries of the Early Modern Period. The lack of inns or taverns in Norway, well documented in the sources, caused important hindrances for travelling. Allegedly, the Church was a central institution when travelling in Norway in Catholic times; hospitality was considered a Christian obligation, and the Church and the monasteries gave shelter and food to travellers and pilgrims, states Olaf Olafsen (Olafsen 1927:144). He claims that hospitals were founded along the most heavily trafficked routes to give lodging, adding that this service ceased with the Reformation in Norway in 1536, when the monasteries and their hospitals were abolished.

Hospitals established by monasteries, in general and elsewhere in Europe, often functioned as inns for travellers – but not so in Norway. The twenty or so hospitals that existed before the Reformation were partly pauper houses, partly hospitals for the sick, or leper institutions (KLNM 6:687ff).

However, if the monasteries have been of less importance for travel in Norway than some have claimed, the ministers all over the country – and the Lutherans to a higher degree than their Catholic precursors – have certainly played a major role. During the first three centuries after the Reformation, the vicarage was an important institution for travellers.

For travellers from the upper classes, the smoky and uncomfortable living rooms of the peasants were not appropriate accommodation. The normal solution was to seek out the vicarages. Or as Absalon Pedersøn Beyer stated in 1570: 'Forsooth, a pious, god-fearing and decent person may well travel from Båhus to Vardøhus without spending a *daler*. Yes, they [the hosts] are even happy to have the honour of eating and drinking with him.' Almost two hundred years later, in 1753, Bishop Erik Pontoppidan joined in: 'Travellers in this country are so rare that they are seldom allowed to pay for their stay'. Actually, most authors of travel accounts from the seventeenth and eighteenth centuries mention their stays at the vicarages.

This hospitality of the vicars is commonly interpreted as a continuation of the medieval monastery tradition, although in a Norwegian context this would be erroneous. As Barbara Ring states with reference to Hanna Winsnes and the Vang vicarage: 'The vicarages all over the country had long ago inherited and for centuries practiced the hospitality of the hospitals of the old Church' (Ring 1924:153).[1] However, the link between the old Catholic Church and the hospitality of the Protestant vicarages must be sought elsewhere.

When the Catholic bishops once a year undertook their visitations of the parishes, as prescribed by law, they were accompanied by a numerous staff, normally around twelve persons, whom the local minister was obliged to lodge and treat. This yearly invasion of guests was not without consequences for the size and the architecture of the parson's or vicar's farm.

Actually the vernacular architecture of the vicarage was subject to regulations which were prolonged in post-Reformation decrees. The *Church Ordinance* of 1607 states that 'aff Arrildstid' – i.e. from time immemorial – the peasants of some districts have been obliged to construct and maintain three buildings at the vicarage and should do so in the future. These buildings were *herrekammeret* (the bishop's chamber) where the bishop resided during the stay, *borgestuen* (where his company was lodged), and finally a stable large enough for all the horses, which was all the more important as the visitations normally took place in the winter time. The function of the three houses was to provide a high guest capacity at the vicarage. These regulations were repeated in Christian IV's Norwegian law of 1687, which means that this remained the legal situation until 1897, when a new law for ecclesiastical farms was passed (Bugge 1918:93-98).

The Lutheran bishops were not as mighty masters as their Catholic precursors had been; neither did they travel with similarly big companies, nor did they set out so often on visitations. Over the years the *herrekammer* ended up as a joint part of the main building, resulting in additional guest rooms and a big parlour. Different decrees maintained, wholly or partly, the obligation on the parishioners, until the late nineteenth century. Bugge correctly points out that the different arguments in the successive decrees show that the lawmakers did not any longer understand the reason for this obligation. As early as in 1604, in the first draft of the *Church Ordinance*, it is stated that the parishioners should provide the ministers with food and beer, lodging and stable room, 'because most of the guesting activities, which happen in our Kingdom, by all those who travel through the Kingdom, mostly take place at the ministers' farms', or, in the language of the day: 'effterdj alt dett meste Giesterie, som her falder i Riget aff alle som fare igiennom Riget, søger allermest til Presterne'.

The wording reveals what had been the usual practice when travelling in Norway. But the draft can probably also be read as an (unsuccessful) attempt on the part of the authorities to force upon the ministers an obligation that they formally never had had.

Hospitable government officials in the countryside

In spite of royal decrees in the seventeenth and eighteenth centuries, the peasant taverns remained few and their standard low. Wayfaring people continued to seek out the vicarages. Until around 1850, taking in at vicarages was the norm for travellers of a certain standing.

From the 1830s, a new group of travellers started exploiting this resource, as it became popular among the students to go on prolonged hikes in the summer time. Or as the historian Ludvig L. Daae (b. 1834) reported:

> In my student days [...] we roamed the valleys to learn to know the countryside. Singing we marched along the main roads. When we arrived at a government official's farm [*embedsgaard*], to which we had neither a letter of recommendation nor a greeting, we just marched into the yard with our student caps on our heads. In most cases the inhabitants came running down to us, inviting us inside and asking news from the capital. And rarely were we dismissed the next day without a toast; we were supposed to need a 'walking stick' on our way, and often enough a second one as well – called 'a spike in the stick'. (L. L. Daae, quoted from Knutzen 1922)

Tradition associates this hospitality with the whole group of government officials or civil servants, and also with the so-called 'proprietors', i.e. the big forest owners, merchants and owners of local industry, who inhabited and exploited big farms and willingly copied the civil servant culture, including the hospitality towards travellers. Especially in the North these proprietors played a major role. Dispersed all over the country, like a thinly spread stratum in the countryside, these farms kept their doors open for travellers of a certain social standing.

During the first half of the nineteenth century, the number of government officials (*embetsmenn*) in Norway was slightly below two thousand, or around 0.7% of the population. Half of them lived in the countryside, and the clergy formed a large majority. The local magistrates (*sorenskrivere*), to take a less numerous group, got their official residential farms at a much later date (nineteenth century). The running of the farm, which was the property of the State, was a part of the minister's revenue. The size of the households was often important, so farming was a necessary skill for a minister, as was household economy for his wife. Also, he was economically responsible towards his successor for the maintenance of the farm buildings.

A traveller of the early nineteenth century who has provided detailed descriptions of his stays at the vicarages, is the Danish admiral Hans Birch Dahlerup. As a lieutenant he visited Norway several times in the years 1804 to 1812. Dahlerup had to pass many a night in the modest abodes of peasants and fishermen, in poor or even miserable conditions, with little or no food and a hard bench or only the floor to sleep on, in the atmosphere of fuming smoke stoves. He knew well the improved conditions offered by the vicarages, which he sought whenever possible. The contrast was enormous:

> How nice it was to enter one of these old-fashioned parlours [of a vicarage] on a winter evening, when the day's journey was over. The fire cracked in a welcoming manner in the heating stove; candles in polished pewter candlesticks were lit all around the room; fine, white sand, mixed with small, finely cut twigs of spruce or juniper, was spread on the floor, giving a very delicate smell which blended with the fragrance of rose petals or other fine incense on the stoves; on the table set for tea the shining copper samovar gave away its steam, the table being covered with a white tablecloth of the best damask. The host and his family were dressed in their best clothes. Such was the hospitality in the Norwegian countryside in those days. (Dahlerup 1908 I:97-98)

Dahlerup has given detailed and amusing descriptions of the reception by the vicarages or other government officials, several of whom, he reports, were offended if travellers of standing passed their farms without paying a visit. A short passage will give an impression of the ambience:

> This is the general picture of those families, with whom I became acquainted on my travels in the less populated and less visited parts of Norway: After the tea there were the tobacco pipes and the punch, while the supper table was set with a busy but silent care. Trout directly from the stream, a mighty veal leg and grouse accompanied by every kind of jam – of red whortleberries, yellow cloudberries,

cherries, red and black currants, was the festive treatment one could always expect. Add to this a bottle of good red wine, and above all, the heartfelt happiness and the delightful excitement and activity that were triggered by the visit of a stranger, affecting everyone down to the humblest servant. If all this did not double the appetite, whetted beforehand by a long day's journey in the sharp winter air, if this did not inspire the visitor to honour the culinary art of the hostess, to drink the host's wine with a double desire, to inspire him to cheerfulness and communicativeness, then indeed the traveller must be an insensitive and ungrateful man. (Dahlerup 1908 I:98-99)

Letters of recommendation were seldom requested, even if some travellers, especially foreigners, used to bring such letters. A recommendation, written by a well-known person, might be quite general in form, addressed 'to whom it may concern', but still function as a door opener throughout the itinerary. Most ministers opened their doors anyway; 'although a complete stranger to the minister' I was very well received, wrote the Danish painter Martinus Rørbye about the vicar in Heddal in Telemark in 1830. (Rørbye 1930:108). Some ministers and magistrates were even known to have given permanent orders to the *skyssskaffer* to bring travellers directly to their residences instead of to the local *skyssskifte* or tavern (Dahlerup 1909 [1811], Nielsen 1909 [1817]). Notes and comments on hospitable vicars are legion in the travel accounts.

At the most sought-after vicarages the influx of travellers could become a heavy charge, and the problem became acute with growing tourism towards the middle of the nineteenth century. Even as early as in 1821, the visitation report from the bishop of Nordland mentions that its position far from the beaten track was considered a resource (*en Herlighed*) for the parish of Saltdalen! Also, popular tradition has handed down stories about sorely tried vicar families. Popular tradition says about the daughters of the vicar in Slidre in Valdres in the 1830s that when they saw travellers approaching on the main road, they ran out and cried to the *skysskar*: 'Drive past! Drive past!' And when the strangers had passed, they happily called: 'Thank you! Thank you!' This vicar was renowned for his hospitality. According to popular tradition, the invasion at his vicarage on the main road between Christiania and Bergen was so important that only the vicar himself and his wife were certain to have their beds to themselves.

Through the memoir literature we know that more than one vicar's wife had subsistence worries and fear of not being able to treat all the guests. One of them was Hanna Winsnes, who, especially in their early years in Trysil, experienced some real crises when provisions were low and visitors poured in (Ring 1924:69-71). The inveterate wanderer Knud Knudsen, who had probably passed a night or two at most of the vicarages in Norway, once noted that he saw the vicar set off at dawn with his fishing gear – probably to secure the day's provision, as several visitors had knocked on his door the preceding day.

When the Swede, Edward Gustaf Fölsch, visited Oppdal in 1817, he wrote about Norwegian ministers in general, and the pastor Rønnow at Oppdal in particular, that 'they pass a lonely life in faraway, desolate places, deprived of the company of other educated people. Pastor Rønnow [...] whose sole pleasure was, he told me, to receive visits from travellers' (Fölsch 1818:108). This leads us to an important aspect of this tradition: the isolation and the need for cultural and social impulses.

Countryside vicars, isolation and solitude

> Far north in Helgeland there is a vicarage, where three young vicar's wives lie buried. They are all said to have died of melancholy. Nothing happens at these vicarages, that's what's so terrible. One becomes 'evil' only to make things happen; a strong desire to do something wrong may fall over you, only to see things happen. [...] How much these northern districts owe those officials, who did not become crushed and destroyed, so to say, by the pressure of loneliness and the depressive isolation [...] (Holm 1923:64, 79)

To understand the extraordinary hospitality of the vicars and the other government officials, their isolated position in the countryside must be considered. Their residential farms were like small islands in an ocean of peasant culture.

These farms, and especially the vicarages, functioned as centres from which culture spread into the countryside; culture in the meaning of both spiritual impulses, material culture and technical innovations, new agricultural methods and architecture, etc. The vicars did much more than spreading the Word! But the officials led an isolated life – sometimes extremely isolated, from their colleagues, from urban culture and from European civilization. Not least in the North the ministers might to some extent 'go rustic' or become *rustificerede*, in the language of the time, from lack of contact with other people than fishermen and a local merchant.

Even in southern Norway some ministers met the same fate. From his innumerable stays at vicarages, the eternal wanderer, hiker and linguist Knud Knudsen mentions that some of his hosts strongly disliked that he or other intellectual guests attended their sermons; 'Rural ministers sometimes 'go rustic', it's as if they become peasants (again), and like the peasants they are afraid of townsfolk and their criticism and harsh judgements' (Knudsen 1980, vol. III: 239-240). This is a recurrent topic in Knudsen's memoirs. He even reveals the names of ministers in whose residences he had lodged and who felt uncomfortable when having to converse with 'a young, educated man, especially one from the capital'.

Slow postal communications contributed to the feeling of isolation. Even far into the nineteenth century many localities had to wait months between the arrivals of mail dispatches with letters and newspapers. The renowned hospitality at the vicarages thus had a clear practical and selfish aspect; a visit from the outside world suspended for a short while the family's exile from civilization, from urban culture, and, if the visitor was a foreigner, from European impulses.

'The worst aspect of our stay in this narrow hole of a fiord, for me and my wife, was to cope with the solitude' This is the opening phrase of the chapter entitled 'Solitude' in the memoirs of pastor Olaf Holm, *Fra en nordlandsk prestegaard* (Holm 1923:60-79). In 1878 Holm came to Tysfjord in Nordland, 'a pot with a lid on' and without other connection to the outside world than by water. The mail took fourteen days from Kristiania, actually more time than between Kristiania and New York. As a telling proof of his 'never suffering injury from an influx of visitors' he mentions that of his two bottles of aquavit, he was able to bring one back – unopened – after seven years in Tysfjord! In other passages, however, he does not hide the fact that more than one pastor had fallen into the habit of choosing the bottle as a weapon against the feeling of loneliness. Holm himself resorted to other tricks when the solitude became overpowering: 'When things got too bad, I closed my book or laid my pen aside in my office, went to see my wife, offered her my arm, and then we made a promenade through all our parlours and living rooms, dreaming that we were marching on – Karl Johan [the main street of the capital]' (Holm 1923:65-66). One can easily imagine how the visit of a traveller would bring a moment of joy to the family.

However, it was not only in the North that the clergy and other officials rejoiced when someone knocked on their door. Diaries and memoirs confirm that the families, all over the country, looked forward to such breaks in the solitude.

The further we go back in time, the more important the visits. Hans Birch Dahlerup, who travelled regularly in Norway between 1804 and 1812, has given a general description from western and southern Norway of his experiences at the vicarages, filled with amusing details and observations. His sympathetic description renders the atmosphere and the joy that visits from the outside world brought to these solitary families:

> Travellers of a certain breeding were so rare in these parts of the country, and connections with the outside world so few, that the lonesome and isolated clergy and other officials enthusiastically practised a hospitality which procured them an evening's entertainment with people of culture and education. These visits also furnished them with news from the cities and the international scene, and it gave an occasion to revive many a cherished reminiscence from the merry days of their

youth and the student years in Copenhagen. These were unfailingly the topics of conversation, when the punch glasses were filled.

The traveller, who brought news, or he who could tell stories and listen to stories, or who knew or was perhaps even related to someone the host had known in his young days, could be certain that his name would be long remembered and mentioned with kind respect in the solitary household. [...]

If the stranger had been the entertainer before the meal, the one who had dominated the conversation and whom the ladies of the house listened to furtively but passionately, slowly tripping around him with their domestic activities, then – at the table – it was time for the host to demonstrate that he too had been a man of the world. He asked if this one or that one was still living, persons in whose house he had been or whose acquaintance he had made as a student in Copenhagen, or if this or that belle, who had once turned his head, was married and with whom, if she had children, what they were doing, etc. Then came the student pranks, the practical jokes they had played on a pedantic or an unpopular professor, the pleasures and amusements in the Norwegian Club, the visits to the entertainment parks, sprees and carousing, street disorders and pecuniary difficulties.

During these tales and anecdotes the respectable housewife folded her hands, and shaking her head with a surprised smile she looked furtively at the grown-up daughters, who modestly looked down and nervously let their fingers play with the edge of the tablecloth, a bit ashamed that their father had been so terribly wild in his young days and even dared to tell all this to the young stranger. And when it was time to break up and go to bed, the host and the hostess accompanied the stranger to the neat and tidy guest room, where the guest bed – the housemother's pride – arranged with sheets of the finest white Dutch linen, a mountain of delicate pillows and the eiderdown coverlet, as light as the winds of Zephyr, awaited the tired traveller.

At the morning coffee the housemother's first question was if the stranger had slept well, if the bed had been made to his satisfaction, if the chamber had been warm enough. It was out of question to start thinking of departure before the traveller had had a good, warm lunch in preparation for the new hardships to come. When finally it was time for departure and the sledge halted in front of the door, there were all the farewells, all the wishes for a happy journey and good health, but not seldom in a melancholic atmosphere of having to part so soon. (Dahlerup 1908:97-100)

Fifty years later a few of these old-fashioned ministers still existed. Aasmund Vinje hit the type in his tale about an old vicar in Gudbrandsdalen, in *Ferdaminni frå sumaren 1860*:

[...] when travellers arrived, this minister was as happy as could be; he even sought out people from the town far away. It was a treat to sit in his parlour, with a toddy and a tobacco pipe and talk about art and science and the capital as it used to be in his days. (Vinje 1939:226)

When Vinje wrote these lines, however, the tradition of finding lodging at the vicar's had come to an end, except in some very remote places. Before discussing the disappearance of a tradition that had lasted three or four centuries, we shall have a look at one of the factors that led to its fall – the emerging tourism in the mid-nineteenth-century.

The vicarage as a summer retreat and a tourist centre

It was essential when setting out on a hike to have good relations at the vicarages. The most fortunate was he who knew the highest number of ministers! (Nielsen 1909:73)

Lom in Vågå and Ullensvang in Hardanger are two vicarages that have achieved a special position in the history of hospitality in the first half of the nineteenth century. Other vicarages have meant more for travellers over a much longer time span, but we know fewer details about these. If Ullensvang and Lom are reputed to be lighthouses of hospitality, the main reason lies in the sources. For Ullensvang, the guest book is preserved, and in the case of Lom, the reputation is mainly due to Elise Aubert's published reminiscences.

The other main reason is that these vicarages, situated far from the main routes, ended up in the centre of the events through the emergence of international tourism in the one case, and of a national fever for hiking in the other. Hardanger became from the early nineteenth century one of the most popular destinations for British upper class tourists, while Lom from the 1840s became something like a hostel for mountain hikers.

Nils Hertzberg was a pastor in Ullensvang from 1804 until his death in 1841. Until 1836 he kept a guest book, as did many ministers. The book lists eighty-nine foreign visitors between 1804 and 1836, but there are several lacunas. The vicarage was also visited by Norwegian students, academics and some 'leisured' travellers from Bergen. Hertzberg's neighbour – the magistrate – also used to grab travellers, so we do not know the total number. Among the eighty-nine foreigners there were fifty-five British, eighteen Germans, seven Danes, four Swedes, four French and one Spaniard (Riis 1884:20).

Ullensvang was not situated on a heavily trafficked route, nor was the Røldal route across the mountains known to a wide public, before the pastor himself wrote an article in *Morgenbladet* in 1829. Until then he had had only one or two visitors every season. Around 1830, however, the number rose to between five and ten every summer, and in the years 1833 to 1836 there was an invasion of between fifteen and twenty foreign visitors every season. (Hertzberg 1929:1929). This increase mirrors a general growth in tourism, but it may also be partly due to the descriptions in the travel account of – among several others – Charles Boileau Elliott (1932). Elliott, who visited Ullensvang in 1830, was an eager advocate of this wild and virgin west coast nature, which according to him matched both the Alps and the Himalayas. With the waterfalls of Vøringsfossen and the glacier of Folgefonna, Ullensvang was a popular destination in this age of European romanticism.

At Lom vicarage, where Julius Aars resided, 'there was a swarm of tourists, Norwegian as well as foreign', wrote the daughter Elise Aubert (b. 1837) in her reminiscences. And she goes on:

> The hospitality of my parents had been tested so often and by so many, that it was by now [around 1850] considered a verified fact. As the taste for travelling and hiking grew, these residential farms still remained the natural haven for the tourists. Along the main routes there were *skyssstasjoner*, sometimes of good quality, but away from the beaten track it was difficult to find good night quarters. Thus the voluntary hospitality came to play a much more important role than today. (Aubert 1909:168)

From Aars' arrival in 1852 until he left in 1863, the vicarage was a 'summer hostel' for hikers, among whom there were many students who made the tour on foot between eastern and western Norway during the summer holidays. They wandered around in the mountains which later were labelled Jotunheimen. The Galdhøpiggen mountain became a great attraction in this period; it was climbed for the first time, measured and found to be Norway's highest peak.

Among the visitors were government officials, artists and foreign tourists. While the foreigners were short of time and hurried along and the elderly visitors tended to follow their planned itineraries, the students settled down and stayed a good while. The students brought life and fun to the vicarage. If they were not acquainted beforehand with the vicar's family, the usual way of introducing themselves was to knock on the door and ask for the keys to the church! (Aubert 1909:162) The result was often an invitation to the vicarage.

Best known among the foreigners is Emily Lowe, who with a supply of food and woollen clothes from the vicarage managed to cross the Sogn mountain to Luster – a passage that was considered daring for two women. Her travel account, however, *Unprotected Females through Norway* (1857), may best be characterised by its 'careless contempt of facts', according to her host's daughter (154).

Aubert does not write about provision problems and subsistence worries. But her description of the housekeeping, the butchering, the baking and all the food preparation, makes it clear that the influx of visitors, on top of a big household, required both a sound economy and good planning. When Julius Aars left Lom, the possibilities of finding other night quarters had become much better. Aars was one of the last to keep up a tradition that in the 1860s was disappearing rapidly.

The end of a tradition

In the 1840s Hanna Winsnes resided at the vicarage of Vang in Løiten, where she lodged and treated travellers – 'warranted or unwarranted' – that were both kin and complete strangers. Or such is the wording of her granddaughter Barbara Ring: 'Everyone who travelled between Trondhjem and Kristiania sought lodging at Vang vicarage, if only with the slightest justification or sometimes none at all, and they were received and treated like a friend of the family.' (Ring 1924:153) Only twenty years later, in 1865, the student (and later professor) Yngvar Nielsen did not dare to knock on the door of vicar Halling, the successor of Aars in Lom. Nielsen had passed a week on milk diet in dairy chalets in the mountains, and his mind was set on the vicar's kitchen and table. (Nielsen 1909:73) However, he observed from a distance another student who was refused at the vicar's door, and he gave up his project. A change had taken place.

Or perhaps more than a simple change. In the years between Hanna Winsnes' reign at Vang and Honoratius Halling's appointment to Lom (1863), the change that had taken place in the infrastructure of travelling and communications came close to being a revolution. *Skyssvesenet* – the posting system – was reorganized, permanent skyss stations with better accommodation possibilities spread quickly, the standard of vehicles was radically changed, and the number of tourists and travellers increased greatly. Important laws governing road building and the *skyssvesen* were passed in the early 1850s, new road standards set, and high quality roads – called *chausseer* – constructed. A number of steam ship routes were started, on the lakes and along the coast, and railroad lines were opened in the 1850-60s. New technologies were applied in all branches of transport and communication, from bridge building to the telegraph, and the modernisation of the field was a main objective for the new ministry (1841) for domestic affairs. Both technologies and mentalities changed – sometimes radically – within this short span of time (Rogan 1986, 1998).

This development had consequences for the lodging traditions at the vicarages, for two reasons. Firstly, modern communications strongly diminished isolation. Secondly, the flux of tourists made it impossible to receive so many guests. When Yngvar Nielsen stated that '[in 1865] it could sometimes be onerous for the vicars' wives and expensive for the vicars to muster all this hospitality' (Nielsen 1909:73), it was indeed an understatement. In most places one could no longer knock uninvited on a vicar's door, unless you knew him well or were close kin.

Among those who were familiar with the vicarage tradition and also with its dissolution, Knud Knudsen holds a special position. He set out on his first hike in 1833, and he went on with long summer hikes for more than fifty years.

Knudsen gained first-hand personal experience of the dissolution of the rural hospitality. We cannot render all his comments on the vicarage tradition, but two episodes are worth quoting. The first one happened in 1852 at Inderøya, where he dropped in at the vicarage in the evening:

> But the vicarage was empty. The doors were open, and it looked as if the inhabitants of the house had been there only a moment ago, everyone at their place. I could not make anything else out of this situation than that they must have fled upstairs or hid themselves in an adjoining boudoir or chamber, in order to avoid a guest who came on foot and not in a carriage. Such a thing had never happened to me in any vicarage [...] But from my own experience in later years – and that of a few others – I don't any longer find it absolutely unbelievable that inhospitality was the reason that nobody turned up. (Knudsen 1980: vol. I:94)

The same happened in Nordfjord in 1860. Knudsen arrived by water to the vicar's boat landing, from where he caught a glimpse of the vicar in the yard. But no one descended to greet him:

> Doors and windows were open, but no human being turned up. I found this strange, to put it mildly. But there was nothing to do but wait, so I sat down on a bench [...] Well, after two or three minutes the eldest son – the chaplain – appeared, then his mother – the housewife, and then more people. As far as I could observe, they did not come in, but down, down from [the bedrooms in] the top storey. That they should be living up there all day was hardly the case, as the living room downstairs was in a normal state. Even the old minister entered the living room, but he kept away from me, and I don't think he talked ten words to me, or not even two, during the about twenty-four hours that I stayed in his house. (*Ibid.*:97)

From the 1860s the tradition of receiving travellers and tourists at the vicarages was no longer observed, except – only on special occasions – in a few remote places. When an English tourist reported in 1882 to *Bennett's Hand-book for Norway* that 'the 'præst' very kindly receives travellers gratuitously and supplies comfortable accommodation' (1882:108), it must be considered a faint reminiscence of an old tradition in what was probably Norway's most isolated vicarage for ten months of the year.

Conclusion

From medieval times up to the middle of the nineteenth century, private hospitality was a precondition for travel in Norway. Due to a sparse population and a dispersed settlement, the conveyance and the lodging of travellers had to be organised on a private basis. Public authorities intervened in the question of conveyance (regulations after 1648 and laws after 1816) but did very little to solve the lodging problem. A main reason was probably that things functioned fairly well, through the unwritten rules and centuries-old practices of private hospitality. Government officials living in rural areas, and above all the clergy, kept spacious houses that served as refuges for travellers from the upper class. The Norwegian clergy was renowned for their hospitality towards wayfaring strangers.

The historical roots of the hospitality should not – or at least not principally – be sought in Christian virtues and a medieval monastic tradition, but in material conditions combined with visitation traditions dating back to Catholic times. The residential farms of the clergy were spacious, due to their obligation to receive the bishop with his large company. Prescriptions regulating the architecture were prolonged into Protestant times.

Another important factor was the isolation of these farms in the countryside. The solitude of these servants of the State, severed as they were from colleagues and from urban culture, is probably the most important reason why the clergy accepted to keep their doors open to strangers and why they performed a degree of hospitality which surprised contemporary foreign travellers. The vicarages and the other official residences were like small islands of breeding and civilisation in an ocean of rural and peasant culture. Any visits from the outside world, any contact with people at their own level, were longed-for social and cultural events. This explains in a nutshell the renowned private hospitality in the countryside. For the travellers, on the other hand, to accept and profit from this hospitality was not only a convenient solution, but also the only way of evading low-standard peasant inns and farms. The vicarage was a safe haven for the upper-class traveller.

With the increase of tourism from the second third of the nineteenth century, however, the open-door policy of the vicars became more difficult to maintain along the most heavily trafficked routes. And with the revolutionary change of infrastructure in travel and communications around the middle of the century, which created new forms of transportation and lodging possibilities and opened up the country to new and steadily more numerous groups of tourists, the renowned hospitality drew towards an end even in the more remote areas of Norway. From the 1860s the vicarages were no longer an option for wayfaring strangers; with a very few exceptions, a traveller could no longer drop in uninvited at a vicarage, unless he was close kin or an old acquaintance.

For more than three centuries travellers in Norway found a safe haven at the vicarages and other residential farms spread out in the countryside. The institution served both parties. The Norwegian clergy were undoubtedly governed by the ethics of hospitality, but their hospitality also served selfish but understandable needs, notably a moment's escape from solitude and the thrills of a taste of the world outside.

References

Aubert, Elise (1909): *Fra de gamle prestegaarde*. Kristiania, Aschehoug.

Bennett's Hand-book for Norway. (1859-) Christiania.

Bugge, Anders (1918): 'Gammel prestegaardskultur tabt i den sidste menneskealder.' *Foreningen til Norske Fortidsminnesmærkers Bevaring*, Årsberetning 1918. Kristiania.

Christie, Elisabeth (ed.) (1967): *Prestegårdsliv*. Vol. I-IV. Oslo, Forlaget Land og Kirke.

Dahlerup, Hans Birch (1908): *Mit Livs Begivenheder*. Vol. I (1790-1814). Copenhagen.

Elliott, Charles Boileau (1932): *Letters from the North of Europe*. London.

Fölsch, Edward Gustaf (1818): *Resa i Norrige år 1817*. Strengnäs.

Hertzberg, Nils (1929): 'Prost Niels Hertzbergs reisebok, ført på Ullensvang prestegård 1806-1841.' *Den Norske Turistforenings Årbok* 1929. Oslo.

Holm, Olaf (1923): *Fra en nordlandsk prestegaard. Oplevelser og skisser*. Kristiania, Aschehoug.

Knudsen, Knud (1980-): *Reiseminner*. Vol. I-VI. Oslo, Det Norske Samlaget.

Knutzen, Knud Olaus (1922): *Dagbøger over Reiser i Norge 1824 og 1828*. Kristiania, Norsk Forlag for Bokkunst.

Kulturhistorisk Leksikon for Nordisk Middelalder (KLNM).

Lowe, Emily 1857: *Unprotected Females through Norway*. London.

Nielsen, Yngvar (1909): *Erindringer fra et Halvt Aarhundredes Vandrerliv*. Kristiania og Kjøbenhavn, Gyldendal.

Nilsson, Sven (1879): *Dagboksanteckningar under en resa från södra Sverige till nordlanden I: Norge 1816*. Lund.

Olafsen, Olaf (1927): *Norsk prestegårdsliv. Kulturhistoriske skildringer fra våre prestegårde*. Bibliotheca Norvegiæ Sacræ. Bergen, Lunde & Co.

Riis, C. P. (1884): 'Reisende i Hardanger i provst N. Hertzbergs embedstid.' *Den Norske Turistforenings Årbok* 1884. Kristiania.

Ring, Barbara (1924): *For hundrede aar siden. Hanna Winsnes og hendes*. Kristiania, Aschehoug.

Rogan, Bjarne (1986): *Det gamle skysstellet. Reiseliv i Norge frå mellomalderen til førre hundreåret*. Oslo, Det Norske Samlaget.

—— (1998): *Mellom tradisjon og modernisering. Kapitler av 1800-tallets samferdselshistorie*. Oslo, Novus.

—— (2004): 'L'auberge du bon secours.' In: Montandon, Alain (ed.): *Le livre de l'hospitalité*. Paris, Bayard.

Rørbye, Martinus (1930): *Maleren Martinus Rørbyes Rejsedagbog 1830*. Ed. Georg Nygaard, Copenhagen.

Sandvik, Gudmund (1965): *Prestegard og prestelønn. Studiar kring problemet eigedomsretten til dei norske prestegardane*. Oslo, Universitetsforlaget.

'Utkast til en norsk Kirkeordinants' (1604), in: Olaf Kolsrud (ed.): *Den Norske Kirkes Mindeskrift ved Reformationens 400-Aars-Jubileum Aar 1917*. Christiania, Jacob Dybwad.

Vinje, Aasmund Olavsson (1939 [1861]): *Ferdaminne frå sumaren 1860*. Oslo, Det Norske Samlaget.

Note

1. All quotations have been translated into English to maximise the number of sources that may be quoted within the space available.

Sweden Discovered and Sweden Invented: the Representation of Sweden in the *Dictionary of National Biography*.

Elizabeth Baigent

Many Britons who forged their way to Sweden in the nineteenth century found a country fresh and raw and a people close to nature. Their writings speak of discovery, of new energy, of new life (Barton 1998; Davies 1999). But the Sweden(s) that these author-travellers discovered for themselves and created for their readers were complemented, contested, or even contradicted by other contemporary literary portraits of the country (Fjågesund and Symes 2003:14). Nineteenth-century readers arguably discovered Sweden as much through creative writing and political literature, which are briefly considered at the end of this paper, or through histories, works of science, encyclopaedias, or dictionaries of national biography (DNBs) as from travelogues.

DNBs flourished in nineteenth-century western Europe (Thomas 2005:15). Sweden, with Wieselgren's *Biographiskt lexicon öfver namnkunnige svenske män* (1835-57), which grew out of Palmblad's *Samtidens märkvärdigaste personer* (1820-1821), was the earliest nation to produce such a dictionary, and Britain, with its *Dictionary of National Biography* (*DNB*) (Stephen and Lee, 1885-1901), was among the most successful (Baigent 1996; Hildebrand 1941; Sylwan 1935; Thomas 2005).[1] The editors of each dictionary presented a view of their nation's history and identity by memorialising some people, and leaving others out, as well as by the tone of each memoir. The nineteenth-century metropolitan men of letters who created the *DNB* were alive to international influences on British life, and liberal in their interpretation of nationality. Their dictionary had as its first entrant Jacques *Abbadie, born in Nay in Bearn, and as its last Wilhelm *Zuylestein, born near Utrecht.[2] The *DNB*'s 28,000 biographical essays have often been analysed to show how the British saw themselves (McCalman 1996; Matthew 1997; Faber and Harrison 2000), and one aspect of their self-image is how they saw others. Though it was hardly a prime reason for its creation, the *DNB* was the first conspectus of British-Swedish relations through history. Its nineteenth-century readers could, through the eyes of the editors, discover how Britons had viewed and interacted with

Sweden and Swedes over many centuries. This paper reveals how Swedish-British relations were portrayed in the *DNB*, its *Supplements* (1911-1995), and its successor the *Oxford Dictionary of National Biography* (*Oxford DNB*) (Matthew and Harrison 2004), with comparisons to *Svenskt Biografiskt Lexikon* (*SBL*) (Boëtius 1918-) and other literature.[3] Many British travel writers who discovered Sweden are themselves memorialised in the *DNB*s, but the dictionaries' broad coverage provides a backdrop against which they and their travelogues can be set.

In the *DNB*, nineteenth-century readers discovered a history of British-Swedish relationships which was rich, but discontinuous, one generation being dominated by movement to the British Isles from Sweden, the next by movement to Sweden from the British Isles. The *DNB* portrayed the earliest contacts between the British Isles and what became Sweden by memorialising Viking adventurers (rather few admittedly from East Norse), as befitted an age when Vikings were in vogue (Wawn 2000). The Viking era was succeeded by a lull and then a change in the direction of flow in the seventeenth century when Scottish adventurers flocked to Sweden in the words of one of them, Sir James *Turner (*b. c.*1615, *d.* in or after 1689), to 'reduce some obstinate countries to order, and force them to submit to the Suedish yoake' (Turner 1829:4), often thereby achieving high military and social rank.

In the eighteenth century the direction of flow changed again. Natural historians forged most contacts, the impetus originating with Linnaeus, but the main results coming after his pupils Daniel *Solander (1733-1782) and Jonas *Dryander (1748-1810) had left Sweden for England, to serve the men driving natural historical discovery: James *Cook (1728-1779) and Joseph *Banks (1743-1820). The coverage was good, but there was a sense of fitness that in 1784 James Edward *Smith (1759-1828) secured for himself (and ultimately the Linnaean Society of London) the library and collections of Linnaeus and his son, Gustav III's opposition notwithstanding. The impact of Linnaeus's binomial classification system was not fully brought out, and the impetus to secure and publish new natural historical information was portrayed as largely British. In this the *DNB* shared the outlook of contemporary travel writers: Davies notes the 'tireless tendency [of British writers] to introduce Sweden as if it were located at the end of one of Captain Cook's voyages rather than just across the North Sea'. This sprang sometimes from travellers' desire to appear intrepid, but it revealed a wider ambivalence about Sweden's status. While Linnaean pupils were clearly part of the European voyaging thrust, Sweden itself was portrayed as undeveloped. This was doubly ironic when commentators followed the method of the scientific tour which Linnaeus had done much to establish (Davies 1999:60, 162, 290; Sörlin 1989), or used unexampled Swedish government statistics to prove the nation in need of development. Sweden is clearly the object of British investigation and improvement in the *DNB*'s coverage of nineteenth-century contacts. Geologist Charles *Lyell (1797-1875)'s uniformitarian insights could explain emergent land round Sweden's Baltic coast, and engineers Thomas *Telford (1757-1834) and Jabez Carter *Hornblower (1744-1814), could solve the country's technical problems.

Men of science are joined in the DNB's coverage of the nineteenth century by travel writers like Henry David *Inglis [Derwent Conway] (1795-1835), who wrote of Sweden one day, Switzerland the next, and Spain the day after. The dictionary's interest was in British publishing and literary history, not the countries visited. The century as a whole was portrayed as a time of limited contact between the two nations, such contact as there was being by Britons opening up Sweden.

Such was the Sweden discovered in the *DNB* by its nineteenth-century readers. Though its authors shared some of the preconceptions of their travel writing contemporaries, the countries they portrayed nonetheless differed considerably. Contemporary travel writers aimed to convey fact, but also to entertain and awake sentiments and sensations. Although they wrote within a genre extending back some centuries, inheriting both practical itineraries and literary expectations, they nonetheless strove successively for novelty, with the result that few accounts commanded sustained readership (Davies 1999:44, 60).[4] The editors of the *DNB*, particularly Stephen, by contrast, felt themselves responsible for a work which, if well done, would endure (Goldman 2006). In this spirit they continued earlier biographical traditions, despite the sometimes very different priorities of their own age (Thomas 2005:22-3), and, unlike many travel writers, never strove for 'moral edification' (Lee, cited in Goldman, 2006). It is then unsurprising that travel books, written for the moment, and the 'remarkably... timeless' *DNB* (Goldman 2006) present differing Swedens.

Although the *DNB*'s editors were no experts on Swedish history and although British-Swedish relations were far from central to their concerns, the portrait they drew is remarkably successful. It typified the high scholarly standards of the work as a whole, the fruits of the editors' liberal inclusion policy; their wide consultations within their metropolitan world of letters; their systematic use of sources such as the British Museum library catalogue; their hard work; their intimate knowledge of the work derived from long and dedicated service; and their chance in the 1901 *Supplement* to include those missed in error. But the coverage of British-Swedish relations, as of British life as a whole, was inevitably patchy. This resulted in part from the editorial team's working method. Starting at A and working through to Z they could not in advance allocate space to each aspect of national life (Matthew 1997:3-4 and cf. Karlsson 2004:218). And without computer technology to give a conspectus of progress and with a change of editor after Stephen's health broke, they could never really know, until they reached the end and it was too late, what it was they were creating. But the patchiness also reflected the period's priorities. Goldman (2006) argues persuasively that the *DNB* escaped or rather eschewed the crude imperialism and nationalism of its age, particularly under its first editor Leslie Stephen: but this does not undermine Matthew's point that the editors' imperial preoccupations left Britain's relationships with non-imperial nations unevenly portrayed (1997).

The *DNB* rapidly established itself as a major scholarly work, but all DNBs date, as people continue to die, new primary sources become accessible, and scholarly standards and interpretations change (Summerson 2006). Just as Swedes were early creators of a multi-volume *DNB*, so they early realised that such dictionaries should meet exacting scholarly standards. *Svenskt Biografiskt Lexikon* (Boëtius 1918-) was established on the initiative of Bertil Boëtius (1885-1974) of Riksarkivet (the Swedish National Archive) who from 1913 campaigned for a DNB of the highest scholarly standards, particularly with respect to primary sources, a need not met by existing dictionaries, pioneering though they had been (Hildebrand 1941; Sylwan 1935; Karlsson 2004:218). Britain's *DNB* was enlarged with *Supplements* to cover those who had died between 1901 and 1995, but enlargement without revision became increasingly unsatisfactory. In 1992 work on an expanded, fully revised, and fully electronic *DNB* began (Faber and Harrison 2002), and the resultant *Oxford DNB* (2004) tells the lives of 50,000 people from the perspective of late twentieth- and early twenty-first-century academe (Thomas 2005). More balanced coverage was achieved through systematic computer analysis of the old and emergent dictionaries, and systematic editorial thinking about who should fill the 14,000 new spaces; and the decision to publish all volumes simultaneously (Matthew 1997).[5] One editorial priority was to revise the *DNB*'s portrayal of Britain in the world (Matthew 1997). The *Oxford DNB* was to show Britain conquered as well as conquering, the British empire contested and ultimately overthrown, and imperial ties co-existing with other international ties, particularly to Europe.[6] This new emphasis was to be effected not least by inviting many non-Britons to write memoirs: some three thousand of the ten thousand contributors to the 2004 edition were from outside Britain (Goldman 2006).

In 1993, as research director of the *Oxford DNB*, I was generously welcomed by *SBL*'s editor Göran Nilzén and his staff, to discuss biographical dictionaries in general, and in particular to learn from Swedish colleagues about their use of illustrations: just as Sweden had the first multi-volume DNB, one of the first DNBs to meet high scholarly standards (and perhaps the first to have a woman editor (Karlsson 2004:224)), so it led the way in illustrating DNBs.[7] Those discussions, discussions with Nilzén's successor Åsa Karlsson, and searches in the CD-ROMs of *SBL* (1997 and 2004), revealed that *SBL* fairly consistently gave more space to British-Swedish contacts than did the *DNB*. In general, however, the Swedish and British dictionaries' editorial priorities were converging. Karlsson writes that the 'storsvensk nationalism' (nationalist aspiration for a Greater Sweden) and 'stadsfixering' (preoccupation with urban affairs) of *SBL*'s early volumes have given way to an altogether more inclusive view of the nation (Karlsson 2004:220). This broadening of the idea of national life is clear too from the *Oxford DNB*. The later volumes of *SBL*, like the *Oxford DNB*, were far readier than their predecessors to record the contribution of tradespeople, manufacturers, and labour leaders and other working class people (Nilzén and Thullberg 1986).[8] Women are treated differently and included more abundantly in each dictionary, reaching very similar proportions of all articles in each. The two dictionaries were also converging in article genre, *SBL* reducing the proportion of articles on families compared with individuals, and the *Oxford DNB* introducing family articles (Karlsson 2004).[9] Just as *SBL*'s present editors continue the work of earlier editors, the *Oxford DNB* built on rather than repudiated its predecessor, a continuity which arguably reflects the fact that both nations can view their twentieth-century histories with some degree of contentment (Goldman 2006 for the British view).

New working methods, editorial priorities, and international contacts mean that twenty-first-century readers of the *Oxford DNB* discover a different Sweden from that discovered by nineteenth-century readers of the *DNB*. A fundamental shift is that attention to the material basis for national life modifies the impression of sharp discontinuities in contact identified by eyes trained mainly on political, military, cultural, or intellectual matters. The *Oxford DNB* shows, for example, that while Bulstrode *Whitelock (1605-1675) famously eulogised Queen Kristina in poetry and music, George (*d.*1692) and William *Hodgkinson (1661/2-1731), iron merchants of Hull, got on with importing goods from Sweden, and John *Jeffreys (*c.*1614-1688), tobacco merchant, continued to export British and colonial goods to Sweden.[10]

The focus on material life has changed the *Oxford DNB*'s portrait of Vikings. Many more Vikings appear in the new edition, and their more rounded biographies reflect the use of historical and archaeological as well as literary evidence to memorialise early figures (Summerson 2006). The greater number of Vikings helps to show Britain conquered as well as conquering (new arrivals include *Erik Bloodaxe (*d.* 954), whose 'career of homicide and plunder [was] remarkable even among tenth-century vikings'), but they also stress material life (through, for example, *Hæsten (*fl.* 882-893) whose 'personal journey from raiding to acculturation and settlement typified the viking age'). New descriptions of settlement and trade temper the previous impression of discontinuity fostered by a focus on raid and conquest.

A similar broadening of focus away from the purely military is seen in coverage of early modern contacts. Between the writing of the *DNB* and that of the *Oxford DNB* Scottish history developed as a recognised academic discipline, and this, and particularly the University of Aberdeen's Scotland, Scandinavia, and Northern Europe 1580-1707 project compelled a reappraisal of the *DNB*'s portrait of early modern contacts (Grosjean 1998; Murdoch 1998; Murdoch 2001; Murdoch and Grosjean database). Murdoch (2001) estimates that 100,000 Britons served in anti-Habsburg armies in the first half of the seventeenth century, of whom half were Scottish – 20 percent of the adult male Scottish population.[11] This astonishing proportion fully justified the *Oxford DNB*'s adding to the already large number of such men included in the *DNB*: but the new coverage is not just more of the same. The *Oxford DNB* shows that these individuals came from families which, like that of James *Spens of Wormiston (*d.*1632), allied their fortunes across several generations to those of Sweden, through military service, marriage, and settlement, recruiting astonishing numbers of ordinary soldiers to the project. The *Oxford DNB* shows that Scotland's history differed markedly from metropolitan England's; that this history affected not only male officers, but their female relatives and the rank and file they enlisted; that unofficial as well as government-led participation in wars has profound cultural, political, and demographic effects on host and native countries; and that unofficial participation was important to metropolitan Britain as well as to Scotland and Ireland. Service in Sweden temporarily rid the English authorities of troublesome Irishmen, and provided employment for Scottish men of upper and lower ranks; but also meant that a corps of experienced soldiers of uncertain allegiance and brutal habit existed in Britain when the civil wars broke out in the 1640s. They could follow Sir James *Turner, mentioned above, in declaring, 'I had swallowed without chewing, in Germanie, a very dangerous maxime, which militarie men there too muche follow, which was, that so we serve our master honestlie, it is no matter what master we serve' (Turner 1829:14). This had a significant impact on Britain's own wars.[12] The *Oxford DNB*'s fuller and more rounded coverage of these men, their followers, and their families, particularly those who settled in Sweden, and those ennobled there, was stimulated by changes in the way the UK's constituent nations see their own history: but it had the effect of changing the way relations with outside nations are portrayed, in this case bringing the British view of British-Swedish contacts closer to *SBL*'s than to *DNB*'s, and stressing the long term nature of contacts originally forged for war.

The *Oxford DNB*, like the *DNB*, shows eighteenth-century British-Swedish contacts dominated by science, but, if the *DNB*'s coverage of science favoured the 'moment of genius' over the 'steady accumulation of evidence' (Goldman 2006), the *Oxford DNB* shows how webs of personal contact, diligent correspondence, and disinterested sharing of knowledge underpinned moments of genius, and indeed that the genius depended on the diligent for the acceptance of his ideas. In the Swedish context, the greater frequency and depth of contact revealed in the new dictionary considerably tempers notions of a sudden 'discovery' of Sweden in the following century. Moreover, the new dictionary's recognition of the importance of Swedes in European science shows an early modern scientific community characterised more by international collaboration than by national particularism.[13]

Swedish and British collaboration is evidenced best in natural history, chemistry, and astronomy. Central to its coverage of natural history is the *Oxford DNB*'s inclusion of Carl *Linnaeus (1707-1778), not to appropriate him for British history, but to reveal the impact of his contacts with Britons.[14] From 1735 to 1736 Linnaeus was employed in Holland by the English banker and director of the East India Company George *Clifford; he visited England in 1736, and corresponded with more than forty Britons. Philip *Miller (1691-1771), superintendent of the Society of Apothecaries' garden at Chelsea; Peter *Collinson (1694-1768), Quaker naturalist; and Johan Jakob *Dillenius (1687-1747), Oxford's Sherardian professor of botany, all Britons by birth or residence whom Linnaeus met in England, were profoundly influential in spreading acceptance of his system. The *Oxford DNB* provides much richer analyses of Linnaeus's pupils Daniel *Solander, who settled in London, promoted the Linnaean classification, catalogued the natural history specimens in the British Museum, and sailed with Banks and Cook to the Antipodes, and Jonas *Dryander, who succeeded Solander as Banks's librarian, producing the *Catalogus bibliothecae historico-naturalis Josephi Banks, baronetti* (5 vols., 1796-1800). These Swedes built on existing British-Swedish links: the Scottish physician Isaac *Lawson (*d.* 1747) helped to pay for the printing of Linnaeus's *Systema naturae* in 1735. The web of British-Swedish contact extended to British North America. Linnaeus's pupil Pehr *Kalm (1716-1779) travelled in England and North America between 1747 and 1751 to gather information and specimens useful to Sweden. In England Kalm's guides were Collinson, Miller, and Virginian naturalist John *Mitchell, and he met Mark *Catesby, a botanist who had spent much time in America. If it does not adopt Sörlin's view (1989) that Sweden, through Linnaeus and his pupils ('apostles' as he called them) led the world in the scientific aspects of natural history (lacking only the funds for extensive overseas voyages), the *Oxford DNB* clearly shows a vital web of international contacts, and sharing of information and material.

It also shows some, albeit limited, scientific interest by Britons in Sweden, rather than Swedish scientists: Alexander *Blackwell (*bap.* 1709, *d.* 1747) and Sir John *Sinclair (1754-1835) were two British agricultural improvers, the first of dubious reputation, who spent time in Sweden learning as much from Swedes as they taught them.

In the coverage of chemistry in the long eighteenth century Jöns Jakob Berzelius (1779-1848) dominates Anglo-Swedish contacts. He was not absent from the *DNB*, but in the *Oxford DNB* we see him more often as master to British pupils (such as Thomas *Anderson (1819-1874)), and the codifier of a system of chemical notation which built on but superseded British predecessors such as that of John *Dalton (1776-1844). The web of international contacts is perhaps best shown by Alexander John Gaspard *Marcet (1770-1822), a Swiss friend of Berzelius resident in Britain, in whose article Berzelius's London visit, English publications, and English influence are noted.

The new dictionary's significantly expanded coverage of applied science recognises both the scientific contribution of tradesmen and manufacturers, and the inherent interest of commerce. We see contacts between eighteenth-century British and Swedish scientific instrument makers who were on the cusp of science and commerce. In 1736 Jonathan *Sisson (1690?-1747) and George *Graham (*c.* 1673-1751) constructed a nine-foot zenith sector, a clock and other instruments for the French Académie des Sciences expedition to northern Sweden under Pierre de Maupertuis to make measurements to establish the figure of the earth. In 1741 Graham supplied further instruments to Uppsala observatory: one was delivered by Daniel Eckström, the Stockholm clockmaker who had spent time with Graham in London and was strongly influenced by Graham's work. The correspondence of optical instrument maker John *Dollond (1707-1761) with Samuel Klingenstierna, professor of mathematics and later physics at Uppsala University, led to experiments which enabled Dollond to produce his important compound lens for refracting telescopes which was free of both chromatic and spherical aberration.

Bringing together science, travel, and commerce were *industrial spies, who have a group article in the *Oxford DNB*. A remarkable number came from Sweden. In an uneasy mix of individual collaboration and international competition, industrial grand tourists to Britain visited industrial premises, their notes and drawings of machines and processes giving unique insight into British mining and manufacture. British manufacturers were ambivalent towards industrial grand tourists. Whilst they sought to keep some processes secret, all were eager to display their facilities and products, with a view to selling overseas, and some, notably Nehemiah Champion (1678-1747) (see *Champion family), retained something of the collaboration which marked earlier scientific contacts (Harris, 1998; Woolrich, 1986). Swedish industrial spies were particularly interested in metallurgy where British advances threatened Swedish dominance. As early as 1696 the Bergskollegium (College of Mines) sent a mining expert, Thomas Cletcher, to inspect copper works at Bristol. Henrik Kalmeter (1693-1750), a mining engineer, was sent to Britain by the Bergskollegium in 1719 and subsequently wrote two important works on the iron industry. Reinhold Rütker Angerstein (1718-1760), a member of Jernkontoret (the Swedish ironmasters' association), traversed England between 1753 and 1755, leaving voluminous notes on commerce and industry. John Ludwig Robsahm (1730-1796) spent a year in England studying metallurgic processes, including the secret process operating at Benjamin Huntsman's steel casting works which was finally uncovered by Benkt Qvist Andersson, a mining engineer who visited England in 1766-7 and who set up near Stockholm the first cast-steel works outside England. While the *DNB* calls these men 'spies', it is arguable that they saw themselves as followers of the Linnaean tradition of investigative journeys with less sinister overtones (Davies 1999:148; Sörlin 1989).

These eighteenth-century scientific and commercial contacts show that the nineteenth-century 'discovery' of Sweden by Britons was neither sudden nor unidirectional, but grew out of established two-way contacts. There was a shift in the nineteenth century to Britons visiting Sweden, rather than Swedes visiting Britons, and the focus of interest for Britons shifted to Sweden, rather than particular Swedes; but the shifts were gradual and incomplete. As Davies argues, nineteenth-century trends did not 'suddenly "create" the Scandinavian tourist... however romantically appealing this conception – it merely *confirmed* a tradition of how the North should be traversed and the worthwhile sites to see' (Davies 1999:108). Memoirs drawn from the *DNB*, with long chronological span and broad thematic compass, epitomise his point.

An important exemplar of continuity is the visit to Sweden in 1799 by (Thomas) Robert *Malthus (1766-1834), the political economist; William *Otter (1768-1840), later bishop of Chichester; Edward Daniel *Clarke (1769-1822), antiquary and mineralogist, and John Marten *Cripps (1780-1843), Clarke's pupil and later antiquary and naturalist. Ironically they went north largely because the Napoleonic blockade – 'the distracted state of public affairs' as Clarke put it (Malthus 1966:16) – prevented their going elsewhere. Clarke cites the additional reason that the northern lands were 'seldom seen by literary men' but it is far from clear that this was an advantage (Clarke 1810-23; Malthus 1800 and 1966). The party reached Sweden, whence Otter and Malthus went into Norway and thence back to Sweden, Otter botanising and Malthus observing industrial sites, people, and landscape. Malthus used these observations and Swedish published statistics in several works including the second (1803) and subsequent editions of his *Essay on the Principle of Population* (1st edn 1798). Population growth, argued Malthus, can always outstrip food production and is brought into balance by societal ('preventive') checks and/or catastrophic ('positive') checks. In Sweden he observed both preventive checks ('The women do not in general marry before 25 & seldom have large families' (1966:72)), and positive checks:

> In the summer of 1799, in the course of a northern tour, I passed through Sweden. There was at that time a general dearth of corn throughout the country, owing to a long drought the preceding year. In the province of Värmland, adjoining to Norway, it approached almost to a famine, and the lower classes of people suffered most severe distress. At the time we were passing through that part of the country, which was in July, they were reduced to two most miserable substitutes for bread; one, made of the inner bark of the fir, and the other, of the common sorrel dried, and powdered. These substances, though made into the usual shape of their rye bread, had no affinity to it whatever in taste, and but very little, I believe, in nourishment, as the effects of this miserable food were but too visible in their pallid and unhealthy countenances. (Malthus 1800)

Sweden had a pattern of late marriage and high numbers never marrying typical of western Europe (Hajnal 1965), and Malthus's visit confirmed his view that delayed marriage was a beneficial preventive check, though, as the then famine showed, it was not completely successful.

Malthus found in Sweden much empirical evidence that corroborated his ideas, and his companions too found that they could learn from their visit.[15] Clark and Cripps went north where Clarke's balloon ascent is well documented as a virtuoso performance. In fact however he spent most of his time in less spectacular study, learning from Swedes in lectures at Uppsala University and the mines of Dalarna, and collecting artefacts which evinced Swedish skill, as well as objects which showed Sweden's natural riches. Clarke was interested in the aesthetics of the landscape and in the technology which allowed the manipulation of natural phenomena. For him the grandeur of nature was complemented by the sublime vistas of industry. He visited Elias *Martin (1739-1818), the Swedish landscape artist who when in England had painted not only conventional landscapes, but also industrial scenes, famously the construction of the bridge at Ironbridge, Shropshire (de Haan 2006), and the naval dockyard at Chatham, Kent (Klingender 1968). He returned to Sweden to execute a similarly wide range of landscapes, including industrial scenes (Hoppe 1933; Lindhagen 1955). Clarke and Martin spanned science, technology, and aesthetics on the one hand, and Sweden and England on the other. Clarke illustrated the third (Scandinavian) part of his *Travels* (1810-1823) with engravings of Martin's dramatic paintings of the copper mines at Falun and the method of raising ore.[16] Not all of this is captured in the brief essays which characterise the *Oxford DNB*, but the tone and content together suggest that scientific, technical, and scholarly knowledge flowed not just from England to Sweden but also in the other direction (Davies 1999:162; Lindqvist 1984:22-33; Davidsson 1975). This tempers the tone of the *DNB*, but the also the idea of a passive Sweden awaiting discovery by later travel writers.

Clarke, Malthus, and Otter were not alone in spanning the eighteenth-century tradition of scientific contact and nineteenth-century travel writing. The chemist Thomas *Thomson (1773-1852) published an account of his visit to Sweden, paying special attention to mineralogy and geology. Sir Arthur de Capell *Broke (1791-1858), regarded now as a literary travel writer, saw himself as a geographical scientist. In 1820-1821 he became probably the first Englishman to travel overland to the North Cape, spending some winter months with the Sami before sledging from Finnmark to Stockholm. His northern experience underpinned simultaneously his claims to be a scientific geographer and traveller, and his metropolitan club life. Broke was a founder member of the Travellers' Club and co-founder and later president of the more serious Raleigh Club. Raleigh Club members in turn accounted for many of the *founders of the Royal Geographical Society (RGS), which positioned geography as simultaneously entertaining and scientific. Broke, fellow of the RGS, personified the intimate nineteenth-century connections between male clubbability and entertaining travel writing on the one hand, and science and science writing on the other (Broke 1823; Broke 1827a and 1827b; Marshall-Cornwall 1978; Stoddart 1986).[17]

Britons pursuing the new sciences of archaeology and ethnography were also attracted to Sweden, this time as a model for how Britons should preserve their past. The Scot John Mitchell *Mitchell (1789-1865), merchant and student of archaeology, natural history, mineralogy, and Scandinavian languages and literature, visited Denmark and Sweden and was inspired by intellectual progress in Scandinavian prehistory, the esteem accorded it by the general public, and the support it received from public funds. It was a model he hoped to emulate at home, through the Scottish Society of Antiquaries, building on the then wave of patriotic interest in the Scottish past. Isabel Frances [Elsie] *Grant (1887-1983) was inspired by Artur Hazelius (1833-1901)'s Nordiska Museet and Skansen, founded to preserve objects, including buildings, from Sweden's threatened folk cultures. After visiting Skansen, Grant developed her vision of a similar museum for the Scottish Highlands which finally opened in 1935, housing Highland and Hebridean objects including reconstructed buildings. As with so many non-literary British-Swedish contacts, the Britons involved were predominantly Scottish: moving in the opposition direction Scots important in Swedish prehistory, such as Alexander Seton (1768-1828), find their place in *SBL*.

If these people are all links with an older generation of travellers, then the new generation of travel writers is also represented in the *Oxford DNB*. To the manly visitor Sweden could offer a bracing climate to refresh the body, solitude to refresh the spirit, a rugged landscape to exercise his mind and body, and an obliging peasantry to satisfy his simple needs. John *MacGregor [Rob Roy] (1825-1892) made a series of solitary cruises in his canoe *Rob Roy*, paddling up rivers and across lakes and carrying his craft overland where necessary. In 1866 MacGregor paddled *Rob Roy* across Sweden. The rivers with their floating logs and the great lakes presented considerable danger, and he enjoyed Vänern so much that he traversed it twice. Overcoming such challenges with British ingenuity and manliness are what interests Rob Roy. In Sweden 'a gladsome buoyancy of spirit in the fine fresh breeze forced me to shout and sing aloud and alone'. 'The two whirlpools on the Göta were easily passed and spectators cheered... I made a tour of the pretty town [of Göteborg] in the canoe, traversing its canals and carrying the boat over obstacles in the streets, until the crowd running after the Rob Roy got breathless in the pursuit' (MacGregor 1867:43 and 174-6). Though Rob Roy enjoys himself in Sweden, the landscape is largely his backdrop, the people his audience, the performance a solo *tour de force*.

As well as attracting the manly traveller, Sweden suited the female professional writer who earned an income appropriate for a lady by writing for women and children. Two such new entrants in the *Oxford DNB* are Selina *Bunbury (1802-1882), who turned her travel experiences into fictional accounts for women and children, and Florence *Caddy (1836/7-1898), who aimed to impart historical, biographical, and scientific information by following in the footsteps of her subject. Her idea was innovative, though its execution in *Through the Fields with Linnaeus* (2 vols., 1887) signally failed to match its potential. Nonetheless, despite some delicate feelings about Linnaeus's sexual classification, she found Sweden a safe but uplifting destination for the serious woman traveller.

Just as Sweden had an ambiguous position in British eyes as both a quasi metropolitan originator of scientific ideas but also a quasi colonial object, ripe for scientifically inspired improvement (Davies 1999:162), she was also regarded with ambivalence by British evangelicals. Considerable numbers of Britons travelled to Sweden as missionaries, in a complex extension of both the imperial missionary project (Hodacs 2003) and the opening up of that country to travellers of all sorts. The *Oxford DNB* begins to sketch these contacts. It includes Joseph *Malins (1844-1926) who helped to build the teetotal fraternal society, the Independent Order of Good Templars, in England and Sweden (Harrison 1971), campaigning with missionary zeal, and Samuel *Owen, (1774-1854), one of the most important of the many Britons who helped to establish Sweden's engineering industry, and the pioneer of the steam vessels from which visitors admired Stockholm's archipelago. In the 1820s and 1830s, with Joseph Stephens and George Scott, he introduced Wesleyanism to Sweden and from 1835 to 1845 he was an important figure in Svenska Missionssällskapet (the Swedish Missionary Society). In 1831 he helped found Kungsholmen's (later Stockholm's) abstinence society, whose newspaper, *Stockholms Nykterhets-Härold*, he published. The coverage of British missionaries to Sweden, however, awaits fuller development in the *Oxford DNB*: George Scott, included in *SBL*, awaits an article; the extensive Baptist mission work in Sweden of Ebenezer *Henderson (1784-1858) and John *Paterson (1776-1855) goes largely unnoticed, and the Swedish work of Wesleyan Joseph Rayner *Stephens (1805-1879) appears important mainly as preparation for the hardships of a British gaol. The inclusion of Agnes Carolina Albertina *Welin (1844-1928), who was hailed by the Swedish established and free churches for her Scandinavian Sailors' Temperance Home in London, shows Swedes helping themselves on British soil; but if we accept the arguments of Hodacs (2003) and Fahey (1996), that Scandinavians became important in sustaining British and international evangelical and temperance work, then fuller coverage of British-Swedish mission in the *Oxford DNB* would round out Britons' understanding of themselves and themselves in the world. In the particular context of the history of British travel to Sweden, it would set missionaries more securely beside pleasure seekers, misery beside natural utopias, and travellers' insistence on the differences between home and abroad, against Hodacs's suggestion that Britons and Swedes came to share the same outlook on contemporary religious and moral questions.[18]

If the *Oxford DNB*'s long time perspective allows us to see that the nineteenth-century 'discovery' of Sweden was no sudden event; and if its glimpses of material life in Sweden allows us to see misery as well as beauty, its breadth also allows us to see that the discovery of Sweden was perhaps less important than its invention by Britons who might never have visited Sweden. William *Watts (*c.*1590-1649)'s *Swedish Intelligencer* (1630-1632) used text and remarkable images to create an enduring icon of Gustavus Adolphus as Protestant hero and liberator. Gustav Vasa, the defender of national, Protestant liberty, was used by Henry *Brooke (*c.*1703-1783) in his tragedy *Gustavus Vasa: the Deliverer of his Country* (1739). Like Watts, Brooke had never visited Sweden, but used it to make a domestic point. To his audience, his glorifying Gustav's elective kingship implied sympathy for parliamentarian powers against royal prerogative. The play further suggested criticism of Robert Walpole and support for Frederick, Prince of Wales, and the patriot Whigs. The political message was so clear that staging the play in Britain was prohibited, but printed copies circulated widely, and it proved especially contentious when staged in Dublin where anti-Walpolian feeling and patriotism were spreading, and where the lesson of Gustav's freeing Sweden from Danish rule resonated with the Irish (Wright 1919). These modern Swedish heroes had equally mythical Gothic forebears. Taken up by enthusiasts such as Robert *Molesworth (1656-1725) in the seventeenth century, the myth of Gothic liberty inspired a succession of British poets, translators, and novelists to write about the north in the following centuries, almost irrespective of whether they had visited it. The invention was most striking in the nineteenth century, when it was also more securely linked to travel, epitomised perhaps by Samuel *Laing (1780-1868), (who, however, castigated Sweden) (Litzenberg 1947; Wawn 2000). Yet just as the Victorian 'discovery' of Sweden in fact grew from earlier, rich travel practices, so the Victorian literary invention of the Vikings built on the eighteenth-century literary invention of the Goths (Omberg 1976), glimpsed in *DNB* memoirs on such men as Thomas *Percy (1729-1811) and Thomas *Gray (1716-1771).

Nineteenth-century Sweden was indeed 'a nation toured, appraised, and textually portrayed by British author-travellers' (Davies 1999:11; Barton 1998), and their 'discovery' of the land could make them view their own in a new light (Fjågesund and Symes 2003). But they were not the only contemporary discoverers of Sweden, nor were their writings read in a vacuum. The conspectus of British-Swedish relations provided by *DNB* and *Oxford DNB* show that literary Britons' 'discovery' of Sweden was rather part of a continuum of contacts; that scientific, technological, and commercial travel blended into literary travel; and that Sweden was as much invented as political archetype by British writers as it was 'discovered' as natural utopia by British travellers.

Acknowledgements

I am most grateful to the staff of the *Oxford DNB* and *SBL*.

Bibliography

Baigent, Elizabeth (1996): 'Nationality and dictionaries of national biography', 63-73 in Iain McCalman, ed., *National biography and national identities*.
Baigent, Elizabeth, Charlotte Brewer, and Vivienne Larminie (2005), 'Gender in the archive: women in the *Oxford Dictionary of National Biography* and the *Oxford English Dictionary*', *Archives* 30:13-35.
Barton, H. Arnold (1998): *Northern arcadia: foreign travellers in Scandinavia 1765-1815*.
Boëtius, Bertil, *et al.*, eds, (1918-): *Svenskt biografiskt lexikon* (CD-ROM, 1997 and 2004).
Bohman, Nils *et al.*, eds, (8 vols, 1942-1955): *Svenska män och kvinnor*.

Broke, Arthur de Capell (1823): *Travels through Sweden, Norway, and Finmark to the North Pole.*

—— (1827a): *A Winter in Lapland and Sweden.*

—— (1827b): *Winter sketches in Lapland.*

Brzezinski, Richard (1991 and 1993): *The army of Gustavus Adolphus* 1: *Infantry*; 2: *Cavalry.*

Caddy, Florence (2 vols, 1887): *Through the fields with Linnaeus.*

Clarke, Edward Daniel (3 parts, 6 vols, 1810-1823): *Travels in various countries of Europe, Asia, and Africa.*

Cornwall, J. Marshall- (1978): 'An early Scandinavian traveller', *Geographical Journal* 144:250-53.

Davidsson, Åke (1975): *Med utländska resenärer i svenska bibliotek.*

Davies, Mark (1999): *A perambulating paradox: British travel literature and the image of Sweden c.1770-1865.*

Driver, Felix and Elizabeth Baigent (2007): 'Biography and the history of geography: a response to Ron Johnston', *Progress in Human Geography* 31:111-12.

Fahey, David M. (1996): *Temperance and racism.*

Faber, Robert and Brian Harrison (2002): 'The *Dictionary of National Biography*: a publishing history', 171-92 in Robin Myers, Michael Harris, and Giles Mandelbrote, eds, *Lives in print: biography and the book trade from the middle ages to the 21st century.*

Fjågesund, Peter and Ruth A. Symes (2003): *The Northern Utopia: British perceptions of Norway in the nineteenth century.*

Goldman, Lawrence, ed., (2005-): *Oxford Dictionary of National Biography* online edition http://www.oxforddnb.com/

Goldman, Lawrence, (2006): 'A monument to the Victorian age? Continuity and discontinuity in the dictionaries of national biography 1882-2004', *Journal of Victorian Culture* 11.1 http://www.oup.com/oxforddnb/info/dictionary/jvc/ (consulted 20 November 2006).

Grosjean, A. N. L. (1998): Scots and the Swedish state: diplomacy, military service and ennoblement, 1611-1660, PhD diss., University of Aberdeen.

—— (2003): *An unofficial alliance: Scotland and Sweden 1569-1654.*

de Haan, David (2002): 'The iron bridge – how was it built?', bbc.co.uk/history/british/ Victorian/ iron_bridge_06.shtml (consulted 14 November 2006).

Hajnal, John (1965): 'European marriage patterns in perspective', 101-143 in D. V. Glass and D. E. C. Eversley, eds, *Population in history.*

Hansson, Sigfrid, ed. (1936): *Den svenska fackföreningsrörelsen.*

Harris, J.R. (1998): *Industrial espionage and technology transfer.*

Harrison, Brian (1971): *Drink and the Victorians.*

—— (2004): 'Comparative biography and the DNB', *Comparative Criticism* 5:3-26.

Hildebrand, Bengt Olof (1941): 'Biografisk historiografi och svenskt biografiskt lexikon. Några huvudlinjer av utvecklingen', *Personhistorisk tidskrift* Årg. 40 1939-40: 138-206.

Hodacs, Hanna (2003): *Converging world views: the European expansion and early-nineteenth-century Anglo-Swedish contacts.*

Hofberg, Herman *et al.* (2nd ed. 2 vols, 1906): *Svenskt biografiskt handlexikon.*

Hoppe, R. (1933): *Målaren Elias Martin.*

Karlsson, Eva-Lena (1991): *Svenska Porträttarkivet 75 år*, *Valör* 5:10-12.

Karlsson, Åsa (2004): 'Kvinnorna i svenskt biografiskt lexicon', 217-34 in Ragnar Björk and Alf W. Johansson eds, *Samtidshistoria och politik.*

Klingender, Francis D. (1968): *Art and the industrial revolution.*

Lindhagen, Nils (1955): *Elias Martin, svenska mästartecknare* [Årsbok för svenska statens konstsamlingar].

Lindqvist, Svante (1984): *Technology on trial: the introduction of steam power technology into*

Sweden 1715-1736.

Litzenberg, Karl (1947): *The Victorians and the Vikings*.

McCalman, Iain, ed. (1996): *National biography and national identities*.

MacGregor, John (1867): *Rob Roy on the Baltic*.

Malthus, T. R. (1st edn 1798; 2nd edn 1803): *Essay on the principle of population*.

—— (1800): *An investigation of the cause of the present high price of provisions*.

—— (1966): *The travel diaries of Thomas Robert Malthus*, ed. Patricia James.

Matthew, H. C. G. (1996): 'Dictionaries of national biography', 1-18 in Iain McCalman ed., *National biography and national identities*.

—— (1997): *Leslie Stephen and the new dictionary of national biography*.

Matthew, H. C. G. and Brian Harrison, eds (60 vols, 2004): *Oxford Dictionary of National Biography*.

Mellin, G. H. (20 parts, 1832-36): *Svensk pantheon*.

Murdoch, Steven (1998): Scotland, Denmark-Norway and the House of Stuart, 1603-1660: a diplomatic and military analysis, PhD diss., University of Aberdeen.

Murdoch, Steven, ed. (2001): *Scotland and the Thirty Years' War, 1618-1648*.

Murdoch, Steven and Alexia Grosjean: Scotland, Scandinavia and Northern Europe 1580-1707 database, University of Aberdeen, www.abdn.ac.uk/ssne/

Nilzén, Göran and Per Thullberg (1986): 'Arbetarrrörelsen i SBL', *Meddelanden från arbetarrörelsens arkiv och bibliotek* 3-4.

Omberg, Margaret (1976): *Scandinavian themes in English poetry 1760-1800*.

Palmblad, F. W. (ed.) (1820-21): *Samtidens märkvärdigaste personer*.

Rydberg, Sven (1951): *Svenska studieresor till England under frihetstiden*.

Sylwan, Otto (1935): 'Svensk biografi i ord och bild', *Samlaren* 15/16: 476-82.

Stephen, Leslie and Sidney Lee, eds (63 vols, 1885-1901): *Dictionary of National Biography*.

Stoddart, David R. (1986): *On geography and its history*.

Strömbom, Sixten (2 vols, 1935 and 1939): *Index över svenska porträtt 1500-1850 i svenska porträttarkivets samlingar*.

Strömbom, Sixten (1943): *Svenska kungliga porträtt i svenska porträttarkivets samlingar: del I Gustav I -Karl XII*.

Summerson, Henry (2006): 'People, places, and shifting perspectives in the *Dictionary of National Biography*', *The Local Historian* 36/2 http://www.oup.com/oxforddnb/info/ dictionary/localhist/ (consulted 20 November 2006).

Sörlin, Sverker (1989): 'Scientific travel – the Linnean tradition', 96-123 in Tore Fränsmyr, ed., *Science in Sweden*.

Thomas, K. V. (2005): *Changing conceptions of national biography*.

Turner, James (1829): *Memoirs of his own life and times, 1632-1670*, ed. T. Thomson.

Wawn, Andrew (2000): *The Vikings and the Victorians*.

Widmalm, Sven (1990): *Mellan kartan och verklighet: geodesi och kartläggning 1695-1860*.

Wieselgren, Peter, ed. (23 vols, 1835-57): *Biographiskt lexicon öfver namnkunnige svenske män: ett tilllägg till Palmblads biographiska lexicon*.

Woolrich, A. P. (1986): *Mechanical arts and merchandise: industrial espionage and travellers' accounts as a source for technology historians*.

Wright, Herbert (1919): 'Henry Brooke's "Gustavus Vasa"', *Modern Language Review* 14:173-82.

Notes

1. The *DNB* (Stephen and Lee 1885-1901), its *Supplements* (1911-95), the *Oxford DNB*

(Matthew and Harrison 2004), and the *Oxford DNB* online (Goldman 2005-) form the primary source material for this essay. Asterisks (*) indicate where a person, family, or group may be found in the above works, which are collectively accessible online via Goldman (2005-).

2. The editors were Leslie *Stephen (1832-1904) and Sidney *Lee (1859-1926). Round them at the *DNB* office in London gathered a group of literary men who worked and dined together. Through the *Athenæum*, the London literary periodical, Stephen circulated lists of those he proposed to include and solicited other names, a process which made the final lists something of a collective judgement by literary men (Harrison 2004: 13; Faber and Harrison 2002:175). While experience at the *DNB* was often a precursor to a British academic career, the Swedish DNBs' editors were from an early date often established academics and academic librarians, though Hildebrand deprecates the lack of archivists and rigorously trained historians among them (1941).

3. Electronic searches of the *Oxford DNB* on 'Sweden' and 'Swedish' produce respectively 760 and 621 individuals who had contacts with Sweden (with some overlap between searches). These numbers change when the dictionary is updated.

4. Davies (1999) shows the interdependence of travellers' experiences and the intertextuality of their writings: their reactions to what they see consciously reinforce, outdo, or contradict those of their predecessors.

5. Karlsson (2004:218) frankly admits that *SBL* is a very different work now from when the first volume was published: simultaneous rather than sequential publication permits a more uniform editorial perspective.

6. Further editorial priorities were to improve coverage of women, commerce, manufacture, applied science, and working-class people, and to include articles on families and groups.

7. Illustrated Swedish DNBs include Mellin (1832-36), Hofberg *et al.* (1906), and Bohman *et al.*, (1942-1955). SBL aims to illustrate all articles using the fine collection in Kungliga Biblioteket, and Svenska Porträttarkivet (SPA). SPA was founded in 1916 under Sixten Strömbom and is now part of Nationalmuseum. Its task is to photograph and catalogue all portraits of those significant in Swedish history 1500-1850. This remarkable record combines information gathered in the field, from Nationalmuseum, and from Personhistoriska samfundet. The resultant index, organised by sitter, distinguishes prime and later versions of portraits, and gives access to the archive's photographs. There are two printed catalogues (Strömbom 1935, 1939, 1943). The manuscript of the second part of the 1943 work is in SPA (Karlsson 1991).

8. Hansson (1936), with memoirs of 4,500 labour leaders, pioneered the biographical treatment of the labour movement, facilitating the inclusion of such figures in *SBL* which, like the *DNB*, relies considerably on pre-existing scholarship.

9. Essays on women comprise about 6 per cent of all articles in early volumes of *SBL* and about 11 per cent in later ones, cf. 3 per cent in *DNB* and 10 per cent in *Oxford DNB*. Both dictionaries change from focusing on women whom men found interesting, to including as well women whom women find interesting (Baigent, Brewer, and Larminie 2005; Karlsson 2004). Whilst family articles in *SBL* primarily memorialise the most prominent families, in the *Oxford DNB* they largely record gentry families who were important locally rather than nationally (Summerson 2006).

10. By a quirk of fate Hodgkinson's estate eventually came to Joseph Banks, whose contacts with Swedish science are described above.

11. Not all were in Swedish service (Brzezinski 1991:14-16 and 1993:19).

12. Turner wrote in part to justify his own vacillating allegiance. Brzezinski (1991:16) considers that such soldiers brought a particular brutality to the British wars.

13. There was of course national rivalry in science, beneath its apparent lofty impartiality

(Widmalm 1990), though perhaps Sweden's lack of imperial ambition made its science overseas more disinterested (Sörlin 1989:100-1).

14. By including Linnaeus, as well as figures such as Erasmus, George Washington, and Karl Marx, Goldman (2006) questions whether the *Oxford DNB* takes inclusivity to its limits. Driver and Baigent (2007), however, suggest that the approach might interestingly be taken further, to include for example a 'British' von Humboldt as a complement to other portraits of him.

15. Clarke's *Travels*, though always written as from Clarke's experience alone, in fact combine his and Malthus's experience for the joint part of their journey, Malthus having, at Clarke's request, sent him the sole copy of his travel journals.

16. This was later to become an established part of the Swedish travel itinerary, but was at this time quite new.

17. Broke's role in these dining clubs is put into odd relief by his apparent distaste at excessive dining in Sweden. I am grateful to Bjarne Rogan for this information.

18. Some pleasure seekers were also missionaries: Rob Roy distributed 1000 tracts in Sweden from his canoe (MacGregor 1867:158-9). Secular Swedish evangelists include Martina Sofia Helena Bergman-*Österberg (1849-1915), feminist and promoter of women's physical education, and (Emilie Augusta) Louise *Lind-af-Hageby (1878-1963), anti-vivisectionist.

From Travel to Tourism: British Travellers to Finland 1830-1900.

Tony Lurcock

In 2002 a reader survey in the *Observer* found that Finland was their readers' most highly regarded holiday destination. Perhaps the only problem facing a traveller today would be whether to take the *Rough Guide* or *Lonely Planet*. It was not always so. Anyone who contemplated travelling to Finland before the last years of the eighteenth century would have found little information beyond the final brief chapter of the *Germania* of Tacitus, written in AD 98. This is how it reads in John Aiken's translation from 1777:

> The Fenni live in a state of amazing savageness and squalid poverty. They are destitute of arms, horses and settled abodes: their food is herbs; their cloathing, skins; their bed, the ground. Their only dependence is on their arrows, which, for want of iron, are headed with bone; and the chace [*sic.*] is the support of the women as well as the men, who wander with them in the pursuit, and demand a share of the prey. Nor do they provide any other shelter for their infants from the wild beasts and storms, than a covering of branches twisted together. This is the resort of youth; this is the receptacle of old age. (Aiken 1777:136-7)

Well into the nineteenth century many British travellers agreed that little had changed. This description, wrote J. T. James, 'is often quoted in allusion to their present habits and character' (James 1816:216). Writer after writer recorded discomfort, disgust and disbelief. Edward Daniel Clarke, crossing from Vartsala to Turku on 2 January 1800, wrote that his journey 'was one of extreme suffering; and perhaps few *English* travellers ever encountered one of greater trial'. 'Yet', he continues, 'any thing was preferable to remaining in the wretched and unwholesome hovel where we had passed the night' (Clarke III: 270). Like other early travellers he found the horrors of the inns even worse than the rigours of the Finnish winter. Summer travelling was no easier: the bugs indoors and the mosquitoes outdoors caused more distress than the blood-curdling temperatures of winter. 'No one, but those who have suffered,' wrote John Carr, 'could believe them capable of producing so much torment' (Carr 1805:193).

These early travellers found the inhabitants of Finland even less attractive than the country itself. 'Unpolished in their manners, and still retaining the vestiges of gothic ignorance, they present not many charms to tempt the traveller,' observed Sir Nathaniel Wraxall (Wraxall 1775:4). Sir Robert Kerr Porter thought that 'their appearance is ten times more savage than the grimmest Russian I ever met' (Porter 1808:79), and Clarke wrote that 'both man and woman, if exhibited in a *menagerie* of wild beasts, might be considered as the long-lost link between man and ape' (Clarke 1823:390). The peasants spoke, in Wraxall's words, 'a barbarous jargon equally unintelligible to a Swede or a Russian' (Wraxall 1775:196). In the whole country it was only the hardiness of the horses that regularly met with praise. Why, then, did these long-suffering gentlemen not stay at home, or at least confine their movements to the well-known resorts of 'civilised' Europe?

There were, in fact, all sorts of reasons that prompted British travellers from the mid-eighteenth century to turn their horses' heads to the North. There was novelty and changing taste. It was no longer 'the grand object of travelling ... to see the shores of the Mediterranean', as Samuel Johnson had claimed (Boswell III: 36). Indeed, the very tradition of the Grand Tour was being questioned, and between 1789 and 1814, in any case, the continental wars made such journeys often hazardous or impossible. There were also many positive attractions in the north: to mention only a few, it attracted scientists ambitious to follow the footsteps of Linnaeus or to see the midnight sun, Romantic travellers looking to extend their experience of the picturesque, and readers of Rousseau hoping to discover noble savages in a state of nature.

Whatever the reason for going there, journeys to and within Finland were not for the faint-hearted. Whether the travellers were going through Sweden to Finnish Lapland, or following the south coast route to St Petersburg, and whether they went in summer or in winter, the journey was arduous. Not that they spared any expense; they were well-off, usually upper-class, sometimes Oxford or Cambridge tutors escorting young men of birth and wealth. They usually took their own carriage, relying on post horses along the way. Winter journeys were by horse-drawn sledge, which was quicker and often more comfortable. This was the pattern for some fifty years.

I have set 1830 as my starting point because it marks a new era in travel and travel writing. This might be termed 'The Age of Steam', which transformed travel in the Baltic as it did elsewhere. John Barrow travelled to St Petersburg in 1830 via Hamburg and Lübeck, and his account contains a fitting introduction to the new age. The first pages are a eulogy to steam travel, and praise the comfort and speed of the journey to Hamburg:

> By means of steam, distant countries are brought nearer to each other; a voyage to Petersburg may now easily be performed in eight days, which by the Baltic in a sailing vessel might be eight weeks. (Barrow 1834:2)

'Speed, convenience, and reliable time-keeping', he writes, have so transformed travel that a man

> may not only himself visit any part of the civilized world approachable by water, but even venture to take his family, great or small, along with him without much apprehension of encountering the delays, the dangers and the difficulties described and dwelt upon by travellers of former days. (Barrow 1834:3)

Barrow and his companion, Mr Rouse, set off from St Petersburg to travel through Finland to Stockholm. They bought a basket-work carriage, long enough to permit lying full-length, which, with a straw mattress and various cushions, 'caused the journey as far as Åbo to be performed with every possible degree of ease and comfort' (Barrow 1834:129). For most of the way the road 'was kept in beautiful order; not a hollow or rut of any description' (Barrow 1834:130), and they accomplished the 418 mile journey in four days. They travelled day and night because they could not contemplate stopping at the post stations, which, 'without one exception, are miserable hovels and totally unfit for any traveller to think of sleeping in' (Barrow 1834:138). As if this were not bad enough, they failed to find anything fit to eat or drink. This long journey takes only a few pages to describe, and dwells mainly on the details of the cheap and efficient posting system. One can say of Barrow that although he noticed many sights which they passed, he never considered stopping for them. He was appalled by the squalid villages where he stopped to change horses, but was favourably impressed with the towns, especially with Hamina, while at Viipuri 'we were agreeably surprised to find ourselves in a fine town wearing all the marks of prosperity' (Barrow 1834:136).

In contrast to their non-stop journey across Finland, they had to wait four days in Turku for a favourable wind. As a consequence Barrow gives quite a detailed account of the city. The picture he presents is very different from what was seen by travellers of the late 1820s; instead of the desolation of a city burned to the ground, he describes the animation of a building site. Their chief entertainment, in the absence of wind, was the theatre; he describes several performances in amusing detail.

Barrow was one of the last travellers to cross to Stockholm by sailing boat, and the last Englishman, of many, to describe the route. The voyage between Turku and Stockholm, which took four days, would never be the same again. He is a transitional figure in the developing history of travel. He arrived by steamer, but once in Finland travelled by traditional means: in his own carriage, using post horses. Like many of his predecessors he regarded Finland merely as a distance to be covered. Barrow was observant, but incurious and impatient; his account of Turku is purely accidental – there was no intention to see sights.

1839 was the publication year of Murray's *A Handbook for Travellers in Denmark, Norway, Sweden and Russia*, which included a twenty-eight-page section on Finland, written by Thomas Denman Whatley, a barrister. Much of this Finland section is his own first-person narrative, and is as much a travel book as a guide, written with promotional enthusiasm:

> The principal object of the following pages is to afford such of my travelling countrymen as are disposed to quit the more beaten paths of southern Europe, and explore the less known, but equally romantic, regions of the north, some useful information as to time and distance, which at present they can only obtain by actual experience. Beyond Hamburg, all is an unknown land; no guide-book contains any account of the Baltic steam-boats, still less of the means and facilities of travelling either by land or water, in the more distant lands of Norway and Sweden. At the steam-packet offices in London, you may learn that an English steamer sails three times a month from Lubec [*sic*] to Stockholm, but no further information may be obtained...

He continues:

> The entire tour of the North can hardly be accomplished in a single summer, without hurrying over too much that deserves a more careful survey, or undergoing such a degree of bodily fatigue as would outweigh the pleasure. (Murray 1839:Preface)

'No journey of the same extent,' he concludes, 'can ... be put in competition with it, either for variety or interest' (*ibid.*). All this presupposes a sort of traveller very different from Barrow, who took four days rather than two summers!

Whatley gives the Baltic steamer timetable for 1838, with three steamers a month from Stockholm to Cronstadt via Turku, Helsinki and Tallinn from the beginning of May. He warns that, despite the timetable, the captains 'have the most independent notions' of when to leave. Until the end of the century passengers on both Baltic and lake steamers complained about this brazen disregard of the published timetable. One delayed traveller from Talinn to Helsinki fulminated against the 'outrageous way in which a steam navigation company takes upon itself to waste the passengers' time' (Gallenga 1882:109); when Mrs Tweedie's steamer from Savonlinna to Punkaharju left early she reiterated incredulously that 'the steamer actually did start twenty minutes before its appointed hour, and no-one then or after made the slightest complaint. Imagine our Flying Scotsman speeding North even one minute before the advertised hour!' (Tweedie 1900:204).

The voyage from Stockholm to Turku took about thirty hours, and onwards to St. Petersburg about eighty hours more. Since the steamers tied up only during the hours of darkness the times were shorter in high summer. We learn from the 1849 edition of Murray's *Handbook* that the post route from Stockholm through the Åland Islands, so graphically described by many of the earliest travellers, 'is but seldom taken since the introduction of *steam* navigation between Stockholm and Abo' (preface). By this time steam had largely taken over the route to St Petersburg as well; travellers abandoned the 'trunk route' from Turku to St Petersburg for the coastal steamer from Turku via Helsinki. 'The most convenient and agreeable mode of travelling in Finland is by sea' Whatley advises (Murray 1849:351). The discomforts and perils encountered on this route, graphically described in many earlier accounts, were now a thing of the past. As if to emphasise this, Whatley writes, 'it is generally believed that ladies cannot travel in Scandinavia; nothing can be more erroneous' (Murray 1849:2), but he advises travellers to 'avoid taking English servants, particularly females,' as they 'would prove a far greater trouble than comfort' (Murray 1849:9).

By 1893 Murray's *Handbook* had reached its seventh edition. A survey of these successive editions shows very clearly the ways in which travel in Finland changed, over a period of about fifty years, from exploration into something which can be recognised as modern tourism. Those who genuinely wanted to explore Finland and find experiences worth recording could no longer be content to hug the south coast or follow the 'trunk route'; they had to head into the interior. As each edition of the *Handbook* added to the number of recommended routes in different parts of the country, they needed to go further and further afield to avoid the popular tourist routes. The new edition of 1865 is the most significant. The substantial changes may reflect the preferences of the new editor, T. Michelle, but they reveal also that a very different type of traveller is now envisaged. The section on Finland (now entitled 'Grand Duchy of Finland') has a lot of background information, notes on the history and language of Finland, and 'A General View of Finland.' In 1839 Swedish had been recommended as the language for travelling, with Finnish described dismissively as 'their own perfectly unintelligible and hopeless tongue' (Murray 1839:5). Now there is a list of Finnish words, phrases, and dialogues, tables of weights, measures and coins, and so forth. It looks like a modern guidebook, written with intelligent and inquisitive travellers in mind.

A principal change in the pattern of travel during this period is the opening up of the lake districts of central and eastern Finland. After Joseph Marshall in 1770 no British traveller recorded a visit to Savonlinna for well over a century, but the coming of the railway soon made Olavinlinna one of the most popular sights in the country. Savonlinna, and later Kuopio, could be used as touring centres with local travel by steamer. The posting system (with a private carriage) was still recommended as 'the best, at least the most comfortable, mode of journeying by land' by Murray in 1865 (Murray 1865:264), and was being extolled by Mrs Tweedie as late as 1896 (Tweedie 1900:230-1). It may have lingered on in remote regions until the 1920s, when the motor-bus came to fill in this last gap in the modern transport system.

Among the principal Finnish attractions now were Kangasala, the rapids at Imatra, and Punkaharju. The same railway system that enabled passengers en route to Russia to pass through Finland without pausing, took tourists into the heart of a land so beautiful that British writers more or less exhausted their superlatives in describing it. Small towns which a few years earlier could be reached only by explorers could now be visited by train, and had a distinct summer season.

As the arrival of steamers on the Baltic made travel easier and cheaper, a very different sort of traveller appeared. The age of the Grand Tour had passed, and the nineteenth century advances in transport left ever fewer opportunities for adventurers or pioneers. Travellers were now mainly middle-class, some of them professional travel-writers simply adding Finland to their list, and writing for readers as comfortably middle-class as themselves. When one compares the late eighteenth century accounts of Finland to those of a century later, another very distinct development can be seen: there has been a change from travellers who write to writers who travel.

It is not until the 1890s that we find travel books devoted exclusively to Finland. For more than a hundred years Finland had provided a chapter or two in a work devoted to Russia, or to a Scandinavian tour. Miss Clive-Bayley and Mrs Tweedie, by contrast, in the 1890s, give no account of their journey – or route, even – to Finland, but begin with their arrival in the harbour, in Turku and Helsinki respectively. From this time on travel books devoted exclusively to Finland proliferated, and become larger, glossier, and more full of photographs.

Before considering the Finland described in books such as these, some account should be given of the only two descriptions of travel in Lapland from this period. Edward Rae was an adventurer, reacting against the bored and unenterprising style of travel which the age of the steamer had engendered. He had ambitions beyond 'finding the best hotel that the place afforded'. 'We live in difficult times,' he writes in his 'Introductory Remarks', 'and young men of initiative are put to their wits' ends for novelties' (Rae 1875:2). 'Travel, like everything else, is beginning to become commonplace' (Rae 1875:3), he continues, but a voyage to the Arctic coast followed by a journey southwards through Lapland was, he considered, a comparative novelty. Rae and his companion left Hull on 2 July 1873, by steamer for Trondheim, and journeyed south from Altenfiord, by horse and boat, to the Gulf of Bothnia. From Oulu they took the coastal steamer to Stockholm. In addition to their portmanteaus they took with them 'stout hampers, as the best means of carrying our food and necessaries' (Rae 1875:4); they would rarely be exceeding walking pace, and so could not depend upon finding regular provisions.

Among the adventures which Rae records were the sauna – his is (I believe) the first British account – and a near-death experience coming down the Kengis cataract in a boat 'like a sinking eggshell' (Rae 1875:91). Unusually for this time, Rae and his companion took a great interest in the Finnish language. They had determined to use Finnish whenever they could, and their attempts to procure a Finnish Grammar in Ostrobothnia are a recurrent comic theme in their adventures. Many earlier travellers had heaped abuse on the Finnish language. Not Mr Rae:

> The Finnish tongue I think is the finest I have ever listened to. I have never been so struck with a language; to hear these illiterate boatmen talk to one another in sounds that rivalled the most beautiful in the ancient Greek, made us jealous, and very ambitious to speak it with them. No weak mincing words, nor coarse gutterals: more dignified than the delicate French: more manly and strong than the soft Spanish. (Rae 1875:75)

They wanted to buy a map of Finland, but 'no one of the booksellers was to be found in Oulu – all were in their country houses. This speaks well for their means' (Rae 1875:116).

One may surmise that by the 1870s the ease of travelling was beginning to produce a reaction. By the end of the century this was unmistakable. The railway had by then reached Tornio, and an excursion to the Arctic Circle had become a bolt-on extra to the standard tour, involving little diversion or inconvenience. C. J. Cutcliffe Hyne was a traveller who had no interest at all in standard tours; the Lapland which he experienced seems as remote and genuinely more dangerous even than that traversed by the eighteenth-century explorers, although throughout his journey he appears calmly unaware that he is crossing 'the last wilderness'.

Like Rae, he sailed from London to Norway, but landed at Vardø, beyond the North Cape. He travelled south-west right across Finnish Lapland, through Neid and on to the Gulf. This route, especially the central part, was considered impossible except in winter, but Hyne belonged to that race of Victorian explorers who always get their way, who outface their guides and servants, and who meet with cool aplomb whatever difficulties and hardships confront them. His whole account is marked by understatement. At Inari they were told that the only possible route to Kittilä was by canoe:

> And we should see, what? Well, we should have an excellent view of several hundred miles of river-bank. And we could post onwards with horses either to Kittilä or else directly down to the sea, in comparative luxury and comfort. (Hyne 1898:87)

This would not do for Hyne: 'We had not journeyed that far, however, to exploit future tourist-routes' (*ibid.*). He ignored all warnings, and simply ordered carriers for the morrow. He describes this stage in two graphic chapters entitled 'Into the Land of Horrible Flies'. At Menesjärvi, which was 'nothing more than the squalid huts of one small family' (Hyne 1898:121), they were offered the best accommodation, the couch in the dairy. They preferred the floor, ate curds, and opened a tin. Hyne is the only traveller from this period who puts one in mind of the great nineteenth-century adventurers in Africa, whether he is constructing a raft with one small axe, bribing and cajoling the natives, or coming to terms with local food.

The fact that Hyne was determined to avoid 'future tourist-routes' probably explains why he travelled in Lapland; in the rest of Finland he would, by 1898, have found it very difficult to avoid them. The title of Mrs Tweedie's *Through Finland in Carts* (1898) suggests that she was some sort of pioneer or trailblazer. She was, in all sorts of ways, and I have no wish to belittle her exploratory spirit, but rough it she did not. The title of her book refers only to the centrepiece of her tour, from Kuopio to Kajaani, but even then it was only the last stage, from Iisalmi, that was made by cart, and her party (she travelled with her sister) was escorted by the son of the Governor of the province. Miss Clive-Bayley records one of her expeditions in a chapter entitled 'To the Wilderness', but her worst privations were a smelly pillow (Clive-Bayley 1895:123), and a farm where she could get no refreshment because earlier sightseers had already 'eaten everything that was eatable' (Clive-Bayley 1895:125). Although Miss Clive-Bayley rather likes to think that she is an explorer of the wilderness, she is in fact much more at home with the comforts of Sortavala:

> The town itself stands on a plain surrounded by hills, and though unimportant in appearance, is evidently flourishing and well-to-do. It is well-situated at the head of the great Lake Ladoga, and enjoys a commanding position, both for commerce and for beauty. The Tourist Club have opened up and laid out a charming park, where we spent some hours the day after our arrival. (Clive-Bayley 1895:199)

Let us pause for a moment at Sortavala, and look at it as an example of what was happening in that part of the Finnish lake district towards the end of the century. As far as English accounts tell, the discovery and commercialisation of the Imatra rapids seem to have been simultaneous. It is a striking instance of that doleful paradox, that tourists spoil remote places which they want to see by the mere fact of visiting them. Imatra first. Miss Clive-Bayley had been warned in advance of the Cascade Hotel; 'people arriving from the East as tourists are generally unable to speak Swedish or Finnish, and are fleeced unmercifully' (Clive-Bayley 1895:159). The visitors viewed the falls first at close quarters, and then from the 'pavilions' in the surrounding woods. Nearby was the English Fishing Club. Mrs Tweedie too was appalled by what man had done there: 'the hand of the Philistine is, alas, to be found even in primitive Finland' (Tweedie 1900:151). She deplored the electric lighting and the modern bridge over the falls, and the litter of 'hideous summer houses' around the area. Later on, in Maanika, she condemned the profusion of 'Aussichsturm' as 'a bane of existence to strangers' (Tweedie 1900:236). Yet her own collaboration in the tourist trend is unmistakable:

> Oh! the joy that night of being in a real hotel, with a real brass bedstead and a real spring mattress, to say nothing of once again seeing a proper sized wash-hand basin and jug. (Tweedie 1900:148)

With the railway connection to Imatra the falls became a short excursion from Helsinki or St Petersburg.

A similar story could be told of Punkaharju, which had been declared a National Park. Rosalind Travers in 1911 wrote how glad she was that she saw it only out of season and in the rain:

> In any other season it would all have appeared painfully *soigné*, those trim black and white railings, the seats, the paths, the rest-houses, the hotel, and the wooden arbour upon Runeberg's Hill, where the poet composed the National Anthem of Finland. (Travers 1911:181)

These developments at Punkaharju were, by contrast, very much to the taste of another tourist, Mrs MacDougall, who arrived in 1907 to find 'a score or more of excursionists upon the bridge, good-tempered uninteresting folk; a very commonplace gathering that a rival steamer from another direction had just deposited there' (McDougall 1908:141). An account of 'A Cruise on Lake Ladoga', published in 1864, demonstrates strikingly another revealing feature of travel: the captain of the steamer tied up so that his passengers could see Kexholm:

> Reaching the last house, nestled among twinkling birch-trees on a bend of the river beyond, we turned about and made for the fortress, – another conquest of the Great Peter. Its low ramparts had a shabby, neglected look; an old drawbridge spanned the moat and there was no sentinel to challenge us as we galloped across. In and out again, and down the long quiet street, and over the jolting level to the top of the sandhill, – we had seen Kexholm in half an hour. (Taylor 1864:181)

Tight timetables, rival firms; both here and at Punkaharju we see very early examples of the exploitation and management of tourists which we associate today with the most popular forms of coach tour, for example in Oxford or Bath. The lake and coastal steamers soon became as great an attraction as the scenery through which they moved. 'All those who have travelled on the boats,' writes Ernest Young, 'are unanimous as to the quality of the accommodation, the cheapness of the fares, and the abundance and variety of the food' (Young 1912:201). 'Delightful lake steamers,' enthuses Mrs MacDougall, 'are found all over Finland, furnished usually with comfortable wicker deck-chairs in which one can laze and revel in the scenery' (MacDougall 1908:59). Harry De Windt considered the steamers 'equal in every respect to those of the Rhine or Danube' (de Windt 1901:27).

Overwhelmingly it was the natural attractions which took tourists to Finland: beauty spots, the wonder of Imatra, and the unspoilt peace of the lakes. The English have too many castles and old churches at home to be much impressed with them abroad. A few man-made achievements did, however, make an impression, most notably the fortress at Suomenlinna, compared occasionally even to the pyramids, and the Saimaa Canal. Nothing, though, rivalled the tar boats as the experience which brought together the forces of nature and the skill of man.

Tar production and export was in the late nineteenth century still a large and important industry in the north, and the mortal dangers involved in piloting the frail boats from Kaajani – or, to be exact, from Vaala – to Oulu stirred the imaginations of all who witnessed them. Some of the most vivid writing from this period is, not surprisingly, found in the descriptions of these journeys down the rapids. 'The journey,' wrote Mrs Tweedie, 'is perfectly wonderful, but should only be undertaken by people blessed with strong nerves and possessed of iron constitutions' (Tweedie 1900:293). George Young describes how, by 1912, the Finnish Tourist Association provided the tar boats! 'They are painted red and yellow, the national colours, and are comfortably cushioned... The greatest number of passengers that can be carried is twelve' (Young 1912:14). This, of course, did not leave room for any tar. Even the times of departure were published, for all the world as if these were excursions from Westminster pier to Hampton Court. It comes as no surprise that the best of the many accounts of descending the rapids is by George Renwick, who, because the 'special boat' for tourists was overbooked decided to 'do the trip in the old way' (Renwick 1911:151).

There is no clearer sign of the change from travel to tourism than the transformation of these terrifyingly dangerous commercial vessels into a tourist attraction. Mrs MacDougall explains how the boats 'are usually booked well ahead', so that those who have not planned their itinerary 'have to content themselves with a place on the ordinary tar-boats' (McDougall 1908:178). In other words, a tourist might be reduced to doing the real thing. By the 1890s 'shooting the rapids' was as common a part of a summer tour in Finland as taking a sauna. Kajaani, where Mrs Tweedie found the beds 'impossible' (one of the ladies had to sleep on a spinet!) quickly put itself on the tourist map; ten years later Rosalind Travers was able to enjoy 'the Public Gardens, the Societetshuset, and all the usual amenities of a town' (Travers 1911:162).

The 'Societetshus' (Society House) was an amenity which sprang up during the nineteenth century, and is still to be found in many Finnish towns, usually now under its Finnish name Seurahuone. It was a purely Finnish phenomenon, with the first erected in Turku in 1811-12. They were instituted during the period of Russian rule, primarily to enable Russian officials and nobility to meet upper class Finns. They were assembly rooms (rather like those which can still be seen in Bath), and only later in the century did they become important as hotels. By the time that tourists were becoming commonplace later in the century, most important towns had a society house ready to accommodate them, and tourists who wanted to be sure of their comfort could head for them as they would today for a recognisable hotel chain (see Ringbom, 1988).

Conclusion

By 1912 Finland was established as a popular, comfortable and inexpensive destination for a leisurely summer holiday. The title of the final chapter of Harry de Windt's *Finland As It Is* is 'How to get to Finland'. None of the routes which he describes in 1901 even hints at roughing it.

> I. *Via* Calais, Berlin, and St. Petersburg. Fare, exclusive of sleeping-car (first class) £16-18/10. (60 hours.) II. *Via* Calais, Copenhagen, and Stockholm (first class) £13- 1/9. (70 hours). *Via* Flushing (first class) £9-5/9. (71 hours). *Via* Hook of Holland (first class) £9-3/9. (74 hours.) III. The Finland Steamship Company ... by sea direct from Hull, ... touching at Copenhagen.... [An] all-the-year-round service by the Arcturus and Polaris, new and powerful fifteen-knot steamers fitted throughout with electric light and with accommodation for seventy saloon, and thirty second class, passengers. These sister-ships resemble miniature ocean-liners, with their broad promenade decks, palatial saloons, and large, airy state-rooms, all amidships. A ladies' boudoir and comfortable smoking-room are also provided, so that the most modern requirements of luxurious sea-travel are fulfilled, while to ensure safety the vessels are divided into watertight compartments. There is first- class cuisine on board, and Finnish customs are observed. (de Windt 1901:288)

These ships sailed every Saturday, and the fare was £5 single and £8 return first class (£3 and £5 second class), with meals charged daily at 6s and 4s respectively. Midweek travellers could take the *Astrea* on Wednesdays to Turku via Copenhagen. Around the turn of the century direct sailings from London were introduced.

As Finland was opened up with the development of steamer and rail communications it became a place for tourists rather than explorers. A tour in Finland was always a summer tour; the only accounts of Finland in winter which I have come across from the whole of this period are from the permanent British residents. Another striking feature of these years is the way in which Lapland disappears almost completely from travellers' itineraries. The reason is simple; the railway went no further north than Tornio. In the 1930s, rail and bus connections opened up Lapland as the popular destination it had been in the eighteenth century.

The three experiences which travellers around 1800 had found most appalling had within a century been transformed into major attractions. Transport had changed from a dangerous necessity to a positively pleasurable experience; accommodation usually meant not a bug-infested hovel but a Societetshus in the next town. Then there was food! Early accounts gave the grimmest picture of Finnish cuisine: sour curds, rancid fish, and bread baked once a year. Mrs MacDougall described an asparagus omelette which she ate (among other delicacies) at the Societetshus in Joensuu: 'the chef of the café Anglais in Paris could not have beaten it in excellency, and I speak from experience' (MacDougall 1908:126).

I have, inevitably, simplified this account of the transition from travel to tourism. The Marchioness of Westminster as early as 1827 enjoyed 'charming' boat trips, and always found 'tolerable rooms' (Westminster 1879:179) in which to stay. More than a hundred years later Jim Ingram arrived in Helsinki wearing hobnailed boots and with five pounds in his pocket, and, as the title of his book records, 'found adventure'. But let us leave Mrs MacDougall with the last word: 'a tour round the Isle of Wight could not be fraught with less peril' (MacDougall 1908:6).

Bibliography

Aiken, John (1777): Translation into English of Cornelius Tacitus, *A Treatise on the Situation, Manners, and Inhabitants of Germany*. Warrington, printed by W. Eyres, for J. Johnson, No. 72, St Paul's Churchyard, London.

Barrow, John Jnr. (1834): *Excursions in the North of Europe, through Parts of Russia. Finland, Sweden, Denmark, and Norway, in the Years 1830 and 1833*. London, Richard Phillips.

Boswell, James (1934-50): *Life of Johnson*. Ed G. B. Hill, rev. L. F. Powell, Oxford University Press.

Carr, John (1805): *A Northern Summer; or Travels round the Baltic through Denmark, Sweden, Russia, Prussia and part of Germany in the Year 1804*. London, Richard Phillips.

Clarke, Edward Daniel (1819-1823): *Travels in Various Countries of Europe, Asia, and Africa. Part the Third: Scandinavia*. London, T. Cadwell and W. Davies .

Clive-Bayley, A. M. C. (1895): *Vignettes from Finland or Twelve Months in Strawberry Land*.

London, Sampson Low Marston & Co.

Hyne, C. J. Cutliffe (n.d.): *Through Arctic Lapland* (1898). Quotations from Collins' Wide World Library edition, London and Glasgow, Collins.

Gallenga, Antonio (1882): *A Summer Tour in Russia.* London, Chapman & Hall.

Ingram, Jim (1951): *I Found Adventure.* London, John Long Ltd.

James, J. T. (1816): *Journal of a Tour in Germany, Sweden, Russia, Poland. During the years 1813 and 1814.* London, John Long Ltd.

Marshall, Joseph (1772): *Travels through Holland, Flanders, Germany, Denmark, Sweden, Lapland, Russia, the Ukraine, and Poland in the Years 1768, 1769, and 1770.* London, J. Almond.

MacDougall, Sylvia (published under the pen name 'Paul Waineman') (1908): *A Summer Tour in Finland.* London, Methuen & Co.

Murray's *A Handbook for Travellers in Denmark, Norway, Sweden and Russia* (1839, 1849, new edition 1865). London, John Murray.

Porter, Robert Ker (Second Edition, 1813): *Travelling Sketches in Russia and Sweden during the Years 1805, 1806, 1807.* London, Richard Phillips.

Rae, Edward (1875): *The Land of the North Wind.* London, John Murray.

Renwick, George (1911): *Finland Today.* London, J. Fisher Unwin.

Ringbom, Asa (1988): *Societetshuset i Storfurstendomet Finland.* Helsingfors.

Taylor, B. (1864): *The Atlantic Monthly*, May, 527-8.

Travers, Rosalind (1911): *Letters from Finland, August 1908 - March 1909.* London, Kegan Paul, Trench and Trubner Co. Ltd.

Tweedie, Mrs Alec (new ed. 1900): *Through Finland in Carts.* London, Adam and Charles Black.

Westminster, Marchioness of (1879): *A Tour in Sweden, Norway, and Russia, with Letters.* London, Hurst and Blackett.

de Windt, Harry (1901): *Finland as It Is.* London, John Murray.

Wraxall, Sir Nathaniel William (1775): *Remarks made on a Tour through some of the Northern Parts of Europe.* London, T. Cadell.

Young, Ernest (1912): *Finland: the Land of a Thousand Lakes.* London, Chapman & Hall.

Engendering a Memorable Place:
Holger Drachmann as Travel-Writer.

Henk van der Liet

> It is no longer the presence of the past that speaks to us, but its pastness.
> (David Lowenthal: *The Past is a Foreign Country*, 1985)

Travel, transportation and border crossings play important roles in the life and work of the Danish author Holger Drachmann (1846-1908). Not only did he travel extensively, at home and abroad, but he also wrote a number of travelogues and essayistic accounts about his travels and journeys. One of the most remarkable of these works is *Derovre fra Grænsen* (From Across the Border), first published in 1877. The book soon became popular and was reprinted many times, even twice in the twentieth century.[1]

This essay begins with a brief introduction to Drachmann and his work. Subsequently it deals with a few early travels which Drachmann undertook in the period around 1871, which is a significant year in Scandinavian literary history (Ingwersen 1992:261ff). Some comments will be made too about the ways in which these journeys are reflected in Drachmann's early works. Finally, attention will be drawn to one specific travel book, the above-mentioned *Derovre fra Grænsen*, because it offers an insight into the way Drachmann mapped out and constructed one particular geographical and mental 'place', the battlefield of Dybbøl in Southern Jutland. This memorable place has since the publication of *Derovre fra Grænsen* been increasingly recognised as a symbolic site of national history, and today it is primarily known for the historical meaning it represents (Adriansen 2003:253).

It is the investigation into the relationship between a text and its defining and constructing of a symbolic and mental topography, which is the implicit goal of this essay. Therefore, some theoretical considerations on the processing of travel experiences, the concept of border crossing in Drachmann's literary work, and what this means for the engendering of collective memory, will also be discussed.

Drachmann's oeuvre

Drachmann made his official debut as a writer in 1872 and was very productive right up until his death in 1908. During most of this period his contemporaries regarded him – as he himself did – as the national Danish poet *par excellence* (Liet 2004a:144). Drachmann's renown was undisputed and lasted until his death. In the decades following his death though, an irreversible decline in his popularity has taken place. Nevertheless, Drachmann's name still has a familiar ring to most Danes. This is to some extent due to his affiliation with the literary movement around the critic Georg Brandes (1842-1927), and the so-called *Modern Breakthrough* in Scandinavian literature. Another reason why Drachmann is still remembered today, and still appeals to the imagination of many contemporary Danes, is his once much-discussed, notoriously bohemian life-style and his tempestuous love life. In the eyes of the public at large, he still is perceived as the modern bohemian poet of his time.

Despite appearances, Drachmann was not just a profligate. His oeuvre is actually one of the most voluminous in all of Danish nineteenth-century literature. Some sixty books and innumerable smaller publications appeared during his lifetime, covering a wide range of genres: poetry, drama, novels, stories, essays, travelogues, journalism, translations, and more.[2] Furthermore, Drachmann was a highly productive visual artist as well. He was a skilful painter, who often illustrated his own works, and in his note- and sketchbooks, words and images are intertwined, often appearing in hybrid generic forms. It is also worth noting, that Drachmann started his career as a painter, and not as a writer. He took his first steps in the literary arena as a journalist, or – more precisely – as a travel writer and chronicler.

Holger Drachmann grew up in the inner city of Copenhagen, in a family distinguished by liberal attitudes and social mobility. Through the activities of his father, who among other things was a ship's doctor, and by rummaging the harbour just around the corner from the parental home, Drachmann, became familiar with ships, sailors, and life at sea from an early age. Later, these themes became the cornerstones of his oeuvre, particularly in his travel writing, and poetry.

After finishing primary school in 1865, Drachmann was enrolled in the Royal Academy of Fine Arts in Copenhagen, where he specialized in marine painting (Weilbach 1896:208). He turned out to be a promising young artist, and when his first paintings were exhibited in public in 1869 his talent was immediately recognized and appreciated. The two paintings that were shown at that first exhibition[3] were the result of the first substantial journeys Drachmann undertook: two trips to the island of Bornholm in the summers of

1866 and 1868, and a European grand tour-like sea voyage to Scotland, Gibraltar, Sicily and back home to Denmark over land from Genoa in early 1867. In 1871 Drachmann visited the United Kingdom where especially the deprived existence of the working class in London made a deep and lasting impression on the sensitive young artist.

On these early trips to Britain Drachmann's writings became more serious, taking root in two radically different sources of inspiration which both originated from these early travel experiences: the sea and modern urban life. Both are thematic complexes that are characterized by instability and movement, by 'flux', to use Stephen Kern's expression (Kern 1998:20). At the same time these topoi are firmly rooted in the fundamental dichotomy between man and nature. In Drachmann's artistic world the iterative, ageless movement of the sea, and the agitated restlessness of contemporary industrial and urban life, are closely related to each other. In London in particular he experienced how huge the cultural and ethical divide between modern industrial society, and the traditional values of his own, rather provincial, Danish frame of reference, actually was.

In 1871, while Drachmann was visiting London, the critic Georg Brandes was attracting huge public attention through a series of lectures on European literature at Copenhagen University. Accidentally, Brandes came across some of Drachmann's essays (Brandes 1907:75) and he felt that they shared the same ideas and hopes for the future. After Drachmann had returned to Copenhagen Brandes went to see him and suggested to him that he should take up writing instead of pursuing a career as a painter (Brandes 1907:76). Drachmann followed Brandes' advice and officially made his literary debut in 1872 with a book of brisk short stories entitled *Med Kul og Kridt* (With Charcoal and Chalk).

These prose-sketches are lively, impressionistic fragments about 'interesting' and picturesque people and milieus the author had encountered on his travels. Sometimes they are mere vehicles for folkloristic interests, using 'exotic' islands such as Sicily and Bornholm as backdrop and local colour. In the context of Drachmann's oeuvre as a whole, they may be seen as the first proofs of his vivid style which characterized his prose throughout his career and, not unimportantly, these early pieces also show the importance of travel as an essential source of inspiration for his writing as such.

Drachmann's real breakthrough as a writer came a few months after his prose debut *Med Kul og Kridt*, with the collection of poetry *Digte* (Poems, 1872). The best known poems in *Digte* were inspired by the experiences Drachmann had during his early journeys abroad, especially to Scotland and London. Among them are poems that are still famous – like 'Engelske Socialister' (English socialists) and 'King mob'. Already in his first collection of poems, some of the themes appear that recur in all of Drachmann's work: a bacchanalian lust for life and natural beauty, a heartfelt sympathy for ordinary people and a romantic awareness of the radical metamorphosis of contemporary culture and society. With the appearance of *Digte*, Drachmann was immediately recognised as the main poet of the Modern Breakthrough.

As mentioned above, Drachmann was also a prolific essayist and chronicler, and his first polemic collection of impressionistic essays, *Derovre fra Grænsen* (1877), is one of the best examples of his work in this genre. *Derovre fra Grænsen* is based on a tour in the Danish-German borderland where the Danish-Prussian war had been fought, and lost, by the Danish forces in 1864. The outcome of the war still cast dark shadows over Danish society in the 1870's, and at the time of its publication the subject-matter of *Derovre fra Grænsen* was still politically highly delicate (Frandsen 1994:87-129). The mere fact that Drachmann dared to touch upon the conflict in his travel account was perceived as a provocation to the liberal political forces, including the Brandesianists. As a result, the more than friendly relations between Drachmann and the supporters of the Brandes brothers began to cool off.

Although patriotism and a barely concealed conservative political agenda pervade the entire text, *Derovre fra Grænsen* also clearly demonstrates Drachmann's artistic skills in depicting the lives of ordinary people in a passionate and original way. This ability is in some way related to his 'discovery' in 1871 of the little fishing hamlet of Skagen, on the northernmost tip of the Jutland peninsula. Here, in a rather remote corner of Denmark, he encountered peasants, fishermen and sailors, groups of people whom he felt were still unaffected by industrialisation and modernity. Soon after Drachmann's 'discovery', numerous artists from all over Scandinavia began visiting picturesque Skagen and some settled there permanently (Svanholm 2001:9-12). Skagen became a highly appreciated refuge for artists and Drachmann often returned to the town.[4]

In addition to making innumerable journeys in his home country, Drachmann undertook dozens of trips all over Europe, and in 1898 he crossed the ocean and went to the United States where he lived for nearly two years.[5] Shortly after returning to Denmark Drachmann married the Norwegian artiste Soffi Lasson (1873-1917), but died in hospital in a seaside resort north of Copenhagen in 1908. His ashes were brought by steamer to the port of Frederikshavn and then transported over land to Skagen.[6] There he found his last resting place in a monumental burial mound, by the sea, due north of the town, where it can still be found (Liet 2004a:151).

Drachmann lived in a period of fundamental change in modern Danish history. In comparison to Britain, Denmark, by and large, was still a pre-industrial society (Jespersen 1994:61-72). The modernisation of Danish society had been slowed down by the consequences of the Danish-Prussian war of 1864 and the persistent power of the dominant conservative political and ecclesiastical elites. During this era of change – roughly from 1870 to 1900 – the political opposition was still frail and badly organised, and the democratisation of society depended heavily on intellectuals. Progressive forces increasingly gained influence through the expanding new media, primarily newspapers and journals, which effectively disseminated their political views on issues such as general suffrage and equal rights for both sexes. Modern newspapers were established in this period, and writers played a crucial role in the process of emancipating journalism, as well as in the overall modernisation of Danish society (Stangerup 1946).[7] It is within this context, i.e.: the rise of new journalistic means in the public arena on the one hand, and the still powerful conservative political elite on the other, that *Derovre fra Grænsen* must be seen. Incidentally, the book became one of Drachmann's greatest successes, also commercially speaking.[8]

From Across the Border

Derovre fra Grænsen was published in the autumn of 1877, and it has the significant subtitle *Strejftog over det danske Termopylæ (Als-Dybbøl). I April Maaned 1877* (Forays into the Danish Thermopylae (Als-Dybbøl) in the month of April of 1877). The book contains a handful of more or less journalistic impressions from a journey Drachmann made in the spring of 1877, to the Danish-German borderland in southern Jutland, i.e. the battleground of the 1864 war against Prussia. This particular part of Denmark had been the object of intense dispute, and the defeat in 1864 had led to deep resentment in the Danish middle class and the bourgeoisie of Copenhagen.

From a semantic point of view Derovre fra Grænsen is a very interesting title, because it deals with the ambiguous concept of 'border' in many ways: the text is about borders, mentions numerous borders, border posts, border police (*gendarmer*), custom-house officers, etc. The text also deals with cultural boundaries and borders that either are being established (through political Germanification of the population) or borders that have to be strengthened and reinforced (to keep Danish patriotism alive under foreign rule). Furthermore, the text itself is in a way a border, and in that respect the paratextual information, the layout, cover design and illustrations, are vital elements.[9]

Intriguingly the title indicates that something – a message? a cry for help? – from the other side of the border urges the reader to respond. The reader of *Derovre fra Grænsen* is initially guided into Drachmann's text by means of a non-textual medium, namely a drawing. It introduces some of the main ingredients of the following text: in the scarce light of sunset we see a slope with a windmill and a kind of obelisk on top, while a steamboat is sailing into a harbour where some masts are sticking up and a large building dominates the foreground. The heavy clair-obscure contours of the clouds in the sky, emphasise the drama of the scenery. The drawing is presumably made by Drachmann himself, as it shows his initials, and this is also the case with the drawing at the end of Chapter 2, which shows the windmill and the buildings surrounding it in more detail. These are the only two illustrations, apart from the vignettes, in the book itself: situated at the very beginning and in the middle. A cover illustration is absent. The drawing, which is placed before the text, is followed by the title of chapter 1, 'Onboard the "Hertha"', and the date: 18 April 1877. For every Dane, this date is crucial information, as it refers to the final assault by the Prussians on exactly that day in 1864. Thus, it can be ascertained that the picture shows the slopes of the Dybbøl battlefield, with the Dybbøl windmill, the Prussian victory monument on top and the castle of Sønderborg in front.[10]

The drawing of a steamboat heading for the coast, the title of the first chapter, the date, the poem that follows and finally the transgression into a third medium or genre, that of the prose narrative itself, are all expressions of the crossing of borders: between natural elements, temporal borders, genre, and between media, etc. The crossing of media borders is finally brought to an end – significantly enough right at the very beginning of the prose text, following the opening poem, and emphasised by a kind of ritualised surfacing of the narrator – by the author telling us *in medias res* that he now has stopped(!) writing: 'Og da jeg var kommen saa vidt, lagde jeg Pennen og gik op paa Dækket' (p. 8; And once I had come so far [i.e. writing these words], I laid down my pen and went up on deck). Does this mean that the text produces itself? Or is it written by history itself?

It is evident that the continuous awareness of transgressing and crossing of borders is vital for a proper understanding of the semiotics at play in *Derovre fra Grænsen*. By elaborating this metaphor and expressing it on a number of levels in the text, Drachmann establishes a parallel to the experiences of immigrants, refugees and – in the case of the inhabitants of the southern provinces of Jutland highly relevant – of people living under foreign rule. For all of these categories of people, the physical crossing of factual borders is often easier than crossing cultural boundaries and the complexity of adjusting to new – culturally unfamiliar – surroundings (Schimanski 2006:42). A number of portraits in *Derovre fra Grænsen*, show that cultural border crossing often is a complicated, time consuming and traumatic process. The reluctance of many Danes in Northern Schleswig to adjust to post 1864 reality, i.e. to accept the fact that they are living in a part of

Germany, is explained as an expression of their patriotism and nurturing of their identity.

Drachmann makes quite a point of emphasising that he is a neutral observer – he even speaks of his head as a 'photographic device' (p. 9). He maintains that he simply wants to be a journalist, who registers things. But the text soon shifts to the present tense, and the narrator is found sitting on the deck of the 'Hertha', pondering the fruitless political quibbling in the (Copenhagen) newspapers, the future of parliament, the constitution and national defence, etc. Drachmann compares the newspapers to batteries of artillery and the political parties to military units, and for more than an entire page he elaborates on these martial metaphors in great detail. Furthermore, he stresses the fact that he is an outsider, a non-combatant, by taking his position on deck – and in between the elements – literally: 'Jeg har i dette Øjeblik ikke de fjerneste berøringspunkter med Land' (p. 12: At this moment I do not have any point of contact with (the main) Land). By doing so he puts two of his main themes in place: the turning of his back on the political quarrels in Copenhagen (the shelling and bombarding of opponents in parliament and in the press), and the taking of a 'neutral' position as a reporter. The latter is immediately rendered questionable though, because of his deeply negative and biased description of the Prussian flag blowing from the ship's stern. His neutrality is undermined even further when he juxtaposes the ship's entering of these foreign waters, with the appearance of thick clouds of sooty smoke from the ship's engine, which cast dark shadows over the water. The narrator does not beat about the bush as he makes it crystal clear that he is entering the realm of darkness, coming from 'det klare, friske Vand her mellem de rige, smilende Øer' (p. 15: this clear and fresh water, between these rich and smiling islands). This is far from an unbiased way of reporting. Nevertheless Drachmann keeps referring to himself as a journalist: 'Jeg har taget min Pen og Papir med, som en anden Korrespondent, der gaar til en Krigsskueplads. Jeg er min egen Korrespondent, mit eget Blad, min egen Opinion. Jeg gaar til en tavs og øde Krigsskueplads i et fremmed Land' (p. 29: I have taken my pen and paper with me, like any correspondent who visits a theatre of war. I am my own correspondent, my own paper, my own opinion. I am off to a silent and deserted theatre of war in a foreign country). By combining the discourse of war with the position of the journalist, time and time again, Drachmann stages himself in the intermediary position of a 'Krigskorrespondent' (p. 29: war correspondent). Because the theatre of operations[11] now is 'silent and deserted', he claims that his special literary talent guarantees him the perfect position to 'opfange hele Stemningens højtidelige Alvor' (p. 25: grasp the solemn gravity of the entire atmosphere), even though it is fourteen years since the real battle took place. This shows how important the notion of

Dybbøl Mølle efter Stormen

Figure 1: Black and white photograph showing the Dybbøl windmill immediately after the assault in April 1864. (Courtesy of the Historical Centre at Dybbøl Banke.)

'atmosphere' is in Drachmann's mission as a poet/journalist. It is through 'atmosphere' that reality presents itself to him in a romantic – dualistic or idealistic – way, dividing the world on two epistemological levels. One level is the reality of aesthetics and natural beauty, while the other is the product of human history – i.e. the sedimentation of time, which establishes various layers of memories, souvenirs, etc. The latter is the dominant level for Drachmann because: 'Ingen kan se Naturskønhederne i en Egn, de er fuld af historiske Minder' (p. 27: Nobody is able to see the beauty of nature in a region so full of historical memories).

The meaning of the word 'memory' in *Derovre fra Grænsen* differs fundamentally from its colloquial usage. For Drachmann memories are not connected to individual experiences, but to collective, involuntary or intuitive understandings of the past. Although it is his first visit to the battlefield and its surroundings, he nevertheless speaks of 'memories'. This visionary element in the author's attitude shows Drachmann's strong affinity with the romantic tradition, but it is also an attempt to define an intermediate stance between the poet-insider (who focuses on subjectivity and introspection) and the journalist-outsider (who deals with objectivity and the outside world). It is remarkable though that Drachmann is fully aware of the fact that these 'memories' actually are mental constructions and forms of representation.

Especially the second chapter of *Derovre fra Grænsen*, 'After sunset', contains detailed descriptions of the landscape around Dybbøl as a theatre of military operations, with trenches, fortifications and troops engaged in different stages of the battle itself, etc. The chapter starts, just like the previous chapter, with a poem. This time the poem describes a battle scene from the 1864 war: a battalion crossing a pontoon bridge, heading for the enemy. The present day poet/journalist Holger Drachmann crosses the same bridge and – in a way – also meets the 'enemy', a group of foreign custom-house officers (p. 31). The text has now changed to prose again, and the first word he hears is significantly enough the 'thundering' German word 'Brückengeld!' (p. 32: bridge toll!). Once he has crossed the bridge, and has entered 'foreign' territory, he notices that many people speak Danish – just as at home – and he is lodged in a 'Danish hotel' (p. 31). Although the narrator now is in a foreign land, he still is at home, primarily because of the language.

Of course the protagonist wants to visit 'Kærnepunktet' (p. 43: the cardinal point) of his journey before nightfall. When he has reached this point – the slopes of Dybbøl hill with the windmill on top – some of the most interesting passages in *Derovre fra Grænsen* follow, containing detailed descriptions of the Prussian monument, an obelisk shaped pillar, which was erected in the vicinity of the Dybbøl windmill to commemorate the Prussian victory over the Danes in 1864 (pp. 51-57). The lyrical and allegorical depictions of the mill and the battlegrounds around it cover approximately twenty pages, in which the mill is personified and the narrator even writes that the windmill 'speaks' to him, while it raises its dark wings to heaven in a dramatic gesture (pp. 60-61). When the Danish 'monument' and its German counterpart are compared with each other, the German pillar is consequently described in negative terms. The shape reminds the narrator of the spike on a German helmet, and the ornamentation is unflatteringly compared to the design of a 'Raubritterburg' (p. 52: a robber baron's castle).

Figure 2: Photograph by Th. Thomsen of the Prussian monument commemorating the defeat of the Danish troops at Dybbøl in 1864. The structure was erected in 1871-1872 on the highest point at Dybbøl and close to the windmill. It was demolished immediately after the end of World War II in May 1945. (By courtesy of the Historical Centre at Dybbøl Banke.)

In the course of the text it becomes increasingly clear that Drachmann is strongly in favour of the erection of a Danish war memorial at Dybbøl too. His text implicitly aims at temporarily supplying such a 'monument', in the sense that as long as a real patriotic war memorial does not yet exist – meaning that as long as Dybbøl is in enemy hands – this text, in its own way, can act as its substitute. Many years later, after the demolition of the German memorial pillar in 1945, and the inauguration of the present 'Historiecenter' in 1992, Drachmann's wishes were finally met.[12]

Judging from the rest of the chapters in *Derovre fra Grænsen*, Drachmann's 'political' mission was to report on the Prussian cultural 'yoke' under which the Danish speaking population suffered. He makes notes of the life stories of the people he meets, and especially the third chapter is designed as an extensive interview, literally with 'the man in the street' e.g. a chimneysweep he meets on the road. These dialogues also offer Drachmann the opportunity to pass on eyewitness reports from the actual fighting in the area in 1864. But his main goal clearly is to draw attention to the fact that many compatriots live under foreign rule. Drachmann makes it clear that the only solution to bring this to an end is to re-establish the pre-war situation, which in some way or other, implies bringing lost territory under Danish authority again. Drachmann does not indicate how this must be brought about, but his textual strategy is to cross the 'real' 1864 border, and to challenge the tenability of the status of a wide range of different borders, both textual and non-textual ones.

It goes without saying that the 1877 situation 'across the border' was hard to accept for romanticists, like Drachmann. The deeply patriotic and conservative tendencies in the text may appear somewhat surprising, if we take into account that Drachmann was one of the advocates of modernity. The really important thing about this journey, and the book about it, is the fact that Drachmann established a new symbol for Danishness, which first in patriotic circles, but later also in Danish society as a whole, obtained general recognition and high status. That symbol is summarized in the name 'Dybbøl'. Today the battlefields and the windmill at Dybbøl are no less than national symbols, and a museum was established at the site in 1992 to commemorate the battle.[13] This museum shows that Dybbøl, and especially the windmill, now part of the museum, has become a symbol of absolute national importance. Virtually every Dane is familiar with the symbolic meaning of Dybbøl. Just like the town of Skagen, it is merely a miniscule spot in the country's surveyable topography. At the same time Dybbøl – and for that matter Skagen too – are important points of reference in the mental and ideological landscape every Dane becomes acquainted with, and is socialised to understand the immanent symbolic importance of. It goes without saying that the pastures and meadows on the slopes og Dybbøl hill, as well as the fishing hamlet of Skagen, already existed long before they were 'discovered' and subsequently promoted as national icons. But how can the role of *Derovre fra Grænsen* in the engendering of the ideological meaning of Dybbøl be understood?

Locations of memory

The French historian Pierre Nora has pointed out some 130 places of crucial interest in French history. His idea was that places, landscapes and so on, in a way could incorporate, or become saturated, so to speak, with history and historical events and in a sense help to save and collectivise memories of the past. Nora looks at certain monuments, landscapes, places, buildings, statues, war memorials, tombs, cemeteries, etc, as places where historical events are symbolised, visualised and concretised. For Pierre Nora and others, these *lieux de mémoire* play a crucial role in the process of keeping the past alive and placing it in collective frameworks of memory.

These 'locations of memory' can also be institutions, certain books, banners, flags, etc. They are concentrated representations of historical events, and, so to speak, symbols that are charged with time and memory. In the introduction to a German work based on Nora's concept of history entitled *Deutsche Erinnerungsorte* (2001), the editors emphasise that 'location of memory' is a metaphor, which originates from classical mnemonics, i.e. from a non-narrative, spatial way of organising cognition, the so-called *loci memoriae* (François & Schulze 2001:18).

The battlefield, and the windmill of Dybbøl have today reached the status of what could be labelled as a *lieu de mémoire*. Furthermore, I think we can easily discern a handful of such 'locations', which play an important role, both in Drachmann's work, and in Danish 'collective memory' in a broader sense. Among them are at least: the village of Skagen (including the burial mound with Drachmann's ashes),[14] the battlefields near Dybbøl (and especially the windmill overlooking the area) and the Danish beaches and seashores as places of reflection and poetical inspiration.[15] In the present essay I only focus on the second 'location' of memory, Dybbøl, because I want to show what Drachmann's role was in the process of establishing this special national arena of commemoration and 'musealisation' of the past.

Drachmann's journey in the Danish-German borderland in April 1877 was a journey in a quasi-no-man's land, an awkward mixture between enemy territory and homeland, an area filled with suppressed history and national trauma. After the Treaty of Versailles (Jones 1970:130-133) it was decided to solve the dispute through a plebiscite in 1920, and as a result large parts of the area became part of Denmark again. Dybbøl has since been turned into a spot resembling a tourist attraction, giving the Danes the opportunity to celebrate their national and historical self-image by sharing a number of collective icons. The battlefields at Dybbøl, and the windmill on a nearby hilltop, are real visual objects, and over the years many trenches have been unearthed or reconstructed. It is nevertheless important to keep in mind that Dybbøl also is a mental construction, and Drachmann's text is one of the original instruments that helped to create it and supply it with ideological content and context (Adriansen 2003:258). Memorising the past implies making (narrative) constructions of the past and tying them to *loci memoriae*. In this case a battlefield and a mill have become locations that help us to understand the past by putting it in a collective ideological framework, and thereby producing identity and a sense of continuity (François & Schulze 2001:14).

The social historian Inge Adriansen correctly asserts in her monumental two-volume work on Danish national symbols that Drachmann's literary image of Dybbøl helped to establish the 'myth' of Dybbøl as the Danish version of the heroic battle at Thermopylae in ancient times, where the

Figure 3: Xylography by N. V. Dorph showing the Dybbøl windmill and the Prussian monument seen from the village of Sundeved. This far less dramatic picture differs fundamentally from the most common iconography. It is the opening illustration of Erik Skram's essay 'Hinsides Grænsen. Nogle Erindringer', published in 1887 in a two-volume anthology edited by M. Galschiøt, *Danmark: Skildringer og Billeder af danske Forfattere og Kunstnere*, Vol. 1, p. 511-569. In 1888 it was reissued as a separate book, entitled *Hinsides Grænsen. Erindringer fra Sønderjylland efter 1864*, but the illustration by Dorph was not included.

Spartans were outnumbered, and notwithstanding their actual loss in battle, became the moral victors because of their heroic resistance against a superior enemy (Adriansen, 2003:251-260). But apart from the text of *Derovre fra Grænsen* itself, and the iconographic effectiveness of the two images in the book of the Dybbøl windmill at dusk, the real reason for the immense success of Drachmann's text may well be the immense popularity of one single poem embedded in the last chapter (pp. 129-130).

This poem is often referred to as 'De sønderjyske Piger' (The girls from North Schleswig) or by its opening line 'De vog dem, vi grov dem' (They slew them, we buried them). The text sings the praise of the northern Schleswig girls who have shown their patriotic disposition by burying fallen Danish soldiers in their gardens and looking devotedly after these graves over the years. These young women personify patriotism and historical continuity. Because they take care of the dead, they are continuously confronted with the past, which also makes them extra motivated not to fraternise with Germans. Soon after the publication of *Derovre fra Grænsen* the poem was set to music by the composer Henrik Hennings (1848-1923). The score and the text were published in the popular journal *Ude og Hjemme* on 14 April 1878, and shortly after the song was republished by the music publisher Oscar Risom in Copenhagen and became widely popular in its own right.[16]

Holger Drachmann was a unique lyrical talent, and some of his verse is among the most beloved by his countrymen. In Drachmann's poetic idiom, everything is in motion. The absence of stability and clear contours in his art reflects the fact that the best of his prose and poetry was written in moods of imminent change and moments of transgression. Thus, it is not surprising that Drachmann also was a frequent – and in some ways obsessive – traveller, looking for new inspirations and thrills all the time. He and many of his colleagues were restless, possibly due to the nervous atmosphere of the era they lived in. Being on the move, and crossing borders, among others social ones, was also specific for fin de siècle literary life, and perhaps we should understand the era's textual heritage within the framework of what Johan Schimanski labels a 'border poetics'.[17]

Drachmann was one of the first artists to 'discover' the fishing hamlet of Skagen, but also as one of the prime promoters of 'Dybbøl' as the national symbol. Today both Dybbøl and Skagen have become places of national interest, with museums dedicated to them, and both places are popular destination for holidaymakers too. Drachmann played a crucial role in the radical metamorphosis of both communities and the way they are perceived by the public at large. Last but not least, Drachmann wrote a number of texts that today are at the very core of the national Danish self-image. These are, apart from *Derovre fra Grænsen*, also the midsummer's song 'Vi elsker vort Land' (We love our country), and the still popular fairytale play *Der var en gang* (Once upon a time) from 1885. In this sense he was one of the main actors in the process of engendering modern 'Danishness', i.e. Danish identity as an element in the nation-building process in the decades after the traumatic defeat in the Danish-Prussian War of 1864. As Per Thomas Andersen recently pointed out again, working with the notion of 'identity' presupposes that we understand it as a narrative (Andersen 2006:8), and Drachmann's *Derovre fra Grænsen* functions precisely as such a narrative gateway to a collective frame of reference on many different levels – textual, paratextual (visual) and even re-contextualised, through the remedialisation of the embedded poem as a song text. Finally, as a travelogue, it continuously crosses and permeates borders whereby it establishes itself as a text and a 'space in-between' in it's own right.

Bibliography

Works by Holger Drachmann:

Med Kul og Kridt (1872). Copenhagen: Andr. Schou.

Digte (1872). Copenhagen: Andr. Schou.

Derovre fra Grænsen (1877). Copenhagen: Gyldendal. (Also used: 10th edition of 1919, and the reprint by Dy-Po Tryk in Sønderborg of 1966.)

Fjæld-Sange og Æventyr (1885). Copenhagen: Gyldendal.

Danmark leve! Blade fra en rejse paa begge Sider af Grænsen (1885). Copenhagen: Gyldendal.

Other sources:

Adriansen, Inge (1997): *Dybbøl Mølle. Monument & museum.* Sønderborg: Museet på Sønderborg Slot.

—— (2003): *Nationale symboler i det danske rige 1830-2000.* Vol. II. Copenhagen: Museum Tusculanum.

Andersen, Per Thomas (2006): *Identitetens geografi. Steder i litteraturen fra Hamsun til Naipaul.* Oslo: Universitetsforlaget.

Bak, Lars H. (2003): 'Tyske sejrsmonumenter på danske hænder. Düppel Denkmal og Arnkiel Denkmal og den danske stat 1918-1950'. *Sønderjyske årbøger 2003,* [= yearbook of Historisk Samfund for Sønderjylland], pp. 7-42.

Bakhtin, Mikhail (1981): 'Forms of Time and of the Chronotope in the Novel', in *The Dialogic Imagination.* Austin: University of Texas Press, pp. 84-258.

Brandes, Georg (1907): *Levned. Et tiaar.* Vol. II. Copenhagen: Gyldendal.

François, Etienne and Hagen Schulze (eds) (2001): *Deutsche Erinnerungsorte.* Vol. I. München: Beck.

Frandsen, Steen Bo (1994): *Dänemark – der kleine Nachbar im Norden. Aspekte der Deutsch-Dänischen Beziehungen im 19. und 20. Jahrhundert.* Darmstadt: Wissenschaftliche Buchgesellschaft.

Geisthövel, Alexa (2005): 'Der Strand', in Alexa Geisthövel & Habbo Knoch (eds), *Orte der Moderne. Erfahrungswelten des 19. und 20. Jahrhunderts.* Frankfurt/New York: Campus, pp. 121-130.

Hennings, Henrik (1878): *'De sønderjyske Piger.' Vexelsang af Holger Drachmanns 'Derovre fra Grænsen' sat i musik af Henrik Hennings,* Copenhagen: Oscar Risom, 1878 [OR118].

Ingwersen, Niels (1992): 'The Modern Breakthrough', in Sven H. Rossel (ed.), *A History of Danish Literature.* [=A History of Scandinavian Literatures, Vol. I] Lincoln & London: University of Nebraska Press, pp. 261-317.

Jespersen, Knud J. V. (1994): *A History of Denmark.* Houndmills & New York: Palgrave Macmillan.

Jones, W. Glyn (1970): *Denmark.* [Nations of the Modern World] London: Ernest Benn.

Kern, Stephen, (1998 [1983]) *The Culture of Time and Space 1880-1918.* Cambridge MA: Harvard University Press.

Liet, Henk van der (1999a): "Haven't You Heard...' Speech and Chronotope in Peer Hultberg's Novel *Byen og Verden*', in *Scandinavian Studies,* vol. 71, no. 2, pp. 207-220.

—— (1999b): "French Fungi': Some Snooping in Holger Drachmann's Letters', in Garton, Janet and Michael Robinson (eds), *Nordic Letters 1870-1910.* Norwich: Norvik Press, pp. 201-227.

—— (2004a): 'Holger Drachmann', in Marianne Stecher-Hansen (ed.): *Dictionary of Literary Biography, Volume 300: Danish Writers from the Reformation to Decadence 1550-1900.* Detroit, etc: Thomson Gale, pp. 142-153.

—— (2004b): 'Holger Drachmann – overgangstidens dobbeltnatur', in Hertel, Hans, *Det stadig moderne gennembrud. Georg Brandes og hans tid, set fra det 21. århundrede.* Copenhagen: Gyldendal, pp. 145-164.

Mortensen, Erik (1990): *Kunstkritikkens og Kunstopfattelsens Historie i Danmark.* Vol. I-II. Copenhagen: Rhodos.

Petersen, Ulrich Horst (2005): *Mens jeg husker det. Essays 2001-2005.* Copenhagen: Tiderne Skifter, pp. 118-138.

Schimanski, Johan (2006): 'Crossing and Reading: Notes towards a Theory and a Method' in: *Nordlit*, nr. 19, pp. 41-63.

Sigmund, Pia (1993): 'Holger Drachmann in America', in: *Scandinavian Studies*, vol. 65, nr. 3, pp. 390-410.

Skram, Erik (1976 [1887]): *Hinsides Grænsen. Erindringer fra Sønderjylland efter 1864.* [Foreword and commentary: Inge Adriansen and Jørgen Slettebo] S.l.: Strandbergs Forlag.

Stangerup, Hakon (1946): *Kulturkampen* I-II. Copenhagen: Gyldendal.

Svanholm, Lise (2001): *Malerne på Skagen.* Copenhagen: Gyldendal.

Ursin, Johannes (1956): *Bibliografi over Holger Drachmanns forfatterskab.* Copenhagen: Gyldendal.

Weilbach, Philip (1896): *Nyt dansk Kunstnerleksikon.* Vol. I. Copenhagen: Gyldendal.

Notes

1. *Derovre fra Grænsen* appeared on 30 November 1877, and within a month a second edition was issued. The book became so popular, that within the first twelve months, seven editions were published. The two most recent printings, in 1919 and 1966, are quite remarkable from a bibliographical and philological point of view. For more details see note 9.

    I would like to thank Marieke Berkhout and Pim van Harten for advice and helpful suggestions on earlier versions of this essay.

2. For comprehensive bibliographies see Ursin 1956 and, in English, van der Liet 2004a:142-144.

3. The titles of these paintings are: 'The beach north of the fishing hamlet Aarsdale on Bornholm', and 'The coast at Granton near Leith'. Both paintings depict coastal scenes – waves, lots of sky, rugged coastlines, in short: the never fixed contact zone between sea and land.

4. Drachmann also often used the locals as models in his work, as for example in the novelette *Lars Kruse* (1879), in the play *Strandbyfolk* (Shoreville People) (1883, revised in 1897) and in dozens of stories.

5. See Sigmund (1993)

6. The funeral procession was attended by thousands of people and immortalised in a series of large oil paintings by Aksel Jørgensen (1883-1957).

7. Among the most influential papers of the day were *Social-Demokraten* (founded 1874) and *Politiken* (founded 1884). Politiken became one of the vital mouthpieces of the cultural avant-garde, in which Drachmann's cousin, the influential politician Viggo Hørup (1841-1902), and Drachmann's former schoolmate, the equally prominent writer-politician Edvard Brandes (1847-1931), were two of the most powerful figures. Ironically Drachmann was banned from the columns of the newspaper, and declared *persona non grata*. Neither his name nor his writings appeared in the newspaper until 1890 (Petersen 2005:118).

8. For publication details see Ursin 1956:17-18.

9.   From a paratextual and editorial perspective it is important to know which text we have in front of us. The first nine editions were identical, but the last but one edition, the 10th, the so-called 're-union' edition of 1919, which appeared in concurrence with the coming plebiscite the next spring, leading to the final establishing of the present Danish-German borderline, later in 1920, differs from all earlier versions. This 10th edition was issued by the same publishing house as all the previous editions had been, Gyldendal. An interesting difference though was the fact that this edition did not contain any of the illustrations or vignettes of the previous editions. Furthermore a cameo-like drawing on the cover of the book is a clear reference to the cover illustration of Erik Skram's *Hinsides Grænsen* (1888). The 10th edition differs also from all other editions, because it has a preface by the author's son, Povl Drachmann (1887-1941), who was a – modestly popular – novelist in his own right and a member of the Danish Parliament for the Conservative Party in the late 1920s. The most recent edition is again an entirely different printing: it was published by the print shop of a local newspaper in Southern Jutland, Dybbøl-Postens Bogtrykkeri, in 1966.

10. The reason these drawings or etchings are noteworthy is that the central image of the windmill, later became one of the strongest and enduring icons of the patriotism connected to the 1864 war. The image of the Dybbøl windmill appeared on memorabilia, souvenirs, special commemoration stamps for veteran organisations, etc., etc. Images of the mill – very similar to Drachmann's drawing – became widely used on the cover of books about the historical events that took place in the area. One of those books actually was Erik Skram's *Hinsides Grænsen*, i.e. the 1888 book publication. The image appeared also on the cover of the 1919 version of *Derovre fra Grænsen*, see note 9.

11. In this case a very appropriate metaphor, because Drachmann – while strolling on the battlegrounds of Dybbøl – reminisces a childhood memory about his first experiences as a theatregoer, *Derovre fra Grænsen*, p. 44.

12. The German triumphal pillar no longer exists; it was destroyed shortly after the end of World War II. See for more information about the German monument, and a picture of it, Inge Adriansen's booklet *Dybbøl Mølle. Monument & museum*, 1997, pp. 12-15 and p. 29. See also: Adriansen (2003:257). The people who blew up the German monumental obelisk actually did precisely what Drachmann had predicted in *Derovre fra Grænsen*: 'i [...] Genoprejsningens Stund vil Mindesmærket blive omstyrtet' (p. 36; in the hour of rehabilitation the monument will be overthrown).

13. I am indebted to the founder and former head of the Centre, Hans-Ole Hansen, for helping me with some of the illustrations for this article.

14. Actually Drachmann himself points at Skagen as a place of national interest, see *Derovre fra Grænsen*, p. 50.

15. With respect to the latter 'location of memory' I would like to add that, although the beach at first may look like a mere literary theme or motive, the floating borderline between sea, sky and land, in combination with Drachmann's famous midsummer night song 'Vi elsker vort Land' (We love our country) is so intensely charged with collective memory, that it justifies to be labelled a *lieu de mémoire*.

16. 'Melodi af Henrik Hennings til Sangen "De sønderjyske Piger"', in *Ude og Hjemme*, no. 28, 14 April 1878, pp. 297-270, the second edition, as a book, was *'De sønderjyske Piger' Vexelsang af Holger Drachmann's 'Derovre fra Grænsen' sat i musik af Henrik Hennings'*, Copenhagen: Oscar Risom, 1878 [OR118]. A few years later, in 1885, Drachmann tried to 'capitalise' on the enormous success of *Derovre fra Grænsen* and the popularity of the embedded song 'De sønderjyske Piger', by writing a sequel, entitled *Danmark leve! Blade fra en Rejse paa begge Sider af Grænsen* (Long live Denmark! Pages from a journey on both sides of the border). Clearly Drachmann aimed at rekindling the mood of 'De

sønderjyske Piger', but the trick did not work and *Danmark leve!* was no success at all.

17. This is a critical tool, which he defines 'as any approach to texts which connect borders on the levels of *histoire*, the word the text presents to the reader, and of *récit*, the text itself, a weave of rhetorical figures and narrative structures' (Schimanski 2006:51).

18. Just for the sake of perspective: Holger Drachmann was not the first to recognise the symbolic importance of the Dybbøl windmill, but he was surely responsible for the effective dispersion of it. After the first Danish-Prussian war, the so-called three-year war (1848-1950), the windmill already had gained some iconographic status, i.e. as a Danish monument of victory!

Hans Christian Andersen: Discovering a Copenhagen Between Fiction and Reality.

Hans Christian Andersen

Introduction

The author Hans Christian Andersen had many 'titles' in the world of publishing: playwright, poet, novelist, translator, journalist, auto-biographer. To these we may add posthumous titles as author of published letters and diaries, as well as titles relating to 'abandoned' careers as actor, dancer and singer and complementary titles of visual artist and touring performer in many private homes, stately homes and castles across Europe, international celebrity and untiring self-promoter.

It is not surprising that if we concentrate on one of these many and varied activities, we are confronted with complexity and the unexpected, and so it is with Andersen as travel-writer. As a contribution to this volume, this chapter explores Andersen's discovery of Scandinavia through his early prose work, his debut as a novelist, *Fodreise fra Holmens Kanal til Østpynten af Amager i Aarene 1828 og 1829* (*A Journey on Foot from Holmens Canal to the East Point of Amager in the Years 1828 and 1829*). Arguably, *Fodreise* shows the young author discovering the literary medium and his own creativity rather than any geographic location and this paper will not dispute this. It is, however, argued that it gives the reader and the student of Andersen's work an insight into his apprenticeship in the travel-writer's workshop and shows him well-integrated among travel-writers of the nineteenth century. Copenhagen becomes the site both of a fantastic journey through a land of the imagination and the location where he exercises his talents as a travel-writer well in advance of his official debut as one.

Andersen was always 'on the move'. This is not only a fact, it is also part of the myth about this almost nomadic artist, for whom the storming steam locomotive and lightning-quick telegraphy became exciting and welcome parts of his contemporary real infrastructure, and air travel and travel through time part of a dreamed-of future. Travel-writing itself occupies a place on the spectrum between reality and the imagined, being part fact and part authorial interpretation. This chapter will see Andersen as a man using a putative form of the genre to 'create' his own identity as a travel-writer and author of imaginative fiction.

The investigation will be based partly on a survey of the development of travel and tourism in the nineteenth century and partly on the development of travel-writing at the time. This will lead to a conclusion about how Andersen raises expectations about his own *future* work as a travel-writer and, at the same time, manages perceptions of what it means to work in that genre. He is, so is my argument, already well acquainted with the basic structures and techniques of travel-writing at this very early point.

The Text Itself: *Fodreise fra Holmens Kanal til Østpynten af Amager i Aarene 1828 og 1829*

This novel is not really Andersen's first published prose work. He had already written and published *Ungdoms-Forsøg* in 1822, under the remarkable pseudonym 'Villiam Christian Walter', which alluded to the young man's two favourite authors, William Shakespeare and Walter Scott and, in a youthful show of ambition, slightly immodestly perhaps, himself in the shape of 'Christian'. *Ungdoms-Forsøg* – which might be translated 'a youthful attempt / experiment' – was a terrible fiasco in terms of sales.

During his school-days, Andersen more or less obeyed his benefactors and steered clear of publication, but once he had matriculated and gained his artistic freedom to create, he promptly set about practising that freedom. Several chapters of the novel under consideration here were published in the prestigious periodical *Kiøbenhavns Flyvende Post* in November 1828, a fact that gave him useful pre-publication publicity. When the novel proper was released, on 2 January, 1829, the first 500 copies were sold immediately. More were printed, and a second edition was in the shops in April 1829 (*Fodreise*, p. 7). That was also the month when Andersen had his first play produced professionally: *Kjærlighed paa Nicolai Taarn eller hvad siger Parterret?* (Love in the tower of St. Nicolai Church, or what does the audience in the pits say?) This was another success, according to Andersen himself.[1] Given that Copenhagen's Royal Theatre was only prepared to put the play on three times, the success was obviously one with limitations, but one cannot blame a young playwright for enjoying any success.

Fodreise fra Holmens Kanal til Østpynten af Amager i Aarene 1828 og 1829 is really a literary joke, the work of a young nineteenth-century punk writer, who seems to set out to write a book that will be shocking and sensational, attracting useful attention in the market-place, and which will do so partly by poking fun at the literary establishment. This was not really a dangerous thing for Andersen to be doing. He was already part of the establishment, whose help he had asked for on many occasions during his early years in Copenhagen, and who had now in a sense 'incorporated' him into the contemporary literary world by giving him an education. He was now, to use a phrase adopted into the Danish language, *salon-fähig*. He was not making any political, pro-democratic or pro-republican statements or in any other way making an anti-establishment gesture. But in his own way, he was 'cocking a snook' at his elders and betters at the aesthetic level and in a manner that would both amuse his readers and entertainment critics.

Fodreise is a kind of travel description or travelogue and it describes a typical nineteenth-century journey on foot – a journey of exploration, as one might say. The journey is of limited geographic extent, starting at the centre of the Danish capital Copenhagen, and extending to the easternmost point of the flat, fertile island of Amager, south of Copenhagen. It is based on real experiences: during his student days, Andersen would walk to Amager to visit his personal tutor,[2] so he knew his way out there and knew the townscape and the landscape a walker would encounter. But beyond that, it is reasonably obvious to the reader that in his depiction of characters in this 'travel description', any resemblance to real persons, living or dead, is entirely accidental and unintentional and the physical surroundings take on qualities that clearly mark this work out as fiction. This Amager of the imagination is a landscape of dream, myth and fantasy, a real landscape merging with fantasy and fairy-tale.

As the title indicates, the journey takes place in the years 1828 and 1829, but this is also a joke. In fact, the journey takes place over a couple of hours before and after midnight on New Year's Eve 1828 and the apparently real time-scale is ironic, lending the kind of fictitious substance to the story which we often find in eighteenth and nineteenth-century prose narrative, such as that of Steen Steensen Blicher.

The narrator is a first-person narrator – 'et fortæller-jeg' – and a creative writer, and critics and commentators are prone to suggest that the narrator is Andersen himself. This seems not to be the case, although it is easy to see why some readers like to think it is. This is certainly not Andersen the man and author, with a Copenhagen address. But the story probably does express Andersen's own deliberations on the nature of writing and of travel-writing and so we shall accept a certain overlap of identities here. Andersen's narrator certainly seems closer to the author himself than Bloom in *Ulysses* does to James Joyce, to draw a parallel to another journey in European fiction that was celebrated recently.[3]

At the start of the Andersen's story, the narrator – and we suspect immediately that it is not a real person – is *made* a writer, and a bad writer at that, by the Devil himself, who is hatching a plot to curse the world with a second deluge, this time not of water but of bad writing. Perhaps in order to demonstrate that he is a creative devil, who can come up with new and original ideas, Satan casts the ultimate curse on both the narrator and an unspecified number of other humans: people who will write but who are no good at it. The narrator (and admittedly one immediately begins to suspect that Andersen himself is somehow at least partly inside the narrator) soon reveals an Andersen-like self-consciousness in the way he presents himself as an author disbelieving his own talents as an author.

This newly-created writer reads a little background literature – not sufficient to make him the well-prepared man of culture that Andersen had now himself become – and then sets out on a journey that he feels *compelled* to embark upon, as a kind of artistic imperative, through the dark and frost-bound streets of Copenhagen, to that virgin country, Amager, so far untouched by any creative writer-cum-traveller. Certainly in Hans Christian Andersen's day Amager did have something of the wild and unexplored land about it, as this is where the capital's gallows stood and it was, until recently, a kind of wilderness close to the heart of the capital. But Amager is also fertile agricultural land, cultivated for many years by immigrant Dutchmen, brought in to improve the agricultural skills of the Danes. This was no true wilderness, rather it was Copenhagen's kitchen garden, romantically agrarian but also just next door to the city-dweller.

The narrator, who is a creative writer like Andersen, sees Amager as a kind of *tabula rasa*, a clean slate on which he can exercise his talent – or demonstrate its absence, as the case may be. However, although the journey he embarks on is full of excitement and challenge, the narrator does not seem to need to do actual authorial work. Although he is carrying his notebook, which is conveniently and unexpectedly to hand at one point in the narrative, the actual book seems to have published itself at a later point and the co-ordination between author and his work has broken down completely at the end of the story, where the readers are asked to complete the work.[4] It seems that the narrative involves, includes and overwhelms the narrator in a series of encounters with very strange people and creatures, encounters that tell us something about Andersen and about writing and culture and not so much about the geography of Copenhagen and Amager. The narrator does make a journey but he is driven along by the flow of the narrative and overtaken by it. Eventually the narrative (as one might say) writes itself.

But the narrator does actually follow a route that we also could follow, as Joyce fans do on 'Bloomsday'. The route takes him from his – Andersen's, the narrator's – flat in old Copenhagen to *Holmens Kanal*, past the Stock Exchange and Chancellery, along the Royal Palace, past the Royal Brewery, over *Langebro* (which takes him an hour to cross and where he is on the stroke of midnight), and finally through one of Copenhagen's old gates – *Amagerport* – to Amager itself, having been let through the gate by St Peter himself.

Once he is there, the geography becomes much less certain, as Amager turns out to be a location out of time and out of space (but it is also the year 1828/1829 and this is an island south of Copenhagen), where ever stranger things happen and where both story and journey eventually reach their end on the shores of the Øresund, the narrow stretch of water that separates Denmark and Sweden.

The narrator's situation is in several respects fluid. He has lost control of his own narrative; and at the same time he has reached the sea, the Øresund, in the middle of the cold, black night. Neither he nor the narrative can go any further. There is no way forward and if we take the narrator's invitation seriously to complete the narrative, we too will be stuck without any real options to develop the plot.

So where have narrator and narrative been? They have partly been in the world of middle-class general knowledge of the time, with its characters and ideas from ancient mythology and contemporary literature and culture, and partly (and to the greater extent, of course) inside the author's fertile and untrammelled imagination.

Let us dive into one or two spots in the novel to see what goes on in this strange world of the night. In *Fodreise*, Copenhagen is connected to Amager by two bridges – these days there are more, but the two that the narrator encounters are still in existence, albeit in more modern versions. But on this particular night, there are only the two and the narrator realises that on this night, the choice of bridge is not simply a matter of convenience or accident. The two bridges are governed, one might say, by two quite distinct principles, embodied by two female allegorical characters. One of these two bridge-spirits, a healthy-looking and beautiful peasant-woman from Amager, tempts the narrator to cross at *Knippelsbro* near the Royal Exchange. The proximity of the Royal Exchange is significant: cross by this bridge, follow this woman, who tempts you with her cornucopia – a basket full of fruit and gingerbread-girls (with bitter almonds for hearts), so beware, young man! – and you go with the principle of materialism and finance.

That is not what a real artist – a man of spirituality – would do and the narrator realises this. So instead he follows the other, a tall, pale and quiet woman, in the direction of *Langebro*, 'Long Bridge'. This other lady, the lady of the mortuary for drowned people, is the pale Heloïse, a much more desirable choice if your heart is set on the finer and more ethereal things of life, as becomes an artist. As happens to Christian in Bunyan's *The Pilgrim's Progress*, the narrator finds himself taking the longer and apparently less convenient (but better) way around to the easternmost point of Amager, and this is clearly intentional on Andersen's part. In fiction, as in real life and on real journeys, decisions must be made about the best way forward, weighing the advantages of taking the scenic route against taking a faster one. Here, the narrator makes the right choice from a moral point of view – *Langebro* is the right artistic and non-materialistic choice – but he then encounters unexpected complications, as one would hope in a good plot.

'Complications' is not a strong enough word for what follows. The narrator falls into a trance, encounters a cat, who is also a mildly frustrated poet, and then, without warning, finds himself projected three hundred years into the future, inside the royal palace, in an ante-chamber crowded with robotic courtiers moving under their own steam.

The narrator moves on to a futuristic theatre, a kind of 360-degree cinema that makes use of all the stage effects of the nineteenth century, devoted to spectacle and vacuous popular entertainment. One senses Andersen's snobbery and resentment at this kind of pre-Hollywood non-art. In fact, Andersen himself is clearly writing for effect and he would always remain in touch with popular art and popular audiences, as his later success as a people's playwright would show.

To take technological 'progress' even further – Andersen lets his narrator enter the library of the future, where each volume has its own dedicated small bird – a parrot or a starling – attached by a silver chain, the bird's task being to pronounce the names of the books, as a precursor, perhaps, to computerised library catalogues.

Andersen includes actual mechanised flight in this chapter in the shape of an air steamship. Steam-driven flight had been attempted – Andersen's idea was not entirely without merit, although it had no future – and although this type of propulsion never worked in real aviation, the notion of motorized airships was less than a century away. At this early point we already see Andersen projecting himself into the advanced technological future that was just around the corner.

Where is the real Copenhagen in all this? Admittedly, Andersen is busier using it as a springboard for his imagination than in exploring it in detail. As he was to create a California of the imagination years later, here he is creating a fantasy Copenhagen. The Danish capital is the reality from which the narrator sets off in order to reach a land of the imagination, and the Amager which he does then explore has little in common with the real flatlands of that island.

After a comical and Kafaesque journey across *Langebro*, he arrives in Christianshavn, that part of the old fortified city that lies on Amager south of

Copenhagen's city centre. At the Amager City Gate, he meets Saint Peter and comes to the realization that Copenhagen is, in fact, Paradise: St Peter guards its gate – *Amagerport* – and gives Andersen a pair of magical glasses that will allow him to see reality differently. This is just the kind of thing an author needs, and it is yet another traditional plot device to which he will return in later narratives: the magical boots in 'Lykkens Kalosker' ('The Magic Galoshes', 1838) that allow their possessor to travel through time and the equally remarkable trunk in 'Den flyvende Kuffert' ('The Flying Trunk', 1839).

If Copenhagen is Paradise, then Amager must be somewhere different, Hell perhaps? The aficionado of Danish literature may remember that the modern author Klaus Rifbjerg uses part of Amager to portray hell in his novel from 1966, *Operaelskeren* (The Opera Lover) an updated version of Mozart's *Don Giovanni*. Although there may be no direct link between Andersen's Amager and the inferno of Mozart/Lorenzo Da Ponte and Rifbjerg, the choice of Amager as non-paradise is, at least, interesting in the literary context. Andersen's Amager is not hell: it is a wonderful playground for the imagination, 'Phantasiens store herlige Tumleplads' (*Fodreise*, p. 87; a wonderful playground for the imagination), where the young narrator seems to be anywhere on earth he might want to be: the Bay of Finland, Novaya Zemlya, the Gobi Desert (where he has tea with the Dalai Lama), the Sahara (going with a caravan to Mecca) or among Eskimos in Hudson's Bay (p. 87). On the one hand, we might say that the narrator has been given the freedom to travel freely in time and space, but more prosaically the author, Andersen, also seems to be including a range of knowledge and information about the world which his school education may have given him. He is travelling in the mind and reviewing the world that is available to the traveller.

It is not hard to understand why the book sold out so quickly in 1829: Andersen is having a wonderful time satirizing contemporary culture and arts. In this literary night-vision nothing is safe or sacred, although it must be said that Andersen is careful not to make any enemies by openly making fun of real people on Denmark's literary Parnassus and imaginary characters from the world of literature. Wearing his magic glasses, he sees a procession of characters from literature: an army of imaginary characters divided into regiments of furious characters, lovers, Lilliputians, even those wounded in battle – in this case characters who have been cannibalized by lesser authors to the point where sometimes only a finger is left of the original. The wounded are tended by doctors, who are literary critics, and the whole army is led by many-headed generals, really the readership, the audience, that many-headed monster. The borrowing of themes, plots and characters from other writers is just part of the methodology of literary creation and has been so ever since

Homer provided the first really good stories to borrow from. But in the world of nineteenth-century travel publication, borrowing from other writers' travel descriptions in order to create new ones became one of the weaknesses of the genre: there was no guarantee that an author had actually visited the country he claimed to be writing about.

Nineteenth-century writers would study their destinations before they set off and would carry useful literature as they went, and Andersen's narrator does both, in addition to carrying a notebook to help him remember. The volume he carries is of one of Andersen's own favourites, the author E. T. A. Hoffmann's *Die Elixiere des Teufels* (*The Devil's Elixir*, 1814/1816), and he intends to use it to help him write his own book, the one we are reading as we follow him on his journey on foot. Fundamentally, *Fodreise* is inspired by Hoffman, and Andersen is paying homage to one of his ideals with his own book, the man who created the kind of work that was frowned on in some critical circles in Copenhagen for its fantastic style, and which would become part of Andersen's own aesthetic armoury in the years that were to follow. It plays little part in his travel description and in that sense it has no place in this chapter.

But the exploration of the world of knowledge, geographical and cultural, is the cornerstone of his later exploration of the real world. As will become clear, general knowledge – in a very specific and socially defined sense – was very much part of travel in the nineteenth century. An exploration of Andersen's own Copenhagen, limited in time and in interest by taking place at night, forms the starting point for what is an early exercise in creating travel literature, and in order to show that, it is now necessary to turn to eighteenth- and nineteenth-century travel literature as such.

Andersen and Travel

'At reise er at leve' (to travel is to be alive),[5] is the phrase that Andersen so famously coined. From his first leap into the unknown, when he left Odense, in 1819, he was always driven to move on, to explore, to visit, to see, to note down, to remember, to write up, sometimes in letters or his diary, sometimes in manuscripts for publication in newspapers, in periodicals, in his own volumes of travel descriptions, or as part of the characterization and environment in novels and tales. The search for material and the urge to travel and experience went together throughout his life.

During his lifetime and career as a tireless traveller, Andersen witnessed the growth of a new infrastructure, with steam ships with vastly improved and predictable timetables and steam trains, that brought one on the (slightly tardy) wheels of steam power from one end of Europe to the other. By the time of his death, in 1875, a phenomenon called *tourism* had come into being and passports had been abolished in most of Europe, enabling the European traveller to go anywhere. If a Dane wanted to see Berlin or Rome he just had to get himself there.

Andersen, as is widely known, saw most of Europe – including a great deal of Sweden and Norway – and a small part of Africa during his lifetime. Travel was part of his life and his career, from his first published travel description, *Skyggebilleder af en Reise til Harzen, det sachsiskse Schweitz etc etc i Sommeren 1831*, published the same year, 1831 (Eng. trans. *Rambles in the Romantic Regions of the Hartz Mountains, Saxon Switzerland etc.*, 1848). Travel provided him with an income, both from sales and from grants which he received, so that as a young man and writer he could also travel and become a man of the world. And, of course, it gave him the additional status of being a known European travel-writer.

The urge to travel and speak about it – and the *methodology* for doing so – is already evident in *Fodreise*. One may, indeed, wonder how he knew, at this early stage, what travel writing was all about.

The Grand Tour

Arguably tourism in its modern form had not been invented in 1828. Andersen would not have been pleased to hear himself described as a tourist in 1828 or subsequently. He travelled in order to learn, his aim was a common one among the educated classes in those times, he aimed for *dannelse*, 'improvement of the mind'. The purpose of travelling around in Europe – unless it were for business purposes or war – was to better oneself. On one of his journeys, in 1866, Andersen writes critically in his diary about the pressures from other, performance-fixated travellers, which the true traveller must resist, the 'evig Snakken om hvad jeg endnu skulde see, og at Engelænderne paa to Dage have været paa flere Steder end jeg i 10 Dage' (endless chatter about what else I had to see and that the Englishmen had been to more places in two days than I in 10).[6]

Andersen saw things differently. Travel was a question of taking one's time, not of seeing as much as possible in the shortest possible space of time. Speed was not of the essence, and indeed high speed was not very easy to achieve. Attitude was also important. In 1833, Andersen wrote to his Danish sponsor, Jonas Collin, complaining about those artists who just move to Rome because it is cheap, not in order to experience the world.[7] To travel was not just to live but also to live with purpose.

The 'model' for travel in the nineteenth century was still that of the 'Grand Tour'. The Grand Tour had been in existence since the sixteenth century. In an English or British context, it developed into a staple part of the education of a young nobleman, who would travel to the Continent for up to two years and follow a more or less set route through Europe.

One man with a great deal of expertise in these matters was the Rev. John Chetwode Eustace. His book, *A Classical Tour Through Italy Anno 1802*, was published and re-published a number of times during the nineteenth century and became a model for this kind of book on useful travel. Eustace stresses the need to prepare oneself properly before embarking on one's journey:

> ... he who believes with Cicero that it becomes a man of a liberal and active mind to visit countries ennobled by the birth and the residence of the Great; who with the same Roman, finds himself disposed by the contemplation of such scenes to virtuous and honorable pursuits, he who, like Titus Quintus devoting the first days of leisure after his glorious achievements, to the celebrated monuments of Greece, embraces the earliest opportunity of visiting the classic regions of Italy; such a traveler will easily comprehend the necessity of providing beforehand the information requisite to enable him to traverse the country without constant difficulty, doubt and enquiry. (Eustace 1815:26-27)

The links with the narrator's approach in *Fodreise* are evident. He also studies before he sets out on his journey, but rather than the classics he studies Nyerup's *Beskrivelse over Kjøbenhavn* and Pontoppidans *Atlas* and brings the aforementioned *Die Elexiere des Teufels* by Hoffman with him on his journey (p. 25). Although Andersen's irony is evident in the choice of Hoffmann, the approach is clearly the recommended one: the narrator is preparing his journey before he sets off. To Andersen's contemporary reader, this kind of preparation for a short domestic journey would obviously seem ridiculous and part of the pastiche, but the actual travel practice must have served as Andersen's model for the approach. Andersen was intellectually prepared for his own grand tours.

The Grand Tour took the traveller on a tour of known and useful destinations and attractions throughout Europe. Paris, even then, was known for art, the ancient cities of Italy had their roots in ancient cultures. The young nobleman would stand, more or less, on the same Forum Romanum as Caesar Augustus; a visit to Pompeii would bring him physically into direct contact with one of the most famous natural disasters of ancient Italy. Andersen does not quite follow the same routine in *Fodreise*. The Royal Brewhouse and the Amager Gate are not on the known itineraries of contemporary guidebooks, although the Royal Palace might well be worth a journey. But Andersen uses locations to structure his narrative and tell us where we are so that we can visualize the 'real' context for his fantastic story and go on the same journey as his narrator does. And in so doing, Andersen does what the printed tourist guide also does: he creates a story out of the urban environment, which could be the guided tour of the highpoints in a city.

Fodreise and Nineteenth-Century Travel literature

Fodreise is, of course, a highly idiosyncratic work. Its language has qualities of speech, the mode which Andersen was to perfect, even pioneer, in his fairy tales from the 1830s onwards. *Fodreise* is also a meta-autobiographical work. The narrator dominates the action. But in that sense, it is typical of the travel book, both of Andersen's own time and of our own: the travel book is part of the autobiographical genre.

In Andersen's own time, we can see the genre developing into sub-genres. Eustace's personal – but informed – recommendations of what to see on the Grand Tour has been mentioned. A very similar but much more secular book is Mariana Starke's 1820 volume *Travels on the Continent*. What she tells us about travel is very like the kind of information that we would want to find in a modern travel guide: where and when to collect your mail, where to cash your bill of exchange and buy your horses, what to pack and how to secure the contents of your trunk from damage during transport.

The step to the modern European travel guide is only short. Mariana Starke's book was published by one John Murray, who would also start publishing guidebooks by the German, Karl Baedeker. Once Baedeker had established himself as a publisher of guidebooks, these and those written by Murray himself would help increasing numbers of travellers find their way around the Continent during the nineteenth and twentieth centuries. They would also be less insistent than the Rev. Eustace that you should have the right kind of experience, but would rather make certain selections among attractions and sights, allowing their readers to choose among these and 'package' their destination to suit themselves.

One last aspect of the link between Andersen and the travel genre must be mentioned, namely that of fiction that describes travel. That is, of course, what *Fodreise* itself is, and as such it is part of a fine tradition in world literature that includes Cervantes and Laurence Sterne. In the nineteenth century, the realistic travel novel – and Andersen is not writing one of those here but he would write others later[8] – became an important example of the kind of novel one could credibly pack in one's baggage as one set out on one's travels. In our own time, Alex Garland's *The Beach* has become the pre-eminent example of the novel that not only describes travel, but considers it a state of mind and a 'way of life', and which seeks to explore the ethical and moral issues that arise from the lives of people engaging in such travel. That takes us away from Andersen for whom travel in *Fodreise* is more a *structural device*. But both Andersen and Garland are creating main characters for whom travel becomes a formative experience; their journeys take them away from the worlds they know – to that extent, we might think we are looking at a kind of 'leisure experience' – but, in fact, travel brings them into a confrontation with their own selves.

Conclusion: Raising Expectations, Managing Perceptions

H. C. Andersen's *Fodreise fra Holmens Kanal til Østpynten af Amager i Aarene 1828 og 1829* is a literary joke rather than a fully formed early modernistic experiment. The author is not engaging in formal experiment, nor is he breaking boundaries in literary creation in order to open new avenues for author and reader alike. He is essentially playing around with literary convention in the way that other authors were already doing in Europe.

However, this does not invalidate the achievement of this early work by one of the world's greatest authors. Andersen may be playing with convention in an almost conventional way, but he knew very well what conventional prose looked like: he had read Scott and was no stranger to heavy prose-narrative. Andersen was able to choose how to write when he created *Fodreise* and his choice was one of being unconventional, playful, imaginative and unpredictable. As we remind ourselves that this is the debut of a young author, we should also acknowledge that *Fodreise* shows him as sharing the behaviour and attitudes of many other young artists before and after him: unruly, excited and exciting, refreshing in his denial of the value of artistic convention. But he also displays the literary and cultural armoury that his reading, education and personal experience had now made available to him. It clearly includes travel-writing. He had an awareness of how one prepares for travel, through study, and how one records one's experiences along the way.

The main character in *Fodreise* is a young writer, 'appointed' by the devil in much the same way that a character was to be 'inspired' by the devil in a later fairy-tale, 'The Snow Queen'. A young writer, much as Andersen himself was at the time, and the structure Andersen uses to launch this young writer on his writing career is that of the journey. Surely this is no co-incidence: travel and travel descriptions would form one of the pillars in Andersen's life's work. Here, he sowed the seeds for an essential part of his creativity and a creativity that would place him at the forefront of travel writing in his own age.

Bibliography

Adams, Percy G. (1983): *Travel Literature and the Evolution of the Novel.* Kentucky: University Press of Kentucky.
Altick, Richard (1978): *The Shows of London.* Cambridge: Harvard University Press.
Andersen, Hans Christian (1878): *Et Besøg i Portugal 1866,* in *H. C. Andersen Samlede Værker* (2nd ed., vol. VIII). Copenhagen: C. A. Reitzels Forlag.

—— (1968 [1860]): *Et besøg hos Charles Dickens*. Copenhagen: Danmarks Apotekerforening.

—— (1940 [1829]): *Fodreise fra Holmens Kanal til Østpynten af Amager i Aarene 1828 og 1829*. Copenhagen: Selskabet for grafisk Kunst og Kunstforeningen i København.

—— (1951; 1974 [1855]): *Mit livs eventyr*. Copenhagen: Gyldendal.

—— (1971-1977): *Dagbøker 1825-1875*, eds K.Olsen and H.Topsøe-Jensen. Copenhagen, Det danske Sprog og Litteraturselskap.

—— (1986 [1831]): *Skyggebilleder af en Reise til Harzen, det sachsiske Schweitz etc. etc. i Sommeren 1831*. Copenhagen: Borgen for Det danske Sprog- og Litteraturselskab.

Andersen, H. C. I. (1992): *H. C. Andersen and Thalia: Love's Labours Lost?* Odense: H. C. Andersen Centret.

—— (1994): 'Hans Christian Andersen: The Journey of his Life' in David Blamires (ed.) *Children's Literature* (Bulletin of the John Rylands University Library of Manchester, vol. LXXVI, No. 3, pp. 127-143.

Baedeker, Karl (1861): *A Handbook for Travellers on the Rhine, from Switzerland to Holland*. London: John Murray; Koblenz: K. Baedeker.

Batten, Charles M. Jr. (1978): *Pleasurable Instruction: Form and convention in Eighteenth Century Literature*. Los Angeles: University of California Press.

Berchtold, Count Leopold (1789): *Essay to Direct and Extend the Inquiries of Patriotic Travellers*. London: for the author. Quoted in Batten.

Black, Jeremy (1992): *The British Abroad: The Grand Tour in the Eighteenth Century*. Stroud: Alan Sutton.

Blicher, Steen Steensen (1920 [1824]): *Af en Landsbydegns Dagbog* in *Steen Steensen Blichers Samlede Værker* (vol. VII). Copenhagen: Det danske sprog- og Litteraturselskab and Gyldendal.

Brix, Hans (1943): *Det første Skridt*. Copenhagen; Carit Andersens Forlag.

Bunyan, John (1965 [1678]): *Pilgrim's Progress*. Harmondsworth: Penguin Books.

Buzard, James (1993): *The Beaten Track: European Tourism, Literature, and the Ways to Culture, 1800-1918*. Oxford: Clarendon Press.

Chapuis, Alfred, and Droz, Edmond (1958): *Automata, A Historical and Technological Study* (transl. Alec Reid). London: B.T. Batsford Ltd.

Dingelstedt, Franz (undated): *Das malerische und romantische Deutschland. Suplement* [*sic*]: *das Weserthal*. Kassel and Leipzig: Theodor Fischer.

Eustace, Rev. John Eustace (1815): *A Classical Tour Through Italy Anno MDCCCII Vol. I*. London: J. Mawman.

Fussell, Paul (1980): *Abroad: British Literary Travelling Between the Wars*. New York: Oxford University Press.

Grønbech, Bo (1971): *H. C. Andersen: Levnedsløb, Digtning, Personlighed*. Copenhagen: Aschehoug.

Hibbert, Christopher (1969): *The Grand Tour*. London: Weidenfeld and Nicholson.

Joyce, James (1922): *Ulysses*. Paris: Shakespeare and Company.

Kilvert, Robert Francis (1960): *Kilvert's Diary: Selections from the Diary of the Rev. Francis Kilvert, 1 January 1870 - 19 August 1871* (new and corrected edition). London: Jonathan Cape.

Landau, G. (1842): *Das malerische und romantische Deutschland. Supplement: Malerische Ansichten von Hessen*. Kassel and Leipzig: Theodor Fischer.

Mead, William Edward (1914): *The Grand Tour in the Eighteenth Century*. Boston and New York: Houghton Mifflin.

Moore, John (1781): *A View of Society and Manners in Italy*. London: W. Strahan.

Murray, John (1852): *A Handbook for Belgium and the Rhine*. London: John Murray.

—— (1875): *A handbook for Travellers in Denmark with Sleswig and Holstein* (4th ed.). London:

John Murray.

Mylius, Johan de (1998): *H. C. Andersens liv dag for dag*. Copenhagen: Aschehoug.

Møller, Tove Barfoed (1995): *Teaterdigteren H. C. Andersen og Meer end Perler og Guld*. Odense: Odense Universitetsforlag.

Rifbjerg, Klaus (1966): *Operaelskeren*. Copenhagen, Gyldendal.

Southey, Robert (1797): *Letters Written During a Short Residence in Spain and Portugal With Some Account of Spanish and Portuguese Poetry*. Bristol: J. Cottle.

Starke, Mariana (1820): *Travels on the Continent, Written for the Use and Particular Information of Travellers*. London: John Murray.

Towner, John (1984): 'The Grand Tour: Sources and a Methodology for an Historical Study of Tourism' in *Tourism Management*, Vol. 5, No.3, pp. 215-222.

—— (1985): 'The Grand Tour: A Key Phase in the History of Tourism' in *Annals of Tourism Research*, Vol. XII, pp. 297-333.

—— (1995): 'What is Tourism's History?' in *Tourism Management*, Vol. VI, No. 5, pp. 339-343.

—— (1996): *An Historical Geography of Recreation and Tourism in the Western World 1540-1940*. Chichester: John Wiley and Sons.

WWW: http://www.rejoycedublin2004.com/

Notes

1. Andersen: *Mit livs eventyr*, p. 103-04.
2. *Mit Livs Eventyr*, Vol. 1, p. 100.
3. 16 June is the day in 1904 on which all the action of James Joyce's novel *Ulysses* takes place, and the centenary of the day was of course celebrated.
4. His notebook appears p. 62, and by p. 109 his own travel description appears magically to have been published, suggesting that he is both experiencing his journey, noting down his experiences and watching the final work coming into being, at one and the same time.
5. *Mit livs Eventyr*, p. 301.
6. *Dagbøker*, 6 August 1866
7. *Ibid*. 21 November 1833.
8. *En Digters Bazar*, 1842.

A Place and a Text In-Between: 'Translation' Patterns in Hans Christian Andersen's *I Sverrig*.

Bjarne Thorup Thomsen

I

In their volume of readings in travel-writing entitled *Writes of Passage* James Duncan and Derek Gregory propose to view travel-writing 'as an act of translation that constantly works to produce a tense "space in-between"' (Duncan & Gregory 1999:4). In re-presenting or re-imagining other cultures or natures travel-writers translate one place into another; this other place is situated somewhere between the foreign place the writers purport to depict and the domestic place whose language – and also often values – they bring to bear on the foreign and in which the main target readership of the travel text is also usually to be found. 'Travel-writing is often inherently domesticating', Duncan and Gregory suggest (1999:5), borrowing viewpoint and terminology from the influential translation theorist Lawrence Venuti.

When considering Hans Christian Andersen's representation of Sweden in his third international travel book, *I Sverrig* (In Sweden) published 1851, the notion of a place in-between seems particularly relevant. In this case, however, the character and direction of the translation process, if we accept the term, is complicated by two factors. First, by the fact that Andersen in the mid nineteenth century was an internationally recognised author who wrote as much for a foreign market, including Sweden, as for the domestic Danish one. His international standing can be exemplified by the facts that, in 1847, his collected works began to appear in Germany, introduced by his first official autobiography in two volumes, *Das Märchen meines Lebens ohne Dichtung*, which in the same year was published in English, in both a British and American edition, under the title of *The True Story of My Life* (Topsøe-Jensen 1975:7). Likewise, soon after its Danish publication *I Sverrig* appeared in English, German, Dutch – and Swedish. In Britain, the text came out in two editions in consecutive years: in 1851 as a free-standing volume entitled *Pictures of Sweden* and in the following year in a joint publication with *The*

Story of My Life – this time entitled *In Sweden*. In assessing Andersen's textual representation or 'translation' of Sweden it is therefore reasonable to assume that the horizon of expectation that governs any process of familiarisation is European as much as specifically Danish.

A second factor that might be expected to inform Andersen's picturing of Sweden and which makes *I Sverrig* stand out among the author's travel accounts is the fact that the writer in this text navigates in a neighbouring country that could be seen as only half foreign and half an extension of home.[1] In the context of Danish travel-writing, Sweden may not constitute an obvious site for an exploration of the exotic.[2] The four other international travel books Andersen published all map out southbound and fairly far-reaching journeys: to Germany in *Skyggebilleder af en Reise til Harzen, det sachsiske Schweitz etc. etc.* (1831; Eng. trans. *Rambles in the Romantic Regions of the Hartz Mountains, Saxon Switzerland, Etc.*, 1848), to the Iberian peninsula in *I Spanien* (1863; Eng. trans. *In Spain*, 1864) and *Et Besøg i Portugal 1866* (1868; Eng. trans. *A Visit to Portugal 1866*, 1972) and as far as Constantinople and the limits of Europe in *En Digters Bazar* (1842; Eng. trans. *A Poet's Bazaar*, 1988). In comparison, *I Sverrig* is unique in the author's work in focusing on inter-Scandinavian travel. In his autobiography, published in Danish as *Mit Livs Eventyr* (The Fairy Tale of My Life) in 1855 – that is, interestingly, eight years after its appearances in German and English – Andersen makes a telling comparison between the southbound and the northbound travel experience. In connection with his looking back on his first Swedish journey in 1837 (he travelled in Sweden six times in total) the author writes:

> Jeg, som kun havde reist syd paa, hvor altsaa Afskeden fra Kjøbenhavn er Afsked med Modersmaalet, følte mig nu *halvt som hjemme gjennem hele Sverrig*, kunde tale mit danske Sprog, og hørte i Landets Tunge kun som en Dialect af det Danske; jeg syntes, at Danmark udvidede sig, det Beslægtede i Folket traadte mig saa levende frem, jeg begreb, hvor nær Svensk, Norsk og Dansk stod til hinanden. (Andersen 1975 [vol. I]:207; my emphasis)

> (Having only travelled to the south before – in which case a farewell to Copenhagen was a farewell to my mother tongue – I now felt *half at home throughout the whole of Sweden*. I could speak my own Danish and heard the language of the country as no more than a dialect of Danish. Denmark, it seemed to me, expanded and I became truly alive to the kinship between the people; I understood how close Swedish, Norwegian and Danish are to each other. [my emphasis])[3]

This passage may on the one hand be read as a form of Danish appropriation of the neighbouring nation space. On the other hand, the concluding lines seem to aim to annul notions of national dominance or expansion by pointing to a pan-Scandinavian popular and linguistic continuum. The basis for either interpretation or 'translation' is, however, that the place visited by the travel-writer has the status of a halfway house between home and away. In considering *I Sverrig*, it must be asked, therefore, if the relative proximity of the 'source' country, as it were, to the homeland of the travelling and translating subject limits its application as an exotic locale.

II

To approach an answer, mention must be made of the relationship between, on the one side, the actual journey the travelogue is based on, including its biographical and historical context, and, on the other side, the travel trajectory as marked out in the text and the recording consciousness operative therein.

Andersen's poetic exploration of Sweden feeds off a three-month trip the author undertook in the summer of 1849, from 17 May to the middle of August (Borup 1944:xii ff.). At a time when Denmark was engulfed by the first of two nineteenth-century wars with Prussia, and his mood depressed, Andersen felt the need for a change of scene, using in a rather modern way travel as a form a therapy. Accepting the encouragement of his Swedish colleague Frederika Bremer to experience more fully the diversity of her fatherland, and in the context of an ideological and political climate in which pan-Scandinavian aspirations were high – not least in a country whose southern borders were being challenged – Andersen decided to undertake a northbound journey. As he states in his autobiography:

> Mit Sind var sygt, jeg led aandeligt og legemligt; jeg trængte til en anden Omgivelse, Frøken *Bremer* talte om sit smukke Fædreland, ogsaa der havde jeg Venner, jeg bestemte mig til en Reise enten op i *Dalarne* eller maaskee til Haparanda... (Andersen 1975 [vol. II]:82)

> (My mind was heavy, I was suffering spiritually and physically, I was in need of a change of environment. Miss Bremer told me about her beautiful homeland and I also had friends there. I decided on a journey either up to Dalarna or maybe as far as Haparanda...)

Of the two possible destinations stipulated here, Andersen did indeed reach the central Swedish district of Dalarna that was to provide the setting for climactic chapters in the travel text. The trip to the Dalecarlian locations of Leksand, lake Siljan and Falun went via Helsingborg in Skåne, Gothenburg, the Trollhättan waterfalls, the Göta Canal, Stockholm, Uppsala, Sala and Avesta. On his return journey, which followed in the main the same route, Andersen visited Motala, Vadstena and Kinnekulle. Modern steamship and 'romantic' horse-driven carriage were his main forms of locomotion.

Significantly, in the published account, impressions from both the outbound and homebound leg of Andersen's journey are condensed into a single travel trajectory, as suggested by the text's working title, *Fra Trollhätta til Siljan* (From Trollhätta to Siljan) (Borup 1944:xiv). This title, furthermore, reflects the fact that the textual or translated route represents a truncated version of the actual itinerary in that the southern-most stage, from Skåne to Gothenburg, has been omitted from the description. The narrative 'gains' resulting from this restructuring may be seen as threefold: First, the singularity of the narrated route rules out the risk of repetition. Secondly, it allows the text to climax and conclude in the most distant of the locales visited by the author. Thirdly, the truncation of the route enables the text to bypass the borderland district of Skåne and the adjoining region of Halland – both, together with Blekinge, part of Denmark until 1658 – and thus privilege topographical and cultural difference over scenery that to Andersen himself, his Danish and possibly also some of his European readership, might border on familiarity. As the desire for distance, the passion for differentness and the quest for uniqueness with its implied fear of repetition are all concepts central to Romantic travel, a reading of the relation between actual and textual journeying may thus contribute to identifying Andersen's travelogue as at least a part-Romantic project. In an illuminating study of Romantic travel Roger Cardinal emphasises that the Romantic traveller 'could assume the role of director and even script-writer of the travel scenario' (Cardinal 1997:136). Following Cardinal, Andersen's translation of his travel experiences into the poetic version provided in *I Sverrig* may thus be seen as indicative of the directorial faculties of the Romantic travel-writer. The result is a text situated in-between the factual and the fictional.

As to the other potential destination mentioned in the passage from Andersen's autobiography quoted above, the author, regrettably, did not make it to Haparanda in the North of Sweden. He was dissuaded from embarking on this venture as he recounts in a letter of 28 May 1849 sent from Stockholm to Henriette Wulff:

> Reisen til Haparanda raade næsten Alle fra, da der vistnok er meget Iis iaar og Farten er angribende, man bruger 7 Dage derop og 7 tilbage og er meest paa aaben Søe, Opholdet der bliver kun tre Dage og saa beror det paa Veirliget, jeg tænker derfor at gaae kun til den sydlige Deel af Nordland, nemlig *Gefle*, see det store Vandfald der og da gaae ind i Dalerne, besøge Fahlun og Kysterne om Søen Siljan see Kortet. (Andersen 2000:559)

> (Almost everyone advise me against travelling to Haparanda since there seems to be a lot of ice this year and the voyage is taxing. It takes seven days to get there and seven back, most of it on the open sea, and it would only be possible to stay three days – and that depends on the weather. So I'm thinking of only going to

the southern part of Norrland – to Gävle, that is – looking at the great waterfall there and then going into Dalarna to visit Falun and the shores of Lake Siljan. See map.)

We shall therefore never know how Andersen's fertile poetic mind would have engaged with the exoticness of places north of the Arctic Circle, if he had actually encountered them. The tension between the poet's travel ambition and his advisers' caution could be seen as emblematic of the difference between a more Romantic desire for a 'journeying-to-the-limits' and a more touristic reluctance to compromise security.

That the north of Sweden remained, in actual terms, a *terra incognita* to Andersen did not, however, prevent him from presenting images of it in the travel account. Thus, the text's opening chapter, 'Vi reise' (We Travel), which reads as a prologue to the work as such, provides a conspectus and stratification of the entire country given from four different bird's-eye perspectives, each mapping a segment of Sweden, including those not covered in the subsequent chapters: a stork thus presents Skåne – "'Sæt Dig paa min Ryg! [...] Du [vil] troe, Du endnu er i Danmark!'" (Andersen 1944b:5) ('Get on my back, [...] you will think that you are still in Denmark.' [Andersen 1851b:3]) – while wild swans are used to guide the reader through a mountainous North soaked in midnight sun. This narrative method prefigures, incidentally, the overriding focus employed in that later and most famous illumination of the Swedish terrain, Selma Lagerlöf's *Nils Holgerssons underbara resa genom Sverige* (1906-07; Nils Holgersson's Wonderful Journey Through Sweden).[4] In Andersen, the opening bird's-eye perspectives read in a wider sense as metaphors for the free recording consciousness that is operative in the text, transcribing impressions of both a literal and an imaginary nature and enabling the poet, as the opening chapter has it, to 'skotte [...] imellem fra Virkeligheden ud over Gjærdet i Tankens Rige, der altid er vort nære Naboland' (Andersen 1944b:6) (glance now and then from reality, over the fence into the region of thought, which is always our near neighbourland [Andersen 1851b:6]).

III

After establishing the flexibility of focus that governs *I Sverrig*, it must be asked what main properties are attributed to the Swedish place Andersen presented to an international readership in a text he himself characterised as 'min maaskee meest gjennemarbeidede Bog' (Andersen 1975 [vol. II]:117) (possibly my most carefully composed book). In the following, we shall attempt to demonstrate that Andersen's 'translation' of Sweden produces a place that fuses together romantic and modern, national and international and, albeit to a far lesser extent, Swedish and Danish. A place truly in-between, therefore.

Let us first focus on the fusion of natural grandeur and modern control of nature in Andersen's imagining of Sweden. In *Writes of Passage* Duncan and Gregory identify as central to romantic travel 'a passion for the wildness of nature, cultural difference and the desire to be immersed in local colour' (Duncan & Gregory 1999:6). They emphasise how the conjunction of Romanticism and industrialism led to a movement away from modernity in a quest for the authentic and the exotic. Also, they stress that in the Romantic project 'travel was no longer an exclusively aristocratic preserve' and was 'most likely to accomplish its goals if it was slow, unregimented and solitary' (Duncan & Gregory 1999:6). In terms of periodisation, Cardinal suggests that 'the golden age of Romantic travel began in 1815, with the lifting of the restrictions on easy movement which had obtained throughout the Napoleonic wars' (Cardinal 1997:137). It went into decline from the mid-century onwards when steam-propelled forms of locomotion enforced 'a very different tempo, while also making travel more affordable and thus more democratic' (Cardinal 1997:148). This, in turn, contributed to creating the conditions for early tourism.

According to this time frame, *I Sverrig* is very neatly positioned at the interface between Romantic travel and tourism.[5] While Andersen shared, as we have already seen, several of the desires feeding into the Romantic travel project, the Romantic traveller's inclination to turn his back on modernity and the industrial is significantly not part of his baggage as a travel-writer in general, nor does it inform *I Sverrig*. On the contrary, the travelogue's concluding chapter XXX, entitled 'Poesiens Californien' (Poetry's California), which may be understood as an epilogue and meta-reflection relevant to the text as a whole, couches the poetic process in terms of technological advance, the discovery of new territories and the extraction of their riches. Borrowing the voices of modern science, transport and communication in a vision of how these vitalise and re-enchant nature, the epilogue formulates its programme for a literature that seeks and finds the romantic in modernity in the following way:

> Og ud over Jorden selv lød Videnskabens Røst, saa Miraklernes Tid syntes vendt tilbage; henover Jorden bleve tynde Jernbaand lagte, og henad disse paa Dampens Vinger fløi med Svaleflugt de tungt belæssede Vogne, Bjergene maatte aabne sig for Tidsalderens Kløgt, Sletterne maate løfte sig. Og gjennem tynde Metaltraade fløi med Lynets Hurtighed Tanken i Ord til fjerne Byer. 'Livet! Livet!' klang det gjennem den hele Natur. 'Det er vor Tid! Digter, Du eier den, syng den i Aand og Sandhed!' (Andersen 1944b:120)

(And the voice of Knowledge sounded over the whole world, so that the age of miracles appeared to have returned. Thin iron ties were laid over the earth, and along these the heavily-laden waggons flew on the wings of steam, with the swallow's flight; mountains were compelled to open themselves to the inquiring spirit of the age; the plains were obliged to raise themselves; and then thought was borne in words, through metal wires, with the lightning's speed, to distant towns. 'Life! life!' it sounded through the whole of nature. 'It is our time! Poet, thou dost possess it! Sing of it in spirit and in truth!' [Andersen 1851b:318ff.])

Thus, global technological appropriation becomes a trope for aesthetic exploration.

It would seem that in *I Sverrig* Andersen sets out to realise this poetic call in relation to a Swedish terrain that is typically perceived as the site of a cross-fertilising intersection of natural and man-made. Appreciations in the travel book of what we might term the Swedish sublime are thus most pronounced when spectacular landscapes, preferably characterised by an imposing vertical axis – of particular exotic appeal to a Danish traveller, one might add – are able to work in unison with the topographical imprints left by human constructions and activity. A case in point is the foregrounded description of the intricate system of sluices at Trollhättan:

Vi stege i Land ved den første Sluse, og stode som i et engelsk Have-Anlæg; de brede Gange ere belagte med Gruus, og hæve sig i korte Terrasser mellem den solbelyste Grønsvær; her er venligt, yndigt, men slet ikke imponerende; vil man derimod betages paa denne Maade, da maa man gaae lidt høiere op til de ældre Sluser, der dybe og smalle ere sprængte gjennem den haarde Klippeblok. Det seer storartet ud, og Vandet bruser til Skum dybt nede i det sorte Leie. Her oppe overseer man Dal og Elv [...]. Gjennem Sluserne stige Damp- og Seilskibe, Vandet selv er den tjenende Aand, der maa bære dem op over Fjeldet; fra Skoven summer, bruser og larmer det. Trollhättafaldenes Drøn blande sig med Larmen fra Saugmøller og Smedier. (Andersen 1944b:6ff.)

(We landed at the first sluice, and stood as [if] it were in a garden laid out in the English style. The broad walks are covered with gravel, and rise in short terraces between the sunlit greensward: it is charming, delightful here, but by no means imposing. If one desires to be excited in this manner, one must go a little higher up to the older sluices, which deep and narrow have burst through the hard rock. It looks magnificent, and the water in its dark bed far below is lashed into foam. Up here one overlooks both elv and valley [...]. Steam-boats and sailing vessels ascend through the sluices; the water itself is the attendant spirit that must bear them up above the rock, and from the forest itself it buzzes, roars and rattles. The din of Trollhätta Falls mingles with the noise from the saw-mills and smithies. [Andersen 1851b:11ff.])

It is noteworthy that the sublime experience is linked to the ascent of the travelling subject and to man's overcoming of nature's height barriers. The role of *peak* experiences, physically and psychologically, in Romantic travel is, of course, well documented. Also, the quote provides the first example – in the simile of the English garden – of the stylistic system of international 'othering' that patterns the text (see section IV).

A more pronounced and programmatic, but also more ambivalent, tribute to the industrial ingenuity of man is given shortly after in the futuristic images of the living machinery in the large metal plant at Motala. Here, the hyperactive and omnipresent '*Blodløs*' (Bloodless) is the somewhat sinister-sounding embodiment of modern technology. While the passage is a high point in the aesthetic embrace of modernity in Andersen's writing,[6] the telling role reversal between the living, dynamic thing and fixated, marginalised man also communicates human fright and loss of orientation: 'Alt er levende, Mennesket staaer kun og stiller af og stopper!' (Andersen 1944b:11) (Everything is living; man alone stands and is silenced by – *stop!* [Andersen 1851b:20][7]). However, rather than engaging in any Romantic avoidance of the industrial, the passage is related to the fantasies of mutations between man and machine that were prevalent in nineteenth-century literature.

Further appreciations of the Swedish natural-industrial complex are found later in the text in the narrator's imagined dizzying descent into the iron mines at Dannemora (chapter XXVIII) and in the polychromatic painterly images of the melting furnaces and copper mines at Falun (chapter XXIII):

Vi vare endelig ude af Skoven, og saae foran os en By i tyk Røg-Omhylling, som de fleste engelske Fabrikbyer vise sig, men her var Røgen grønlig, det var Staden *Fahlun*. (Andersen 1944b:97)

Fra Smelteovnene skinnede Ilden i grønne, gule og røde Tunger under en blaagrøn Røg... (Andersen 1944b:98)

(We made our way at length out of the forest, and saw a town before us enveloped in thick smoke, having a similar appearance to most of the English manufacturing towns, save that the smoke was greenish – it was the town Fahlun. [Andersen 1851b:251]

The fire shone from the smelting furnaces with green, yellow and red tongues of flame under a blue-green smoke... [Andersen 1851b:253])

This could be described as an immersion in local *industrial* colour. A recurring topos in the text, the combined land- and techno-scape conveys the assumption that there is no unbridgeable gulf between the natural and the constructed domains.

A particular stylistic pattern instrumental in reinforcing this linkage is in evidence in the text. In order to communicate the visual properties of human constructions the narrator employs naturalising similes as in the following representation of a long-distance view down into a mining area: 'de mange Aabninger dernede ind til Schachterne see ovenfra ud som Jordsvalens sorte Redehuller i Leerskrænterne' (Andersen 1944b:98) (the many openings below, to the shafts of the mine, look, from above, like the sand-martin's dark nest-holes in the declivities of the shore [Andersen 1851b:254]). Conversely, when appreciating natural phenomena, a recurring stylistic emphasis in the travel book is put on the constructedness of nature: the features of Kinnekulle's steep and rocky hillside are, for example, summed up in terms of architecture and perceived as fragments of a ruined castle:

> Lag paa Lag ligge Steenblokkene, dannende ligesom Fæstningsværker med Skydehuller, fremspringende Fløie, runde Taarne, men rystede, revnede, faldne i Ruiner; det er et architectonisk Phantasispil af Naturen. (Andersen 1944b:18)

> (The red stone blocks lie, strata on strata, forming fortifications with embrasures, projecting wings and round towers; but shaken, split and fallen in ruins – it is an architectural fantastic freak of nature. [Andersen 1851b:41ff.])

In keeping with the poetical guidelines laid out in the travelogue, Kinnekulle's topography is thus figured as a borderland between reality and fantasy, between natural and man-made – and between present and past. The combined effect of the complementary tensions between signifier and signified exemplified by the two quotes given here is the joining-up of the Swedish terrain by annulling traditional oppositions between natural and socio-cultural. It is a two-way stylistic translation process that, just like the more thematically oriented observations offered earlier in this section, suggests that in the treatment of place in *I Sverrig* nature-romantic and cultural-industrial can indeed coalesce.[8]

IV

Another form of fusion that informs the text throughout is the forging together of national and international. The travelling narrator's inclination to perceive and present Swedish places in terms of their similarities to European or 'Oriental' prestige locations climaxes in the Stockholm section (chapters XI and XII). In the description of the capital, Norrmalm's streets are 'berlineragtige' (Andersen 1944b:48) (Berlin-like [Andersen 1851b:135]); Strömparterren is 'i Smaat, i meget Smaat, Stockholmernes *Villa reale*, vil Neapolitaneren sige; det er i Smaat, i meget Smaat Stockholmernes "Jungfernstieg", vil Hamborgeren fortælle' (Andersen 1944b: 47) (The Neapolitans would tell us: It is in miniature – quite in miniature – the Stockholmers' 'Villa Reale'. The Hamburgers would say: It is in miniature –

quite in miniature – the Stockholmers' 'Jungfernstieg.' [Andersen 1851b:134]). And when visiting Djurgården, 'er [man] i Borghesernes Have, man er ved Bosporus og dog høit i Norden' (Andersen 1944b:51) (We are in the Borghese garden; we are by the Bosphorus, and yet far in the North [Andersen 1851b:144]). Likewise, a bit further north, Uppsala Cathedral er 'som *Notre-Dame*' (Andersen 1944b:59) (like Notre Dame [Andersen 1951b:167]). Such inscribing of the foreign is, however, by no means confined to capital or central place settings. Even the chapter focused on the small town of Sala, which is an excellent meditation on provinciality, stillness and absence, makes use of an international referencing: 'det var stille, som paa en skotsk Søndag, og det var en Tirsdag' (Andersen 1944b:68) (It was as still as a Scotch Sunday – and yet it was a Tuesday [Andersen 1851b:191]). The relatively frequent occurrence, incidentally, of references to Scottish matters in the travel book should undoubtedly be understood in the context of the prominent international position occupied by Scottish literature in the late eighteenth and early nineteenth centuries with figures such as Burns, Macpherson and Scott (the latter one of Andersen's role models as a novelist).

The Swedish terrain thus becomes a mirror image of 'canonical' international locations whose renown may have literary or non-literary origins. Just as landscapes or townscapes may be viewed through a part-naturalising and part-'culturalising' lens (see previous section), they appear as palimpsests of local and foreign. This particular type of translation would seem to have a three-fold function. Firstly, it is Andersen paying his compliment to Sweden. Secondly, it is a reader-oriented device that familiarises the country to an international target audience, in which case, interestingly, foreignisation equals domestication.[9] Thirdly, it is the travel-writer demonstrating that he is conversant with a large range of geographies. More fundamentally, the international inscribing is in keeping with what seems to be a common endeavour in Andersen's travel-writing, namely to emphasise the contiguous aspects and porous borders of places, to assert the comparability and similarity of locations that may be physically far apart, and to challenge binary oppositions of familiar and foreign, home and away, north and south. Thus, while in *I Sverrig* Stockholm may be envisioned with reference to the Bosporus, as shown above, in *En Digters Bazar*, which contains Andersen's interrogation of the 'Orient' and climaxes in Constantinople by the Bosporus, the roles of literal and figurative place are reversed:

> Jeg sagde ham, at jeg fandt Beliggenheden at være den skjønneste i Verden, at Skuet langt overgik *Neapels*, men at vi i Norden havde en Stad, der frembød noget meget beslægtet med *Constantinopel*. Og jeg beskrev ham *Stockholm...* (Andersen 1944a:266ff.)

(I told him [a Turkish official] that I found the situation the most beautiful in the world, that the view far surpassed that of Naples, but that we in the North had a city that offered something very much like Constantinople. And I described Stockholm... [Andersen 1988:127]).

Such reversals suggest that the tireless translation of places into other places in Andersen's travel-writing is more than a pedagogical or self-affirming device: it is a process that calls into question the very notions of original and translated, source and target, literal and figurative.

V

While there is a high incidence of international appreciation of the Swedish space in *I Sverrig*, any specifically Danish appropriation is conspicuous only by its absence. Likewise, the travelling Danish subject has, in terms of self-contemplative material, a very limited presence in the travel book (it plays a considerably more restricted role than in *En Digters Bazar*, for instance). Andersen intended the text to be his paying-back of a debt of gratitude to the Swedish nation for its positive reception of him and therefore he directed its focus clearly onto the country in receipt of his textual thank you, while minimising the representation of the psyche of the traveller.

One chapter which will be given brief concluding consideration, however, provides a telling and symbolically charged exception to the general withdrawal of the first person singular from the text. Chapter XVIII entitled 'Midsommerfesten i Leksand' (The Midsummer Festival in Lacksand [*sic*]) is in several ways a culmination point in Andersen's tribute to Sweden. It depicts how thousands of people converge on the town of Leksand in Dalarna to go to church and spend midsummer together. While the chapter is a celebration of local folk culture, the presentation is governed by a pronounced carnivalesque dynamic whereby prostestant becomes catholic, north becomes south, and periphery becomes centre. In this carnival of cultures and colours the Danish visitor also, through his appearance and through his artistry, makes his contribution to the exoticisation of the local (again, the occurrence of Scottish and 'Oriental' emblems is noteworthy):

Som jeg sidder i min Stue, kommer Vertindens lille Datterdatter ind, et net lille barn, der var lykkelig ved at see min brogede Natsæk, min skotske Plaid og det røde Saffian i Kufferten; jeg klippede i Hast til hende, af et Ark Papiir, en tyrkisk Moskee med Minareter og aabne Vinduer, og hun styrtede lyksalig afsted. (Andersen 1944b:78)

(As I sit in my room, my hostess's granddaughter, a nice little child, comes in, and is pleased to see my parti-coloured carpet-bag, my Scotch plaid, and the red leather lining of the portmanteau. I directly cut out for her, from a sheet of white paper, a Turkish mosque, with minarets and open windows, and away she runs with it – so happy, so happy! [Andersen 1851b:222])

These poignant images of the foreign visitor also read as reflections of Andersen the travel-writer whose pictures of Sweden by means of intricate systems of fusion and othering portray a place that integrates Romantic and modern, natural and cultural, local and global.

Bibliography

Ahlström, Gunnar (1958 [1942]): *Den underbara resan. En bok om Selma Lagerlöfs Nils Holgersson.* Stockholm: Bonniers.
Andersen, H. C. (1851a): *I Sverige*, trans. Lars Månsson. Stockholm: Alb. Bonniers förlag.
—— (1851b): *Pictures of Sweden*. London: Richard Bentley.
—— (1944a [1842]): *En Digters Bazar*, ed. Knud Bøgh, in *Romaner og Rejseskildringer*, vol. VI, ed. H. Topsøe-Jensen, Det Danske Sprog- og Litteraturselskab. Copenhagen: Gyldendal.
—— (1944b [1851]): *I Sverrig*, ed. Morten Borup, in *Romaner og Rejseskildringer*, vol. VII, ed. H. Topsøe-Jensen, Det Danske Sprog- og Litteraturselskab. Copenhagen: Gyldendal, pp. 1-122.
—— (1975 [1855]): *Mit Livs Eventyr*, vols I-II, ed. H. Topsøe-Jensen. Copenhagen: Gyldendal.
—— (1988 [1842]): *A Poet's Bazaar. A Journey to Greece, Turkey and up the Danube*, trans. Grace Thornton. (New York: Michael Kesend Publishing.
—— (2000 [1878]): *Breve fra H. C. Andersen*, ed. C. St. A. Billc and Nicolaj Bøgh. Copenhagen: Aschehoug.
Borup, Morten (1944): 'Indledning', in Andersen (1944b), pp. IX-XXIII.
Cardinal, Roger (1997): 'Romantic Travel', in *Rewriting the Self. Histories from the Renaissance to the Present*, ed. Roy Porter. London and New York: Routledge, pp. 135-155.
Duncan, James and Derek Gregory (eds) (1999): *Writes of Passage. Reading travel-writing*. London and New York: Routledge.
Jensen, Carsten (1996): *Jeg har set verden begynde.* Copenhagen: Munksgaard Rosinante.
Thorup Thomsen, Bjarne (1995): 'Maskine, Nation og Modernitet hos Andersen og Almqvist', *Tidskrift För Litteraturvetenskap*, 1995, vol. 2, pp. 27-46.
—— (2004): 'Lagerlöfs relative landskaber. Om konstruktionen af et nationalt territorium i *Nils Holgersson*', *Edda. Scandinavian Journal of Literary Research*, 2004, vol. 2, pp. 118-135.
Topsøe-Jensen, H. (1975 [1951]): 'Indledning', in Andersen 1975, pp. 7-23.

Notes

1. This should be qualified by adding that to most people at Andersen's time the closeness between the countries would have been an imagined affinity rather than an actually experienced one. Morten Borup points out that it was a rarity that Danes travelled to Sweden as tourists around the middle of the nineteenth century. If Danes ventured north, Norway (Denmark's union partner between 1380 and 1814) remained a more likely

destination (Borup 1944:ix).

2. Morten Borup stresses that in the age of Romanticism the dominant direction chosen by independent Danish travellers was towards Southern countries and characterises Andersen as 'den første Dansker, der poetisk opdager Sverige' (the first Dane to discover Sweden poetically) (Borup 1944:xvii).

3. Translated by my friend and colleague Peter Graves. When no other source is given in the following, translations into English are by Peter Graves.

4. In his stimulating monograph on *Nils Holgersson* entitled *Den underbara resan* (The Wonderful Journey) Gunnar Ahlström demonstrates that, while a direct influence from *I Sverrig* on Lagerlöf's text cannot be established, an indirect connection is possible through an intermediary Swedish text, 'Det okända paradiset' (1875; The Unknown Paradise) by Richard Gustafsson. Inspired by the opening of *I Sverrig*, Gustafsson's tale depicts how a small boy from Skåne is taught to appreciate the paradisal properties of his nation by a migrating swan that carries him through the country from south to north. Gustafsson's tale was later in a slightly modified form incorporated into the standard textbook for the teaching of Swedish at elementary school level. This textbook, in turn, was used in the preparatory classes at the school in Landskrona, Skåne, in which Lagerlöf taught for ten years (1885-95) (Ahlström 1958:110ff.) (Cf. also note 8).

5. In an interesting passage the narrator, when answering a fellow traveller's question of who he is, seems to be gesturing towards a notion of 'ordinary' travel: 'En sædvanlig Reisende, [...] en Reisende, der betaler for Befordringen' (Andersen 1944b:13) (A common traveller [...] a traveller who pays for his conveyance [Andersen 1951b:25]). This statement, incidentally, forms part of the motto quote used in Carsten Jensen's highly acclaimed contemporary travel account *Jeg har set verden begynde* (1996).

6. Another high point is, of course, the famous chapter in *En Digters Bazar* entitled 'Jernbanen' (The Railway), which is a stylistically and thematically not dissimilar interrogation of contemporary cutting-edge technology. For an analysis of this chapter, see Thorup Thomsen 1995:27ff.

7. While the accuracy of this translation leaves something to be desired, it does in a general sense capture the main tension conveyed in the original passage.

8. In terms of embracing the Swedish natural-industrial complex and interweaving natural and cultural components of the national terrain there is, incidentally, considerable congruence between *I Sverrig* and *Nils Holgersson*. See my discussion of the latter text in Thorup Thomsen 2004.

9. A very similar method of familiarising a country through international references is used in relation to Denmark in Andersen's second novel *O.T.* (1836), cf. my discussion in Thorup Thomsen 1995:30-37.

Art and Commerce in
Hans Christian Andersen's
A Poet's Bazaar.

Elisabeth Oxfeldt

Introduction

The original intention with this essay was to lay out Hans Christian Andersen's poetics with an emphasis on the travelogue's title. *En Digters Bazar* (1842; *A Poet's Bazaar*) has until recently been regarded as a well-chosen indicator of the text's content and form. In terms of content, it conjures up a sense of the exotic and sensual, and in terms of genre, it suggests a series of unconnected portraits and impressions. As noted in one Danish literary history: 'systematik er ikke denne rejsendes anliggende' (Baggesen 1984:141; systematization is of no concern for this traveller). Yet what tends to be overlooked is the degree to which Andersen through this title signals a commercialization and commodification of not only art, but also the cultural Other. The first part of this chapter will thus regard the text from a nineteenth-century point of view – that is, read it within its own historical horizon – and focus on what I will call Andersen's bazaar poetics.

The second part of the essay was inspired by the Andersen bicentennial. In the case of 'Andersen 2005' and the so-called worldwide celebration, 'art and commerce' remains a relevant title. Now, however, it must be applied to the commodification of Andersen. In the years around 2005, the Danish media held up Andersen as a cultural icon symbolizing innocence and cross-cultural openness. *A Poet's Bazaar*, in particular was promoted as a model and inspiration for attaining friendship and understanding between Danes and Arabs. Yet one could just as well read the text focusing on its Orientalist and Euroimperialist aspects. The second part of this chapter, therefore, situates *A Poet's Bazaar* in the ideological landscape emerging between two poles: between that of a radical postcolonial stance where all white, European, male travellers are seen as suspect imperialists, on the one hand; and that of a national, overly self-congratulatory project on the other.

Bazaar Poetics

A Poet's Bazaar covers nine months of travel in 1840 and 1841 during which Andersen went from Denmark, down through Germany to Italy, Greece, and Turkey, and then up the Danube river to Budapest, Vienna and Prague, and finally back to Denmark through Germany. The travelogue is divided into six geographical sections presenting the journey chronologically. Each section, in turn, is divided into short chapters containing a hotch-potch of genres, ranging from lyrical depictions to fairy tales, poetry, prose poems,[1] short stories and dialogues. Andersen, in fact, makes an explicit point of his romantic goal of breaking through previously established genre conventions. In terms of content he is up against earlier travel accounts; Goethe for instance, he muses, has already described the Roman carnival to completion, rendering each new depiction superfluous (Andersen vol.I:173). Andersen, in turn, provides but a sketch on this subject matter – a solution pointing to form as one of his main strategies for originality. A few pages later he introduces a chapter subtitled 'En Dialog' (A dialogue) with the following claim to originality: 'Man har faaet Reisebeskrivelser paa saa mange Maader, men som Dialog troer jeg endnu ikke' (one has received travelogues in so many forms, but still not as dialogue, I believe). He then depicts a day trip from Rome to the countryside from the point of view of the horses drawing the carriage (Andersen vol.I:178).

Clearly, the travel account is intended to prove Andersen's status as a romantic poet, engaging the reader in constant games of formal experimentation, changing points of view, and temporal shifts. Brimming with metapoetic reflections, Andersen also emphasizes his aim of embracing modernity. *A Poet's Bazaar* is ultimately situated at the intersection of fantasy, feeling and reason; West and East; tradition and modernity; poetry and prose; art and commerce. In each of these constellations, it is the latter term that breaks with earlier romanticism, i.e. the emphasis on reason, travel to the Orient, modernity, prose and commerce.

When it comes to a modern aesthetic, the most commonly cited passage in *A Poet's Bazaar* is Andersen's enthused depiction of his first railway journey. Various scholars have pointed to this textual celebration of the steam engine and the newly constructed railway prefiguring Johs. V. Jensen's turn-of-the-century modern(ist) aesthetics. The depiction culminates in poetic insight, with the narrator contemplating the role reason now must play in poetry: 'i Poesiens Rige ere ikke Følelsen og Phantasien de eneste, der herske, de have en Broder, der er ligesaa mægtig, han kaldes Forstanden' (Andersen vol.I:44; in the kingdom of poetry, feeling and fantasy are not the only rulers; they have a brother, equally powerful, called reason).

Yet in order to illuminate a broader range of aspects of Andersen's poetics,

I would like to focus on the metapoetic reflections derived from modern, romantic music. Franz Liszt's concerts in Hamburg constitute an aesthetic frame in the travelogue, with Andersen attending these both on his way out and his way back. Liszt's boundary-breaking artistry thoroughly impressed Andersen who saw and heard in the composer's performance of 'Valse Infernale' the need to combine genius with technical skill:

> Vor Tidsalder er ikke længer Phantasiens og Følelsens, den er Forstandens, den tekniske Færdighed i enhver Kunst og i enhver Haandtering er nu en almindelig Betingelse for deres Udøvelse [...]. Alt Technisk, saavel det Materielle, som det Aandelige er i vor Tid i sin høieste Udvikling. (Andersen vol.I:36)

> (Our era is no longer that of fantasy and feeling, but that of reason. Technical skill in every art form and in every trade is now a common prerequisite for their execution [...]. Everything technical – both materially and spiritually – is at its highest point of development in our era.)

This statement recaptures the emphasis placed on rationality in the railway conclusion, but Andersen then goes on to establish a link between art and geography, implicating the modern poet's reliance on travel. Europe and the Orient, we find out, are of equal importance for the artist. They always have been, one may argue, but what Europe and the Orient refer to has changed. Rather than emphasizing Europe's cultural cradle in the South – especially Rome – Andersen's reference is to Europe's industrial and economic centres in the North. Liszt's capacity boldly to define the limits for art in his time is tied to his visits to London, 'denne Maskinernes store Verdens-By' (this great world-city of machines), and Hamburg, 'dette europæiske Handels-Contoir' (Andersen vol.I:35-6; this European trade-office). The Orient, on the other hand, is in the process of slipping from a realm of pure fantasy – that of *A Thousand and One Nights* – to one that the traveller will visit and experience as reality.

Andersen's interpretation of Liszt's music captures this ambivalence towards the Orient as a geographical site as well as a state of mind. As a means of introducing the reader to his text, Andersen-the-narrator presents Liszt's performance as an overture to Andersen-the-traveller's journey. In Liszt's 'Tone-Billeder' (tonal images), he foresees the entire journey, from leaving the well-known to arriving in the unknown: 'Toner jeg ikke kjendte, Toner jeg ei har Ord for, tydede paa Orienten, Phantasiens Land, Digterens andet Fædreland!' (Andersen vol.I:38; tones I did not know, tones for which I have no words, indicated the Orient, the land of fantasy, the poet's second homeland!). Thus, the modern romantic poet is one who travels, and in opposition to his Grand Tour predecessor, he does not seek out the great sites of antiquity. Rome and Athens no longer serve to educate the traveller by showing him what he perceives as his own cultural heritage – his historical Self. Instead, the traveller seeks out his modern Self in Europe's big cities, as well as his cultural Other in the Orient. Technology, trade and fantasy combine as the traveller, in short, absorbs the influences from the geographical sites representing each. This is the new, and I am admittedly misrepresenting the situation by presenting it as an either-or when it is, in fact, a both-and. Andersen travels during a time of transition and he pursues both the traditional and the modern, the European historical Self as well as the European modern Self and cultural Other. The mid-nineteenth-century means of transportation alone would make it impossible to ignore the Grand Tour aspect of his journey.

If we turn to the development of Andersen's titles for his travelogue, we see that they similarly reflect a shift in emphasis – from insisting on the newest aspect of his travels to more sober-minded consideration of their in-between status. Andersen's original working title for the travelogue was 'Orientalske Aftener' (Oriental Evenings)[2] – a title that seems overly zealous if not preposterous for a journey lasting a total of nine months, of which just eleven days were spent outside Europe, in the so-called Orient. It could of course be justified by the notion that the Orient represents a state of mind: the actively poeticizing fantasy accompanying Andersen throughout his journey. Andersen's final title, though, with its emphasis on the bazaar captures the extent to which *A Poet's Bazaar* is situated in a transitional era.

Traditionally, critics have focused on the exotic aspect of the bazaar – on how 'Bazarbilledet giver associationer om et fjernt, eksotisk marked med alle dets sanseoplevelser' (Baggesen 1984:141; the image of the bazaar provides associations of a distant, exotic market with all its sensual experiences). Yet, according to the text itself, the bazaar is not merely an exotic Other located in opposition to the European Self. Rather, it is a site where East meets West, and where each nation has its own quarter. In the end, the bazaar is seen as functioning as a world of graspable dimensions lending itself to a comparative ethnographic study – entirely in the vein of the world fairs built ten years later. These world fairs, we may note, end up reflecting Andersen's aesthetics more thoroughly, incorporating the last of Andersen's poetic components, namely technological innovation. But rather than pointing to how the bazaar chapter can be read in relation to Andersen's world-fair depictions, such as 'Dryaden' (The Dryad, 1868), I want to dwell on the bazaar title a bit longer.

In signifying a meeting ground between East and West, a 'bazaar' reveals the preconditions for this meeting, namely trade. A bazaar is, after all, a market where people come to buy and sell goods. In using this as his title, Andersen suggests not only how his own work is *like* a bazaar, containing a vast variety of literary goods, but also how it is the object *of* a bazaar – a commodity for sale in and of itself. At the time of publication, this implication provoked aesthetic annoyance. Noting the unpoetic aspect of the term, *Fædrelandet*'s critic insisted that 'bazaar' was not a suitable name for a poetic work, 'thi Industrien og Poesien ere uensartede Størrelser, som ikke lader sig bringe under ens Benævnelse' (quoted in Topsøe-Jensen 1975:242; for industry and poetry are of incongruous dimensions and cannot be brought under a common term).

However, as the above depiction of Liszt shows, Andersen saw modern technology *and* financial trade as components of a modern romantic aesthetic. And in Constantinople's Grand Bazaar he saw the poetic aspect of commerce, as well as the commercial aspect of poetry. This latter point – the commercial aspect of poetry – would remain a point of deliberation in Andersen's oeuvre. We recognize the theme from Andersen's 'Skyggen' (The Shadow, 1847), for example, where poetry – in the shape of a woman – lives isolated, above a series of shops. This depiction, too, points to the commercialization of poetry, which has to pass through a type of market place to find an audience.

Finally, with regards to the commercial aspect of the bazaar title, Andersen's own opportunity to travel to the Orient was entirely dependent on modern economics and trade interests. When Andersen visited Constantinople, the Ottoman Empire had just become an open market through the Anglo-Turkish Commercial Treaty of 1838. In the following years, similar agreements were made with other European countries, including Denmark – a fact of which Andersen was entirely aware, and of which he informs his reader in a footnote.

Thus Andersen's travels and texts are embroiled in nineteenth-century economics and politics and may be read as products of – and as contributions to – European imperialism and Orientalism. This is where I want to move on to the second part of my essay in order to look at *A Poet's Bazaar* from a late twentieth and early twenty-first-century point of view, emphasizing recent concerns with cross-cultural meetings.

The National Hero

As mentioned above, the narrator of *A Poet's Bazaar* clearly has the potential to be read as both tolerant and prejudiced, honest and dishonest, politically innocent and politically implicated. To illustrate the span of these ideological readings, I will first consider the celebratory hype which emerged in Denmark in connection with Andersen's being launched as a world-wide icon by the HCA 2005 Foundation, and, more popularly, being elected as 'Alle Tiders Største Dansker' (The Greatest Dane of All Times) by the readers of *Berlingske Tidende*.

Jens Andersen has – especially since the publication of his two-volume Andersen biography in 2003 – emerged as a natural Andersen expert in the public arena. In this context he often emphasizes Andersen's open and friendly attitude towards the Arabic world based on a scene in *A Poet's Bazaar*. The scene is one in which Hans Christian Andersen encounters a Persian on the deck of a steam ship. The two recognize each other from a previous stretch of journey, and feel a sense of comradeship based on their recent common background. They exchange fruits, then phrases. Andersen points to the starry sky and recites the first line of *Genesis* in Hebrew. The Persian, in turn, answers in English: 'Yes Sir! verily! verily!' Andersen concludes the depiction of this scene with the following words: 'Det var hele vor Conversation. Ingen af os vidste mere; men gode Venner vare vi!' (Andersen vol.I:236; That was our entire conversation. Neither one of us knew more; but we were good friends!).

In the depiction, the key ingredients consist of reciprocity: the exchange of objects, words, greetings, and the conclusion that the two are friends. Jens Andersen's conclusion is that Andersen is a person from the nation's past whose historical example can be held up as an ideal for cross-cultural understanding, openness and communication. In his article in *Berlingske Tidende* (2 May 2004) celebrating Hans Christian Andersen's being voted 'Alle Tiders Største Dansker', Jens Andersen sums up the meeting with the Persian – referred to as a 'kærligt kulturmøde' (an affectionate cultural encounter) – with a plea to the rest of the nation: 'Vi kan jo forstå hinanden – og mødes på trods af kulturelle, politiske og religiøse forskelle. Hvis vi altså tør. Det turde H. C. Andersen' (We are, after all, able to understand each other – and meet despite cultural, political and religious differences. If we dare, that is. Hans Christian Andersen dared).[3]

While I find celebrating Andersen and inspiring Danes to be open in their encounters with Arabs and the rest of the world entirely commendable, the reading of the above scene strikes me as odd. Andersen no doubt captures the traveller's momentary goodwill and eagerness for meaningful exchanges. But the abundance of exclamation points – in the Persian's line and not the least Andersen's concluding remark – also suggests irony, and an understanding that the two are but momentarily staging or playing at something that can be called a friendship. As Andersen so openly admits: after the exchange neither of them knew more about the other. Andersen knows nothing about the Persian, and nothing about Persian culture, history or language. Nor has the Persian gained any insight into Andersen's culture. And neither feels bad about it. Promoted as a model for cross-cultural openness and understanding, the scene functions well as a feel-good anecdote (*en skåltale*) when presented to a Danish audience at the beginning of the twenty-first century. Yet, as an exemplar it hardly leads to a greater understanding of the Arabic world – either for Andersen then, or for Danes today.

The Seeing-Man

Postcolonial theory, then, might provide a corrective to what may appear too unilaterally as a national heroic traveller's innocence and openness abroad. For this, I will turn to Edward Said's *Orientalism* (1978) and Mary Louise Pratt's *Imperial Eyes* (1992). Andersen is often depicted as 'et se-menneske' – a man with the ability to visually absorb his surroundings and turn these scenes into writing. According to the traveller in *A Poet's Bazaar* himself, the main purpose of his travels is seeing. He writes:

> Paa Reisen maa jeg tumle mig fra Morgen til Aften, jeg maa see og atter see! man kan jo ikke bestille Andet end pakke hele Byer, Folkefærd, Bjerge og Have ind i Tanken; altid tage, altid gjemme, der er ikke Tid til at synge en eneste Sang! (Andersen vol.II:158)[4]

> (While travelling I have to romp about from morning to evening, I must see, and always see! One cannot but wrap entire cities, peoples, mountains and oceans into one's thoughts; always take, always store, there is no time to sing a single song!)

In *Imperial Eyes*, however, Pratt stresses how 'seeing' is never an innocent act. The position of travelling outside Europe to see, she insists, is inextricably linked to imperial conquest: 'Only through a guilty act of conquest (invasion) can the innocent act of the anti-conquest (seeing) be carried out' (Pratt 1992:66). Her point, then, is that anti-conquest and seeing rather than constituting innocent acts, are strategies used by travel writers in an attempt to distance themselves from the project and guilt of empire. 'Anti-conquest' refers to 'the strategies of representations whereby European bourgeois subjects seek to secure their innocence in the same moment as they assert European hegemony' (Pratt 1992:7). To what degree then, we may ask, do Andersen and his travelling protagonist assert European hegemony in Turkey? To what degree is Andersen Pratt's 'seeing-man', defined by Pratt as 'the European male subject of European landscape discourse – he whose imperial eyes passively look out and possess' (*ibid.*)?

Given that world trade and capitalism are viewed as pillars of European imperialism, Andersen is, of course, guilty. He would not be travelling to Turkey were it not for Europe's interest in the Ottoman Empire as a trading partner. The European representatives would not be there to host him. Similarly, he would not be in a position to bring knowledge about the Orient to a European reading audience, if Europeans did not view the Orient as something to be known and that could be known.

Pratt argues, further, that not only passively possessing eyes, but also the depiction of reciprocal vision – i.e. the exchange of curious glances – is fundamentally imperialistic. Reciprocity, she argues, 'has always been capitalism's ideology of itself' (Pratt 1992:84). Thus, any kind of reciprocal gesture, such as Andersen's exchange of glances, fruits and phrases with the Persian, is rendered suspect. In her chapter on sentimental travellers, Pratt writes about Mungo Park's *Travels in the Interior Districts of Africa* (1799) – a travel account she holds up as her exemplary text in the sentimental travel genre.[5] In her reading of this text and its narrative strategies, she establishes a link between sentimental travel literature and Euroimperialism; sentimental travel literature is structured around a narrative of reciprocal exchanges, which in turn mirrors capitalist ideology. Again a link between art and commerce is established – this time by the postcolonial theorist associating European travelogues with imperialism.

Pratt's reading is full of sharp observations and her material is historically relevant and interesting. The problem, however, is the level of generalization. As Mungo Park's *Travels* is presented as the quintessential European sentimental travel account, we are led to believe that *A Poet's Bazaar* should be read in the same way. Pratt's insinuation ends up turning every sentimental traveller and travel writer into a suspect, exploitative capitalist based on the argument that this is what the traveller is, if he – in his narrative – presents himself as someone aiming for reciprocity in the contact zone. In Andersen's case this seems extremely reductive, moralistic, and in need of a historicizing and individualizing corrective.

Reading Andersen, one is best served, I think, by finding a nuanced position that allows for a twentieth-century critical perspective, placing his text in a greater global context, while also allowing for an understanding of Andersen as a nineteenth-century individual human being. As such, I will point to two of his qualities, deserving special attention: his nationality and his profession. Andersen was a Dane, and it is simply Occidentalizing to insist on a monolithic territory called Europe. Postcolonial theorists, including Said and Pratt, use the term Europe to signify England, or England and France, and in some instances England, France and the U.S.A. This practice only emphasizes the marginality of non-great colonial powers such as the Scandinavian countries – with 'non-great' used as a modifier to signal that Denmark, of course, did possess colonies, but had none of the world-wide power and influence of England, for instance. Theories of Orientalism and Euroimperialism ought to be inflected by nationality – as it is already in the process of being inflected by race, gender and social status.

What becomes interesting in terms of nationality is to examine the relationship between the European periphery and the European center. During the course of the nineteenth century, the attitude of Scandinavian travellers towards nationalism versus Europeanism (a.k.a. universalism or cosmopolitanism) changes. While travellers at the turn of the century (such as

Hamsun, who went to Constantinople in 1899) wish to distinguish themselves from the French and English, Andersen finds it entirely natural to disregard his Danishness abroad. In Constantinople, he lives at the *Hotel de la France* where he feels at home since it offers European luxury and German, French and English newspapers (Andersen vol.I:106). He refers to other Europeans as *Frankere* and clearly identifies with, and accepts, all expressions of French culture. He compares the Grand Bazaar with Palais Royal in Paris, he notes that Sultan Mahmud overthrew the Jannisaries and established French discipline and clothing (Andersen vol.I:86), and he discusses Lamartine's *Voyage en Orient* with Europeanized Turks (Andersen vol.I:108).[6] It never occurs to Andersen to make a special case of his Danishness or to insist that the Turks should approach him as a Dane. We may say that Andersen in the 1840s is subject to the same marginalizing logic that governs present-day postcolonialism. Yet, the purpose of downplaying the European periphery is different.

Part of Andersen's undertaking is to travel and write himself into a European context. His dedications at the beginning of each section in his travelogue strongly indicate this legitimizing project. Yet, again Andersen is caught in a time of transition. Fraternizing with great European men may have been a natural feature of the classical Grand Tour during the age of high romanticism, but by the time Andersen travels and writes, references to Johan Ludwig Tieck, Felix Mendelssohn Bartholdy and Franz von Liszt as 'my friends' were frowned upon by a Danish reading audience. The cosmopolitan project clashes with that of nationalism, and viewing oneself from the center rather than from the periphery simply comes across as conceited.

The second aspect of Andersen's individual identity upon which I want to comment is Andersen's profession as a poet. Pratt's exemplary sentimental traveller, Mungo Park, was commissioned (by the London-based *Association for Promoting the Discovery of the Interior Parts of Africa*) to explore West Africa as a potential market for British goods (Pratt 1992:69). Officially, then, he travelled as an economic explorer, with the connection between art (his travelogue) and commerce being entirely overt. Andersen on the other hand travelled as a literary explorer and was not instructed and paid by anybody to search out a market for Danish goods. While Mungo Park may be exemplary of British colonial adventurers, Andersen may at best be exemplary of peripheral European travellers.

Poeticizing Strategies

Finally – with regards to Andersen the poet – I want to make a point of Andersen's poeticizing strategy, and insist on the reader's responsibility vis-à-vis ambivalent texts. Andersen's method in writing what is often termed poetic realism consists of *seeing* and what he calls *remembering*. Seeing supplies the realistic aspect of his travelogue and is the main purpose of his travels, as we saw in the quote above on his manic seeing. The quote, however, continues with a reflection on the second aspect of his writing process – his remembering:

> Det [digtningen] kommer nok, veed jeg! indeni syder og gjærer det, og naar jeg saa er i den gode Stad Kjøbenhavn og faaer aandelige og legemlige kolde Omslag, saa skyde Blomsterne frem! (Andersen vol.II:158)

> (It [poeticizing] will come, I know! Inside things are seething and brewing, and when I am back in the good city of Copenhagen and have some cold compresses applied to my body and soul, then the flowers shoot forward.)

Writing in the romantic vein is described as a three-fold process, consisting of seeing, of inner seething and brewing, and of applying cold compresses. While the final cold compresses function as a metaphor for applying cold reason and structure to the amassment of visual material, the feverish state of inner seething and brewing refers to Andersen's remembering. The memory associations may be factual or fictional, and may be of a personal or historical kind. In southern Europe, remembering often consists of projecting figures from classical literature onto Italian or Greek landscapes, while in Turkey it consists of recalling scenes from the Old Testament, from classical Greek literature and from *A Thousand and One Nights*. Andersen's first view of the Asian coastline outside Smyrna, for instance, activates memories of Moses' and Jesus' lives, Homer's songs, and Oriental fairy tales (Andersen vol.II:64). When applied to the Orient, this memory process constitutes what Said, in short, has termed Orientalism.

According to Said, 'every writer on the Orient [...] assumes some Oriental precedent, some previous knowledge of the Orient, to which he refers and on which he relies'(Said 1978:20). His criticism is that this process allows the nineteenth-century European traveller to claim authority over the Orient in its present state: 'At most, the 'real' Orient provoked a writer to his vision; it very rarely guided it' (Said 1978:22). Andersen no doubt Orientalizes the Orient – just as he Hellenizes Greece – yet, it is also worthwhile noticing his moments of surprise, when the 'real' Orient in fact does guide his description. Sailing to Constantinople, for example, he observes a young, animated, story-teller on deck and concludes: 'her var en lystighed, ganske forskjellig fra hvad jeg havde tænkt mig hos den gravitetiske Tyrk' (Andersen vol.II:72; here was merriment quite different from what I had imagined regarding the solemn Turk). The Turks similarly surprised Andersen with their honesty in financial matters: 'Tyrkerne ere de meest godmodige, de ærligste Folk' (Andersen vol.II:77; The Turks are the most good-natured, the most honest of people).

If we compare Andersen's associative process in the Orient with that in southern Europe, we find that the Orient activates memories and projections linked to notions of Oriental eroticism and Mohammedanism (as he calls Islam). Time and again, realistic depictions of poverty, brutality, death, and the grotesque are suspended by harem and houri fantasies. A chapter titled 'En Tyrkisk Skizze' (A Turkish Sketch) includes a reflection upon this aestheticizing process, and serves as a particularly illustrative example of Andersen's poetic realism. Over the course of one page, a scene of poverty metamorphosizes into an erotic fantasy. Specifically, the poet turns a poverty-stricken street – with dogs fighting and ripping at a carcass, and with little children running around half-naked, playing on the corpse of a bloody, skinned horse – into a turban-clad Turk's fantasy about his extreme sexual vigour, his harem, and his climactic praise of Allah (Andersen vol.II:94-95).

Andersen is well aware of the challenge this aestheticizing project has presented, and proudly delivers a metapoetic reflection, laying his poetics out as a three-step process. First he presents the seen: 'Jeg giver Billedet, som jeg har seet det' (Andersen vol.II:94; I render the picture as I have seen it). Second, he struggles to demonstrate his poetic genius by finding beauty even in this scene. 'Men findes her ingen Straale af Poesi i hele dette Uvæsen!' (But is there no ray of poetry in this entire nuisance!), he asks rhetorically. Third, after having activated his memories, he is able – in true romantic fashion – to evoke nature's capacity to create an organic whole:

> Jo, thi jeg husker de store Viinranker, der ved enkelte Huse strække deres tykke Stamme op ad Trævæggen, og brede sig som et Løvtag hen over Gaden til Naboens Huus, som den pynter med sit Grønt! (Andersen vol.II:95)

> (Yes, for I recall the great vines, that stretch their thick stems up along the wooden wall of the individual houses, spreading like a roof of leaves across the street to the neighboring house, which it then decorates with its greenery!).

The natural aspects creating harmony are of an outer and inner kind. While the trees create a physical connection between the houses, the gazes from young Turkish women create an erotic link between the street's inhabitants and the traveller: 'Jeg husker den veltilgittrede, høiere Etage, der omslutter Qvinderne og skjuler dem for den Fremmedes Blik! her er poesi!' (*ibid.*; I recall the well-barred, higher floor, surrounding the women, hiding them from the stranger's view. Here is poetry!). The phrase clearly reveals that 'remembering' for Andersen means fantasizing and *not* recalling facts – *not* seeing; after all, how would he be able to see women hidden from his gaze?

The scene is telling for Andersen's poetic realism in which two seemingly incommensurable narratives coexist: that of a cruel, everyday reality, and that of a kind, metaphysical eternity. Andersen's equally short tale, 'Den lille Pige med Svovlstikkerne' (1845; The Little Matchgirl), shows how common this antithesis is for Andersen's poetics, but it also points to the distancing mechanism applied to the Oriental variants. Telling two stories simultaneously in 'The Little Matchgirl' the narrator ends up leaving a double imprint upon the reader's retina: that of a girl dying in Copenhagen's streets and that of the same girl being reunited with her grandmother in heaven. This is somewhat similar to the narrative strategy we find in 'A Turkish Sketch'. As readers we are left with an image of everyday poverty and one of eternal bliss. In the context of Orientalism, however, an important difference between the two tales is a shift in perspective. The two stories in 'The Little Matchgirl' are told by the same narrator. 'A Turkish Sketch', on the other hand, relies on a disavowing shift in perspective. In the final paragraph, the original poet-narrator's voice slips into the Turk's fantasy, rendering this in quotation marks. The quotation marks serve to further reinforce the distance between the fictional Turk and the autobiographical narrator – a distance that nonetheless comes across as strained.

Throughout the Orient section, Andersen uses the Turk's thoughts, dreams, intoxications and poetry as narrative vehicles for his erotic fantasies. It is as if the Orient allows – or forces – Andersen to play with his own inner Turk. Often, Andersen simply comes across as a dirty old man viewed with current eyes. An encounter with a six-year-old Turkish girl turns into a fantasy about riding away with her on a horse once she has turned into a grown virgin (Andersen vol.II:75). The above-mentioned sight of the impoverished opium-smoking Turk turns into thoughts of entering his intoxicated imagination in which the Turk gets ever more excited – 'jeg bliver ellevild' (Andersen vol.II:95; I am going wild) – wanting to embrace not just his wife, but ten or twelve of them (*ibid.*). At Scutari graveyard Andersen cannot see an old man without projecting Orientalist thoughts of harem lust onto him. Moments later, an allegedly passionate young man passes by, and of course, his thoughts are the same. He, too, must be insatiable and dream of non-stop lovemaking ('elskov'): 'Hvilke Tanker flyve gjennem hans Sjæl – ! Ja det er en Tyrk!' (Andersen vol.II:98; What thoughts flutter through his soul – ! Indeed, that is a Turk!) Through whose soul, one may ask, and who, here, is a 'Turk'?

When it comes to poetic realism, Andersen's romanticizing tour-de-force may seem nauseatingly escapist. Yet, as indicated above, the reader is informed of Andersen's aestheticizing project and is able to judge for himself. In the reader's mind, Andersen has planted dual images of social outrage and faith in a higher sense of justice, and even if the harmonizing image always leaves the last imprint and thus has the advantage of greater impact, Andersen cannot be accused of blindness vis-à-vis reality.

Conclusion

Space does not allow me to go into further analysis of Andersen's seeing and the Euroimperialist and Orientalist aspects of his travelogue. Suffice it to say that read with present-day sensitivity to cross-cultural encounters, *A Poet's Bazaar* does at times shock. Andersen's objection to female slaves being locked up in a cage, for example, is surprisingly poeticizing and erotic rather than political: 'Tilhyl ikke de smukke, hvide Qvinder, Du gamle hæslige Karl, dem ville vi just see, driv dem ikke ind i Buret, vi skulle ikke, som Du troer, skade dem med onde Øine!' (Andersen vol.II:83; Do not cover up the beautiful, white women, you old disgusting man. We just wanted to look at them. Do not force them into the cage. We would not, as you believe, hurt them with evil eyes!). Here is a direct and absolutely disconcerting claim to innocent eyes. Similarly, it is disturbing when Andersen enters Muslim sanctuaries such as the Aya Sofia, fantasizing about filling the mosque with Christian hymns, and then objects to the angry looks *he* receives as an outsider. 'Det er sælsomt at vandre herinde, fulgt af Bevæbnede, betragtet med vrede Øine af de Bedende, som vare vi banlyste Aander' (Andersen vol.II:84; It is strange to walk in here, followed by armed men, observed with angry eyes by those praying, as if we were banned spirits). Seen with contemporary eyes, Andersen is not as politically correct as those preparing for a popular celebration of Andersen's bicentennial would have it. But his travelogue cannot be reduced to an example of Orientalism and Euroimperialism either. As the title suggests, *A Poet's Bazaar* reflects the polyphony of a market place. These voices have different geographical origins but cannot transcend time. And like his idol, Franz Liszt, Andersen can go against the conventions of his time – he can strike many chords, but given the restrictions of history, most of these will sound somewhat familiar even if played with unprecedented virtuosity.

Bibliography

Andersen, Hans Christian (1975 [1842]): *En Digters Bazar*, 2 vols. Copenhagen: Lademann.
Andersen, Jens (2004): 'På hat med verden', in *Berlingske Tidende*, May 2.
Baggesen, Søren (1990 [1984]): 'En rendestensunges dannelse: H. C. Andersen' in: *Dansk Litteraturhistorie*, vol. 5, 2nd ed., ed. Peter Holst. Copenhagen: Gyldendal.
Handesten, Lars (1992): *Litterære rejser – poetik og erkendelse i danske digteres rejsebøger*. Copenhagen: Reitzels.
Pratt, Mary Louise (1992): *Imperial Eyes. Travel Writing and Transculturation*. London: Routledge.
Said, Edward (1978): *Orientalism*. New York: Vintage Books.
Topsøe-Jensen, Helge (1975): 'Efterskrift' in Andersen (1975), vol.2. Copenhagen: Lademann.

Notes

1. For example: 'En lille Fugl har sjunget derom' (Andersen vol.II:68-69).
2. Helge Topsøe-Jensen, 'Efterskrift' in Andersen vol.II:235.
3. Earlier in the article, Jens Andersen delivers an equally positive outlook on Hans Christian Andersen's ability to face other cultures without prejudice:

    > H. C. Andersen var en tolerant rejsende. Han havde formidabelt let ved at krydse grænser, også i forhold til trosretninger og politiske systemer, uden nogen stor frygt for det fremmede. Hvor Danmark og danskerne i vor tid ofte har nærmet sig det øvrige Europe og – især – mere fremmede folkeslag og religioner med en flagstang af forbehold, ja der overskred Andersen gang på gang denne voldgrav mellem 'os' og 'dem' i 1800-tallet. (*Berlingske Tidende*, 2 May 2004)

    > (H. C. Andersen was a tolerant traveller. It was formidably easy for him to cross boundaries, also in the case of religious beliefs and political systems, without any great fear of the foreign. Whereas Denmark and the Danes of our time often have approached Europe, and especially more foreign peoples and religions, flagging their reservations, Andersen repeatedly overstepped this moat between 'us' and 'them' in the 1800s.)

    In a study of Danish travelogues, Lars Handesten passes similar judgment upon the traveller in *En Digters Bazar*: 'Andersen er åben og møder mestendels den moderne verden, de fremmede skikke og mennesker ganske fordomsfrit – kun den katolske kirkes alt for materialistiske ritualer får et par protestantiske drag over nakken' (Handesten 1992:37-38; Andersen is open and for the most part he encounters the modern world, the foreign customs and people quite unprejudiced – only the excessively materialistic rituals of the Catholic Church receive some Protestant slaps).
4. This depiction does not stand uncontested. While Andersen presents his travelling 'I' as an active seer in the travelogue, his travelling companion in Italy – H. P. Holst – wrote a letter home, accusing Andersen of not observing anything at all:

    > Gud veed forresten, hvad han vil foretage sig i Grækenland og Constantinopel, thi en latterligere Maade end han bruger sin Tid paa, skal man vanskelig kunne opvise. Han seer Intet, han nyder Intet, han glæder sig over Intet – han gjør ikke andet end skrive. (Quoted in Topsøe-Jensen 1975:232)

    > (God knows what he will do in Greece and Constantinople, for it would be difficult to spend time in a more ridiculous manner than he does. He sees nothing, he enjoys nothing, he rejoices at nothing – he does nothing but write.)
5. 'Park's *Travels* richly exemplifies the eruption of the sentimental mode into European narrative of the contact zone at the end of the eighteenth century' (74-5).
6. Furthermore, he communicates with Italian and French-speaking Turks (Andersen vol.I:104), and he refers to 'our' Danish consul – who is Italian (Andersen vol.I:106).

Notes on Contributors

Hans Christian Andersen has worked for Newcastle Business School (part of Northumbria University) since 1991, lecturing in Cultural Tourism. He specialises in travel descriptions (with particular emphasis on Hans Christian Andersen) and literary tourism, and is researching the links between travel literature and the early development of the modern tourist industry. He has also published on Hans Christian Andersen's literary works (his fairy tales and works for the theatre), and writes regularly on modern British heritage attractions.

Elizabeth Baigent is Reader in the History of Geography at the University of Oxford. From 1993 to 2003 she was Research Director of the *Oxford Dictionary of National Biography* (2004) and had particular responsibility for travelers and explorers. She was a Leverhulme Visiting Fellow at the University of Stockholm 1984-5 and has published on Sweden and Swedish America.

Sumarliði Ísleifsson has been a member of the Reykjavik Academy since 1999. He is the author of several books and documentaries on political history and Icelandic images and identities, including *Island framandi land* (1996, on Icelandic images) and *Saga Stjórnarráðs Íslands I-III* (2004, History of the Icelandic Government Offices, author and editor). He is currently writing and editing the history of the Icelandic trade unions and is one of two project leaders for the research project 'Iceland and Images of the North'.

Henk van der Liet is Professor of Scandinavian Languages and Literature at the University of Amsterdam, and is a member of the literary committee of the Danish Arts Foundation (Statens Kunstfond). His publications include numerous articles in the field of Scandinavian literature of the nineteenth and twentieth centuries, with a special emphasis on Danish literature, as well as *Kontrapunkter. En studie i Poul Vads skønlitterære forfatterskab* (1997). He contributed to *Danske digtere i det 20. århundrede I-III* (Gad Publishers, 2000-2002), is editor of the Dutch-Flemish journal *Tijdschrift voor Skandinavistiek*, and is publisher and editor in chief of the book series Amsterdam Contributions to Scandinavian Studies. At present he is working on a study of the works of Holger Drachmann.

Tony Lurcock recently retired from St. Clare's College in Oxford, where he has taught English literature for many years. He began his academic career in Finland, as lecturer in Helsinki University and then Åbo Akademi. Although his academic work has been mainly in the fields of biography and eighteenth century literature, he has for forty years been compiling a comprehensive account of records of British travellers in Finland, which he hopes will eventually be published.

Wendy Mercer is Senior Lecturer in French at University College London. Her publications include a book on Balzac, editions of works by Léonie d'Aunet, articles on various aspects of nineteenth-century French and comparative literature, especially the reception of German Romanticism in France, and ninteenth-century travel writing. A biography, *The Life and travels of Xavier Marmier (1808-1892): bringing world literature to France* is forthcoming (Oxford University Press).

Astrid E. J. Ogilvie is a fellow of INSTAAR (Institute of Arctic and Alpine Research) in Boulder, Colorado, and holds honorary positions at the Stefansson Arctic Institute, Akureyri and the Climatic Research Unit at UEA, Norwich. She is Professor of Anthropology at Hunter College, City University of New York. She works primarily in the fields of climate and environmental history in North Atlantic regions, but has broad interdisciplinary interests within the human dimensions of global change. She has published some seventy articles, and is currently working on two books within the field of climate and society, as well as leading research projects in Iceland, Norway and Canada.

Elizabeth Oxfeldt holds a Ph.D. in Scandinavian Studies from U.C. Berkeley. She has worked as a Danish lecturer at Oslo University for four years and is currently employed at Vestfold University College. Her main research interests are postcolonialism and interaesthetics. Her publications include *Nordic Orientalism. Paris and the Cosmopolitan Imagination 1800-1900* (Museum Tusculanum Press 2005) and various articles on Hans Christian Andersen's fairy tales, travelogues and drama in *Kritik*, *Animation Journal*, *Spring*, and in her anthology *H. C. Andersen – eventyr, kunst og modernitet* (2006). She is currently writing a book on Scandinavian travel writing from 1840 to 2000. The present article is an initial version of the book's first chapter.

Bjarne Rogan is Professor of Cultural Studies, University of Oslo. His main research fields include material culture & consumption studies; transport history & tourism; littoral culture & fisheries; language, culture & communcation; museology and the historiography of European ethnology.

Anne-Kari Skarðhamar is Associate Professor at Oslo University College, Faculty of Education. Her publications include *Poetikk og livstolkning i Christian Matras' lyrikk. Med et tillegg om Matras og færøysk lyrik*k (2002), *Fyrvokteren ved verdens ende og hans laterna magica. Ti artikler om William Heinesens forfatterskap* (2005), *Periferi og sentrum. Tolv artikler om færøysk litteratur* (2006), books on teaching literature, articles on children's literature and on descriptions of childhood in Nordic literature

Bjarne Thorup Thomsen is Senior Lecturer in Scandinavian Literature at the University of Edinburgh. He was a co-editor of *Dansk litteraturhistorie* (Gyldendal, 1983-85) and has published widely on Scandinavian nineteenth- and early twentieth-century literature. He also has a research interest in early Scandinavian cinema. His most recent monograph is *Lagerlöfs litterære landvinding* (Amsterdam Contributions to Scandinavian Studies, 2007). He is editor of *Centring on the Peripheries. Studies in Scandinavian, Scottish, Gaelic and Greenlandic Literature* (Norvik Press, 2007) and a special Hans Christian Andersen issue of the journal *Scandinavica* (autumn 2007).

Andrew Wawn is Professor of Anglo-Icelandic Studies at the University of Leeds. His books include *The Iceland Journal of Henry Holland 1810* (London, 1987), *The Anglo Man: Þorleifr Repp, Philology and Nineteenth-Century Britain* (Reykjavik, 1991), and *The Vikings and the Victorians: Inventing the Old North in Nineteenth-Century Britain* (2000).

Marie Wells was W. P. Ker Lecturer in Norwegian at University College London until her retirement. Her main research interests have been nineteenth- and twentieth-century Norwegian literature, with a special interest in the work of Henrik Ibsen. Articles on Ibsen have appeared in *Scandinavica*, *Edda* and *New Comparisons*. She is currently translating *Bondestudentar* by Arne Garborg, to be published as *The Making of Daniel Braut* by Norvik Press in the autumn of 2008.

C. CLAIRE THOMSON (ED.)

Northern Constellations
New Readings in Nordic Cinema

What happens when a camera gets trapped in a Swedish elevator, or when the body of the tourist meets the snow of an Icelandic winter? How is Lars von Trier re-working Carl Th. Dreyer's images of flesh and spirit for a digital age? How can filmic space re-negotiate local, national, and global forms of belonging?

Northern Constellations features interventions from leading cinema studies scholars and Scandinavian specialists from the UK, the US and the Nordic world. Engaging with contemporary film and cultural theory – particularly on affect, embodiment, memory, place, interculturality, and realism – the essays explore the potential of cinema to map space, body, and community. Older Nordic classics by Carl Th. Dreyer, Ingmar Bergman and Victor Sjöström are re-interpreted in constellation with the themes and concerns of established and emerging contemporary filmmakers, including Lars von Trier, Aki Kaurismäki, Liv Ullmann, Suzanne Taslimi and Max Kestner.

As the seventh art forges on towards its second century, *Northern Constellations* bears witness to the fertile interdisciplinarity and maturity of the discipline of film studies, and celebrates the diversity and dynamism of film-making in the Nordic world. It should appeal to the general cinema-goer as well as to film scholars and students. The volume includes black-and-white illustrations, and each chapter is supported by bibliographical references.

ISBN 978 1 870041 63 8

UK £16.95
(paperback, 248 pages)

For further information, or to request a catalogue, please contact:
Norvik Press, Department of Scandinavian Studies, University College London,
Gower Street, London WC1E 6BT, England
or visit our website at www.norvikpress.com